# SAVE THE HEADACHE OF MANUAL ENTRY

## THE PROGRAMS ARE AVAILABLE ON DISK!!!

Put the power of the programs in the dBASE BOOK OF BUSINESS APPLICATIONS to use in your business without delay and forget the manual entry of 210 pages of dBASE$^{T.M.}$ command files. All applications are available on one disk for the IBM PC or PC compatible computers with at least 320K of disk storage. To order, enclose $34.95 plus $3.00 shipping for a diskette in IBM PC (PC DOS 1.1) format.

Method of Payment   \_\_\_\_ Check   \_\_\_\_ MasterCard   \_\_\_\_ Visa

Credit Card Number _____

Exp. Date _____

Name: _____

Address: _____

_____

City, State, Zip _____

ISBN 0-8359-1241-8

Mail to:
Prentice Hall, Inc.
200 Old Tappan Road
Old Tappan, NJ 07675
Att.: M.O.B.

# The dBase™ Book
# of Business Applications

Michael J. Clifford

A Reston Computer Group Book
RESTON PUBLISHING COMPANY, INC.
*A Prentice-Hall Company*
Reston, Virginia

*Library of Congress Cataloging in Publication Data*

Clifford, Michael.
   The dBase book of business applications.

   Includes index.
   1. dBase II (Computer program)   2. Business—Data
processing.   I. Title.
HF5548.4.D22C55     1984        650'.028'5425        84-9852
ISBN 0-8359-1242-6

Editorial/production supervision and
interior design by Camelia Townsend

© 1984 by Computer Essentials, Inc.
*A Prentice-Hall Company*
Reston, Virginia 22090

10   9   8   7   6   5   4   3   2   1

PRINTED IN THE UNITED STATES OF AMERICA

# Contents

# Acknowledgments

My heartfelt thanks go to Bob May who introduced me to dBASE II and to Jim Stephan of Reston Publishing who audaciously suggested that this book be written.

Further thanks are due to Paul Shirley for his ideas and to the kind support from Ron Miller and Jim Burdette of CompuShop of Georgia.

This book would not be possible without the editing and support of my business associate and partner in life, Sandy Murray, to whom this book is dedicated.

# Preface

Information is critical to the survival of every enterprise. Business practices and innovative ideas are only as good as the operating procedures and information that support them. Quality information is marked by its accessibility and by the clarity with which it facilitates timely and tough decisions. A vital resource, quality data boosts productivity and provides the automated enterprise with a competitive edge.

The microcomputer revolution began several years ago and shows few signs of waning. Many advanced programs that were previously tailored for larger computers are now available for the microcomputer.

Data base software, supercharged electronic file cabinets, have expedited the microcomputer storage and retrieval of business data. The dBASE II data base manager is one of the most popular software packages ever sold. Acting as both a file cabinet for beginners and a programming language for the experienced, dBASE II allows unrivaled flexibility to meet the full needs of your organization.

*The dBASE Book of Business Applications* is written for:

- Computer non-professionals who wish to develop their own information systems for their business.

- Managers who wish to instruct subordinates in the use of dBASE II in their offices.

- Trainers of dBASE II who wish to use the applications as models for instruction.

- Students of programming and operation of common business software.

- Anybody who is interested in automating office procedures and maximizing productivity.

Henry Ford, when criticized about the limited color options of his production vehicle, replied, "Any color is fine, so long as it is black." Microcomputer software has allowed the average person to possess a computing ability unthinkable just a few years ago. Software programs have been written for use by a mass market of computer users who do not profess to be computer programmers. Many software designers have complied by preparing programs that primarily emphasize the most widespread needs common to the average business consumer. You may be sacrificing the unique processing needs of your enterprise when buying generic Model T software.

The *dBASE Book of Business Applications* emerged from two years of requests from business people who attended our dBASE II classes. All attendees shared the desire to manage their own data, develop their own procedures, and be dictated not by the common denominator of a canned package of business software but by the custom needs of their enterprises.

The *dBASE Book of Business Applications* is strictly about business. This book answers the inevitable question by the recent purchaser of dBASE II: Now that I own this popular software program, how do I use it to solve my problems? With this book you'll be able to:

- Manage clients and prospects; account for money you owe to others and others owe to you (accounts payable and receivable); maintain an inventory and update it from invoices written; create numerous electronic file cabinets by following simple prompts; compute expense accounts expenditures; graph a display; and calculate dates and durations.

- Run some of these popular business applications without any detailed knowledge of dBASE II. Just type in the code and read the Operations Chapter in each section.

- Modify each program to *your* needs by following the suggested Modifications and Embellishments.

- Use the dBASE II programming techniques from the TECH TIPS throughout the book and the Technical Tutorials at the end of each section.

Training courses in computer usage have just become widespread. Classes in the use of dBASE II have tended to stress fundamentals. This has left many of the students knowledgeable of simple commands, which facilitates use of dBASE II at the conversational level. Armed with this, many students have attempted to design the fullblown applications that were the original motivation for the purchase and use of dBASE II.

Follow-up contacts have revealed that classes alone are not sufficient to ensure rapid implementation of dBASE II in the office. Most people require time and practice to assimilate the fundamentals before the routines can be conceptualized, developed, debugged, and polished. The need for office software is urgent, yet the time-consuming prospect of developing a program from scratch discourages many potential do-it-yourselfers. The manager may be prevented from minding the business while the development progresses. Both time and money can be lost.

*The dBASE Book of Business Applications* solves this problem. Applications are presented that can be immediately installed and operated. Modifications can be made as time permits and your dBASE II skill improves.

Why wait until you're a dBASE II expert to have custom programs running in your business? *The dBASE Book of Business Applications* is the perfect companion to any other dBASE II tutorial or class you may have taken.

# SECTION ONE

## dBasics of Business

An overfilled closet was the center of a continuing sketch on the Fibber McGee show many years ago. A pack rat by nature, Fibber piled other junk outside the door, just waiting its turn to be crammed into the already bulging depository.

Small business is suffering from the Fibber McGee phenomenon: information overflow is severely taxing the average office. Seldom is management of information satisfactory; better letters could be written, more effective methods to track prospects could be developed, and the cost of maintaining an inventory could be decreased.

Many specialized software programs accomplish these tasks admirably. All make assumptions about the need of the average business user. However, many programs have no provision to adapt to the unique needs of a particular business—you must adapt to the designs of the software engineer, not the dictates of your business.

The software program dBASE II by Ashton-Tate remedies the problem. dBASE II is a database management system (DBMS)—a supercharged electronic file cabinet. Information can be entered into the computer, manipulated (invoices posted, inventory calculated), and printed out according to *your* needs.

Extremely powerful DBMS programs were established for large computers several years ago. The technology has now been applied to microcomputers and is available to the average user (a non-programmer) with moderate resources.

Enterprising pioneers built stereos in the 50s, constructed furniture in the 60s, and remodeled homes in the 70s. The microcomputer has ushered in the 80s with data-do-it-yourselfers, self-reliant people who process their own information. Rather than depending upon the often cumbersome services of a data processing department, the contemporary office member can manage data in his or her own way, according to the unique requirements of the enterprise.

The *dBASE Book of Business Applications* has been designed expressly for this adventuresome do-it-yourselfer. Applications in Sections one, two, three, and five manage clients, money, and material by using dBASE to process text, numbers, and graphs.

Section one contains introductory information and can be skipped by readers familiar with dBASE application programming. Others, however, are encouraged to review the basic concepts and the installation notes.

# 1

# BASIC CONCEPTS
# AND ORGANIZATION

## dBASE II HAS
## TWO OPERATIONAL LEVELS

dBASE works on two levels. The first is often called the *keyboard, command,* or *conversational* level. The keyboard level of operation can satisfy most of the simple applications that may arise. Users may define their informational needs and enter the data into the computer in accordance with a basic but easily learned series of prompts. Once done, the data can be extracted by one-line commands. Both prompts and commands can be learned in about two days of study and practice.

dBASE can also be used to develop powerful and flexible computer programs. The dBASE commands are written to command files which, when executed, can fulfill virtually any office application. The same clear and comprehensible commands used at the conversational level are used when programming. As a result, dBASE II requires far less time and effort than other software to produce a useful program.

## EVERYBODY WANTS TO GET
## INTO THE ACT: PARTICIPATORY
## PROCESSING

The ease of use of the first level and the comprehensiveness of the second level allows business people to use a new approach to office computing: participatory processing.

3

In the past, end-users (managers, specialists, clerks) who wished to automate the processing of their information were required to submit requests to the professional data processors. The experts of the care and feeding of large computers were compelled to custom design reports and programs, which often competed with other priorities. Moreover, data processing professionals, while highly skilled in programming, often did not fully comprehend the complexities of the requester's business, and the turnaround time often far exceeded the deadline for timely data.

Participatory processing is the sharing of computer processing and procedures by all or most of the recipients of the processed data. End-users of the finished product bear some or all responsibility for entry and processing of the data. People best able to formulate the problem also manage the processing, which has been greatly simplified. The advent of the microcomputer and software has allowed end-users to compute directly without the need for outside assistance.

Participatory processing implies that responsibilities for processing be delegated to the staff members who are most familiar with the meaningful data that will be produced. Mistakes can be found and reports can be revised immediately because the same person both operates the computer and uses the results processed from it. The need and reliance on the Data Processing Department is diminished or circumvented. Reams of data can be transformed into meaningful reports to support daily decisions in a competitive enterprise, without the need and delay due to intermediate assistance.

Not all staff will be computer programmers in a business that follows the principles of participatory processing, but virtually everybody will acquire keyboard experience. Staff members may assume three roles: users, tweakers, and micro-managers.

Users are the operators of the program. Cursory knowledge of the program's operation is the main prerequisite. Fundamental computer usage is the only other necessity; this includes typing on a computer keyboard, handling and backing up diskettes and hard disk drives, and use of a printer and computer keyboard.

Tweakers are casual students of dBASE II who possess beginning or intermediate comprehension of dBASE II commands and procedures. They may be relied upon to make minor modifications to each existing program if backup copies are made and if thorough testing of the modified program is done.

Micro-managers are entrusted with the major modifications, design, sizeable embellishments, and trouble-shooting of each program (if necessary). Continued operation ultimately rests with the designated micro-manager of the particular program.

Unlike the traditional specialization of processing, each staff member may occupy several of these roles, depending upon the office, the computer program, and the computers. One may be the manager of the dBASE II mailing list program, another may oversee the accounting software, and so on.

# HOW TO USE THIS BOOK: THE STRATEGY OF IMPLEMENTATION

This book is organized by applications. Each application section has segments that consist of the following:

1. An Operations segment explaining the use and appearance of the program.
2. Installation and Inner Workings segment. The code and its operation are explained. TECH TIPS briefly highlight techniques that can be used in other programs. Modifications and Embellishments are outlined to tailor the system to your needs.
3. A Technical Tutorial at the end of each section that discusses in depth many powerful dBASE II techniques used to program the system.

The *dBASE Book of Business Applications* may be used in different ways. Each of the systems and subordinate programs may be typed in and operated immediately. The programs in this book may be used just like any commercial software—just type in the code and operate.

Other uses may be found according to the interest and responsibility of each reader. The person responsible for installation needs to read only the corresponding chapter in each section. Casual students (tweakers) of dBASE II programming will profit from the Inner Workings in that chapter as well. Users need only to read the Operations chapter. Chapters 1 and 2 expose users to procedures of dBASE in an office and should be read by all.

The most requested applications by our students have been included in this book. These are customer prospect management, accounts payable, accounts receivable, and graphics display. Each reflects major types of business software:

- Sales/Marketing
- Administration/Planning
- Accounting/Finance
- Inventory Control

*Table 1-1. Recommended Reading by User*

|  | Chaps. 1–2 | Operations | Installation/ Inner Work | Technical Tutorial |
|---|---|---|---|---|
| Users | X | X |  |  |
| Tweakers | X | X | X | X |
| Micro-managers | X | X | X | X |

The flexibility and power of dBASE II is ideally suited for each use. The conversational level may be used by all staff members for "quick and dirty" answers needed during the daily conduct of business. The ability of the language and the flexibility of dBASE II allow dBASE II to grow with your needs. This text features programs for each area of need as outlined in table 1-2.

Choose the application or applications that interest you, and determine which role you and your staff members will assume. The designated micro-manager will install the program listings on your computer and start operation. Major modifications can then be made by the micro-manager, and minor alterations can be made by others once the skeleton routine is operating smoothly.

Each system is operational without modification. Due to brevity, not every conceivable feature (help menus, prompts, report options) has been included, but the programs that are included can be greatly enhanced and easily modified. In order to do so, the micro-manager and preferably other staff should know the fundamental commands. Many training centers are located throughout the country which offer dBASE II seminars. Introductory books are available that detail the conversational commands.

Become familiar with the operation, make a list of possible improvements, and follow the suggestions for tailoring the program to your specific needs. You will quickly be relieved of the tedium of manual procedures. Automate your enterprise with a microcomputer, dBASE II, and *The dBASE Book of Business Applications!*

## Table 1-2.   Enclosed Applications, Data Managed, and the Technical Tutorials

| Software Type Manages | System Name | Chapter(s) | Technical Tutorial |
|---|---|---|---|
| Clients | MAILFORM | 3–5 | Chapter 6 |
| Material | INVENT | 7–8 | |
| Money | INVOICE | 9–10 | |
| | PAYBILLS | 11–12 | Chapter 13 |
| | EXPENSE | 14–15 | |
| Files | INIT | 16 | |
| Dates & Durations | DATEMENU | 17 | |
| Decisions | dPLOT | 18 | |

# 2

# MATING YOUR PROGRAMS
# WITH dBASE II

## THE OPERATING ENVIRONMENT

This text contains files which, when entered into your computer and run with dBASE II, will operate as described. You will first need a version of dBASE which fits your computer system and its operating system. Both, along with the other hardware, constitute the operating environment of your computer system.

Ashton-Tate has released dBASE for many computer environments. Currently, dBASE will run on the most popular operating systems: CP/M and PC-DOS (and its generic equivalent, MS-DOS). A version for Apple's Macintosh computer should be available soon.

Command files written for one environment should run on others if dBASE is installed properly. Subtle differences, however, have been noted between the IBM-PC compatible version of dBASE and the CP/M version. In addition, several versions of each have been produced. Version 2.4, released in the middle of 1983, was used to develop the programs. Check with your dealer to ensure that you have the latest issue for your computer.

Every program has been tested by several users on different CP/M and IBM-PC compatible computers, for both version 2.3B and the latest 2.4 version. All have run without difficulty.

If you have other than a CP/M version of dBASE, please consult the additional installation notes in the Appendix.

# ENTERING PROGRAMS ON THE DISK

All the applications are composed of several files. Most are command files, which end in the CMD extension (PRG on the MS-DOS version). These and the other program files (reports) should be placed consistently on a chosen default drive. Operators with two disk drives may wish to store all program files on the A drive and data on the B drive. Owners of hard disk drives may wish to place all dBASE files on the hard disk. In all cases, two utility programs (DTVERIFY and INIT) are placed on drive A with the dBASE program purchased from Ashton-Tate. Suggested configurations are summarized in table 2.1.

Each application will look for the INIT program, which will inform your main menu of the locations of other program and data files (drive A or B). You will need to enter the locations only once.

The dBASE text editor may be used to enter each command file. To enter MAILFORM.CMD, type

```
MODIFY COMMAND mailform
```

The screen will erase and the cursor will appear in the upper left of the screen. The lines of dBASE code may then be entered.

Entering the code exactly as it appears in the book is highly recommended if correct operation is to be ensured. Limited storage on your disk drives may require, however, that the comments and spaces used liberally in the code throughout the book be omitted to conserve space. Comments are statements preceded by an asterisk (*). Comments clarify operation to the reader of the dBASE II code, although the program itself is not altered by the comments in any manner. Comments may also follow the ENDDO, DO WHILE, and ENDIF commands. Spaces between lines and words also clarify but do not alter operation. Each program has lines of code grouped by function. The code groups are separated down the page by blank lines. The code is further indented across the page. The blank lines and spaces are for comprehension by the reader and are not required by dBASE to operate.

## Table 2-1.  Placement Options for dBASE Files

| CONFIGURATION | dBASE II software* | Utilities | Program Files | Data Files |
|---|---|---|---|---|
| 2 Disk drives (option 1) | A | A | A | B |
| 2 Disk drives (option 2) | A | A | B | B |
| Hard disk** | A | A | A | A |

*dBASE II main and subordinate programs from Ashton-Tate.
**Assumes that drive A is the main disk drive; substitute as necessary.

```
CODE WITH
SPACES, COMMENTS
AND BLANK LINES              COMPACTED CODE
SET TALK OFF                 SET TALK OFF
                             DO WHILE .NOT. EOF
DO WHILE .NOT. EOF           IF A=B
  IF A=B                     STORE C TO B
    STORE C TO B             ENDIF
  ENDIF A=B                  ENDDO
ENDDO WHILE .NOT. EOF
```

Complete typing of each command file. Once done, exit by using the command CONTROL-W to write the file to the program disk.

A word processor or text editor may also be used to enter the command files. You must place the extension .CMD (or .PRG for PC-DOS and MS-DOS versions) after the filename. Be sure to use the provision in your word processing program for computer programs. Wordstar designates this as the 'N' document mode (versus the 'D' document mode). Other word processors have similar options.

The applications may be tested once the program files have been entered. Use the DO command and the name of the main menu. To invoke the MAILFORM system, type the dBASE command DO MAIL-FORM. Carefully check that the performance is as described in the Operations segment of each section.

You may need to debug until operation is satisfactory because computers are unforgiving of mistyped code. The newest version of dBASE II has a traceback feature. With this feature, the command file with the error is printed on the screen—an invaluable aid in detecting the bug. If the bug is still not found, or if you possess an earlier version, place the temporary commands SET talk ON and SET echo ON just below the DO INIT statement in the main menu of an application. Run the program again and note where the program bombs. The problem will most likely be in last line of code just echoed to the console. Check, revise, remove the diagnostic, and save the corrected command file.

## STANDARDS AND PROCEDURES: THE HUMAN ROLE IN THE SYSTEM

Standards of operation must be established once the system is operating. Procedures are as essential as hardware and software to the processing of data. The manager should establish standards for the following:

- *Program alteration and operation.* People who have responsibility for design should be identified. Alteration may be done by others, but only if the alterations are well documented. Operators should also be identified. All others should be prohibited from using the application program.

- *Backup.* Your data may be one of the company's most vital resources. A stray electrical impulse may be very costly. Clearly designate staff and procedures for backing up program and data files. Procedures are recommended in Section II.
- *Dates.* Dates are used flexibly by humans, not computers. Many different formats exist and are outlined in Chapter 17. Two conventions will be used throughout: the recognizable MM/DD/YY format and the YY/MM/DD format for comparing intervals between two dates. VIEWDATE will refer to the format easily readable by operators and FILEDATE will refer to the format to be placed into the file for comparisons.
- *Printer margins.* A printer shared by many people will often print paper of many different widths during the day. Standardize the left margin on all printed forms by permanently fastening the paper guide with tape.

Implementation of standards and procedures will assist in the smooth operation of each program in this book.

## A WORD ABOUT SELECTED COMMANDS

A review of two powerful commands used by programs in this text is necessary because they are not adequately described in the User's Manual. The commands are the "Holy Macro" and the INDEX command.

### The Holy Macro

A macro is one of the most powerful commands in dBASE and is often used at the beginning of every application. The macro symbol (&) tells dBASE to treat a memory variable in a special way, by not taking it at face value. The *contents* of a macro are considered not as text, but as a command.

Macros are used for two purposes. Special information may be sent from one command to another about the general operation of the program. A common method to assign default drives flexibly is to ask the operator to choose a desired default disk drive, then assign the drive by using the SET DEFAULT TO command.

```
STORE 'B' TO dfdefault
@ 6,5 SAY 'Data Disk Drive' GET dfdefault
READ
SET default TO &dfdefault
```

The operator has a choice to override the assumed assignment of the drive B and replace it with another. The contents of dfdefault (A,B,C,D) are passed to the SET command by the macro symbol (&). An error message will result if the SET command is used without the macro preceding the memory variable.

The macro also allows the abbreviation of a detailed and long command and assigning the command to a memory variable. A command

DISPLAY ALL FOR datepaid > '02/01/84' .AND. datepaid < '02/29/83'

can be STOREd to a memory variable, called *example*. The long command need not be typed again. To accomplish the same purpose, invoke the macro:

CODE                   WHAT dBASE SEES

? &example     DISPLAY ALL FOR datepaid . . . (etc.)

dBase will expand the memory variable example, substituting for the contents the command that was STOREd to it.

## Indexing on Multiple Fields

The INDEX command, unlike the SORT command, allows arranging records on more than one field. SORT will allow a file to be organized by one field, for example, the last name field of a file. Usually, this may be sufficient. Frequently, however, a program needs to account for ties. Observe a typical mailing list file structure and contents.

| STRUCTURE | | CONTENTS | |
|---|---|---|---|
| firstname,c,12 | | 00001 | Alphonse T. Zachary |
| middle,c,1 | | 00002 | William W. Williams |
| lastname,c,15 | | 00003 | Alphonse Q. Zachary |

The SORT command will not further sort two records if the contents of the sorted field key is identical for each, i.e., the two records containing the last name of Zachary. Alphonse T. Zachary will be listed before Alphonse Q. Zachary simply because the first was (coincidentally) entered into dBASE II before the other.

The INDEX command, however, will order the arrangement by all three fields with the expression:

INDEX ON lastname + firstname + middle TO [*index file name*]

The SET INDEX TO, followed by the name of the index file, will produce the desired order.

```
00003    Alphonse Q. Zachary
00001    Alphonse T. Zachary
00002    William W. Williams
```

Two major purposes are accomplished. First, similar items are grouped by one or more fields. The Alphonses cluster together and Williams is alphabetically ordered to the bottom of the list. Second, ties on all but identical data are broken if additional fields are specified in the indexing expression. The use of a middle name will organize Alphonse Q. always to precede Alphonse T. for the same last name.

The use of macros and indexing on multiple fields are techniques that are used in most of the applications of this book. The first application, MAILFORM uses both extensively.

MAILFORM assists your staff in the contact of prospects and clients. MAILFORM is an example of a dBASE II program that is easily entered and that automates tedious office procedures. MAILFORM creates a client file and allows all staff to run the MAILFORM program to print the standard reports or to access the CLIENT file at the dot-prompt level for quick and effortless custom queries.

# SECTION TWO

# Communicating with Clients

A disciplined strategy of communications with clients and prospects is essential to business success. Opportunities do not occur easily; prospects often call when workers are occupied or otherwise distracted. A busy office allows ample opportunity for messages to the staff members to be mislaid. Sales, patients, or clients can be lost simply because leads were committed to memory and not to a computer. That lost phone number may be the big lead that got away.

## PROSPECT MANAGEMENT: STONE AGE STYLE

An office or clinic that is not automated or computerized is vulnerable to two nemeses: confusion and paper. Let's examine a typical case of how *not* to conduct communication with potential customers.

Barnaby Bumbler works in the sales division for Stone Age Products, a fabricator of granite furniture. Four models are offered: The Stonehenge Special, the Penultimate Pyramid, the Rock of Ages, and the Pitcairn Group. The first two are recliners; the last two are sofas.

Mr. Bumbler is out of the office on calls about half the time. Other sales and clerical staff take messages and leave them on his desk. He returns to confusion.

Barnaby had received ten messages, which resulted in the following sales:

### The Bottom Line: Stone Age Sales

| Number of messages | Sale? | Result or reason |
| --- | --- | --- |
| 4 | No | Illegible due to coffee and doughnut stains. |
| 2 | No | Callers needed sofa immediately. Staff people did not question prospect. Caller bought from competitor. |
| 1 | No | Tried to return calls six times. Once reached, caller wanted a contribution to the indigent stonecutters' union. |
| 1 | No | Caller wanted quick answer to simple question: Do we sell beds too? (We don't). |
| 1 | No | Major client called about possible government contract they warned us about six months ago. Forgot to call last month about this lead. Missed deadline by one day. |
| 1 | Yes | Sold the Pitcairn Group. |

The Stone Age costs of conducting its business were evident. While all of the calls were returned, substantial sales were lost by the failure to communicate. The greatest efforts were expended to reach prospects that were interested the least. Several prospects could have remained active if the purpose of the caller had been made known and the other clerical and sales staff assisted them. One sale was lost simply because Mr. Bumbler forgot to call back a client to check a lead five months after the opportunity became known.

Mr. Bumbler has also lost business by not regularly communicating with his steady customers. Many of his competitors are sending out monthly newsletters and promotional announcements. One competitor, the Rock Ridge Retailers, had already obtained many clients from Stone Age Products by the publication of its newsletter, *The Rock Ridge Rocker.*

The costs for Stone Age's primitive sales strategy are high. The uncoordinated non-method of communicating with clients and prospects results in a stone cold business for Stone Age Products.

# STEPS TO AUTOMATE COMMUNICATION

A systematic series of steps for communicating with business candidates greatly improves office efficiency by doing the following:

1. Categorizing the callers by interest and product.
2. Generating a uniform report to the manager daily.
3. Eliminating the haphazard collection of notes, replacing them with a consistent and coordinated data storage.
4. Automating the time-consuming clerical functions to allow more time for the pursuit of sales.

Each step is necessary, and each can be easily implemented with dBASE II.

## Categorizing Callers by Interest and Product

How interested is the caller? This is the basic question in sales. Is he or she a hot prospect, a casual caller, or has the lead gone cold? Is the interest in the business in general, or is the attention focused on one product or service? A good salesperson rapidly assesses (qualifies) the caller to answer these questions. The flowchart on page 17 outlines one method of qualifying a caller.

## Uniform Reporting to the Sales Manager

Salespeople often operate independently. Reports submitted to the manager vary widely in detail. Leads may be worked twice or opportunities missed due to no coordinated sharing of information by salespeople.

Uniform reporting of leads to a central authority serves to reduce problems.

## Computerizing the Paperwork

The tireless memory of a computer can quickly replace the haphazard notes. The computer can prompt the operator to request from the caller other valuable information as well as the name. All of these can be retained for permanent storage and easily retrieved, and no sales will be missed by losing a critical phone number.

## Automating Clerical Functions

All sales require persistence. The constant communication requires disciplined scheduling for follow-up contacts; letters and promotional announcements often are profitable. Computers excel at these mundane tasks.

# PROSPECT MANAGEMENT: THE MAILFORM METHOD

A systematized communications program consists basically of messages and reminders. dBASE II is unexcelled at working with words and storing data. The application in Section II, MAILFORM, is designed to automate the calls to your office by clients and prospects about your product or service. Computerized records of leads are retained, and the outgoing mail is organized.

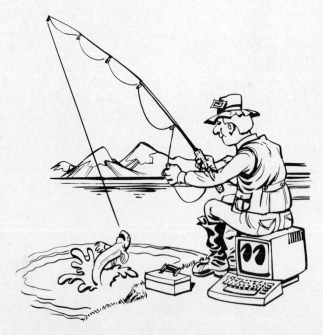

Your Staff Concentrates on Reeling in the Clients

Flowchart of Marketing Steps

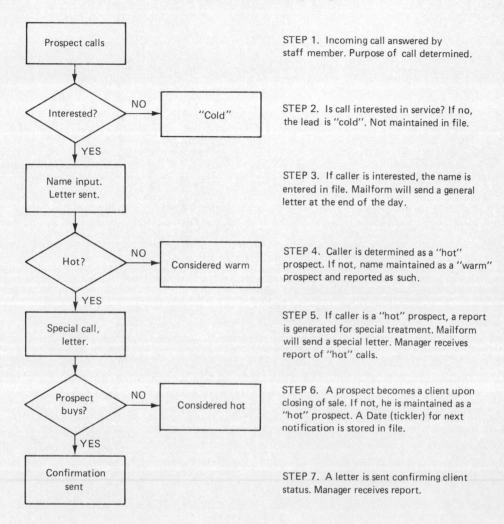

STEP 1. Incoming call answered by staff member. Purpose of call determined.

STEP 2. Is call interested in service? If no, the lead is "cold". Not maintained in file.

STEP 3. If caller is interested, the name is entered in file. Mailform will send a general letter at the end of the day.

STEP 4. Caller is determined as a "hot" prospect. If not, name maintained as a "warm" prospect and reported as such.

STEP 5. If caller is a "hot" prospect, a report is generated for special treatment. Mailform will send a special letter. Manager receives report of "hot" calls.

STEP 6. A prospect becomes a client upon closing of sale. If not, he is maintained as a "hot" prospect. A Date (tickler) for next notification is stored in file.

STEP 7. A letter is sent confirming client status. Manager receives report.

MAILFORM was designed originally as a program to boost sales, but it has also been applied to medical and consulting practices. In all of these applications, the MAILFORM system encourages the prospecting and retaining of clients. Inquiries about your product or services are tracked and reported daily to the manager. Your computer and dBASE II manage the paperwork. Your staff concentrates on reeling in the prospects, clients, or patients.

# 3

# TRACKING PROSPECTS
# AND MAINTAINING CLIENTS

MAILFORM is based upon a series of distinct marketing steps that occur when a prospect first calls. The response to this caller should lead to a purchase of your product or service. Casual inquiries are distinguished from hot prospects and the prospect is qualified by the degree of interest in a given product or service.

Designed for businesses that deliver services, MAILFORM organizes telephone inquiries and produces individualized letters. Callers are also tracked as they progress from casual inquiry to confirmed sale. To build your business, MAILFORM does the following.

*Qualifies Callers.*   Prospective clients are categorized by their degree of interest in your product or service: casual inquiry (WARM) or likely purchase (HOT). COLD prospects are discarded.

*Generates Reports.*   New and prospective clients are reported daily to the manager.

*Maintains Client Information.*   All information is maintained on existing clients in the same dBASE II file.

*Automates Mail.*   Letters, reminders, and promotional notices can be sent automatically to the appropriate clients. Dates for subsequent contact can be entered as well.

## Stone Age Products Revisited

MAILFORM may not solve all of your problems in dealing with the public, but the daily mundane tasks are greatly minimized. Compare Stone Age's business if MAILFORM and other automated procedures had been implemented a few months before.

Barnaby again leaves for a few days. During this time, every time that a prospect called who was interested in a product in his service area, other staff members requested key information and entered it into the computer. Five calls were received the first day and five the second. Barnaby was handed the prospect list shown in Figure 3-1 by the manager when he returned.

The reports quickly inform Bumbler about which calls to return and what tactic to pursue. Stone Age recorded the sales shown in table 3-1 as a result.

Sales were generated by MAILFORM not only by the immediate calls, but also from the leads maintained in the TICKLER file. A TICKLE report last month had reminded Barnaby about a conversation last year with a government official. Bids for a large furniture contract were to be solicited six months in the future. Bumbler had instructed MAILFORM to prompt him in five months to compete for a slice of the action. The TICKLE report allowed him a month to prepare the bid. An initial letter of interest was automatically generated, and Barnaby had signed it and submitted it with the bidding, with apparent lucrative success.

### Table 3-1. Stone Age Sales with MAILFORM

| Number of messages | Sale? | Result or reason |
|---|---|---|
| 1 | Yes | Sale of Pitcairn Group. |
| 1 | Yes | Sale of Rock of Ages. |
| 1 | Yes | Sale of Stonehenge Special. |
| 1 | No | Can't buy now. Will be TICKLED and called in two months. Moving into house. |
| 1 | Yes | Caller needed sofa immediately. Was going to buy elsewhere. Stone Age threw in free ashtrays to close sale. |
| 1 | Yes | Caller needed recliner immediately. Was going to buy elsewhere. Stone Age lowered price, added same-day delivery. |
| 1 | No | Did not return call. Contributed to the indigent stonecutters' union last year. |
| 1 | No | Caller wanted quick answer to simple question: Do we sell beds too? (We don't). No need to return call; other staff answered the question. General brochure sent out. |
| 1 | Yes | Major client called to reward government contract. Paperwork for bid completed and sent last month. |
| 1 | Yes | Sold the Pitcairn Group. |

TODAY'S PHONE LISTING FOR PROSPECTS AND CLIENTS

| TITL | FIRST | LAST NAME | COMPANY | WORK PH. | HOME PH. | IN | QU | NOTES |
|------|-------|-----------|---------|----------|----------|-----|-----|-------|
| Mr. | Granite | Bedrock | Tower of Power | 432-847-8273 | 404-377-5273 | PA | S | Bought a trivet |
| Mr. | Charles | Pickens | Bide-A-Wee Nursery | 512-902-0922 | 504-434-9383 | PB | H | Just bought house |
| Ms. | Charles | Jones | Federal Gov't | 435-924-9309 | 435-827-8431 | PA | H | Bid contract |
| Ms. | William | Fossil | | | | | | |

*Figure 3-1.* Stone Age Sales Report (Partial List)

The calls were made, the sales were achieved, and several of the clients were TICKLED to be checked on at some future date. Barnaby planned his next itinerary, using the MAILFORM geographic report. He left the office with a steep commission in his pocket and the assurance of many more.

Within a very short time, the sales division was commended for its large increase in sales. Barnaby was appointed sales manager of the new Mastodon Icebox Division.

## SUMMARY

Both the non-automated and automated systems involve cost. Failure to implement a coordinated system of client communications costs time, sales, and aggravation. On the other hand, dBASE II and MAILFORM build sales, automate notification, and allow the staff to concentrate on selling and servicing.

# USING THE MAILFORM SYSTEM

To invoke MAILFORM, simply enter dBASE II from your computer's operating system and type DO MAILFORM. The computer will ask for the location of both the data (CLIENT) and other files, and the date. The following will appear on the screen as shown in Figure 4-1.

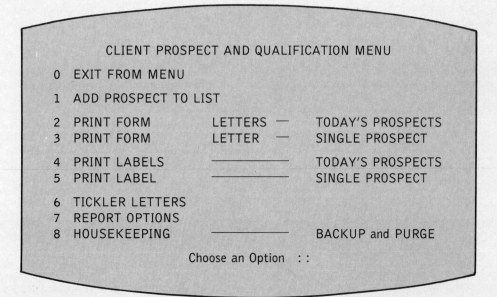

Figure 4-1. Operator's View of Mailform Menu

The main menu allows selection of the program's features. Each menu option activates (calls) another command file. Once processed, the menu is again displayed.

- Option 0 exits from dBASE II and restores the user to the operating system.
- Option 1 allows the operator to enter information into the computer while talking with the prospect on the telephone. No paper is needed.
- Option 2 prints an individually addressed letter. MAILFORM will choose a letter to print, according to the designated interest of the caller.
- Option 3 addresses and prints one selected form letter for a designated client.
- Option 4 addresses labels to all new prospects.
- Option 5 reprints a label for which a record number is entered.
- Option 6 is the TICKLER menu. A chosen letter will be sent to all prospects and clients after the allotted period.
- Option 7 offers a subordinate menu of reports. The names of prospects and the daily sales are summarized.
- Option 8 allows the operator to back up the files and eliminate data about leads gone cold.

## ENTERING CLIENT DATA: OPTION 1

Data is stored consistently on clients and prospects to serve several purposes. Phone numbers and addresses are collected to allow easy contact. A date for next contact is used by the TICKLER option to allow reminders to be generated later. Above all, the prospect is categorized by his degree of interest in any given product or service.

You are first asked to enter the next date that the client should be contacted. This is the TICKLE date. If none is required, enter today's date again. Once done, the MAILFORM entry screen is displayed (see Figure 4-2).

When answering telephone calls, each staff member should request the necessary information shown on the screen from the caller. The arrow and the RETURN keys allow movement to all the items on the screen, in any direction. As a convenience, the first letter of each of the name and address items will be forced to upper case. Numbers only will be accepted for the phone items. Enter the usual Mr., Ms., for the Title item. Entry is required, even if the staff member is on a first name basis with the caller. The form letter will not produce a polished heading without it. Always enter a last name, otherwise, MAILFORM will assume you wish to exit. MAILFORM recognizes this as the signal to return to the

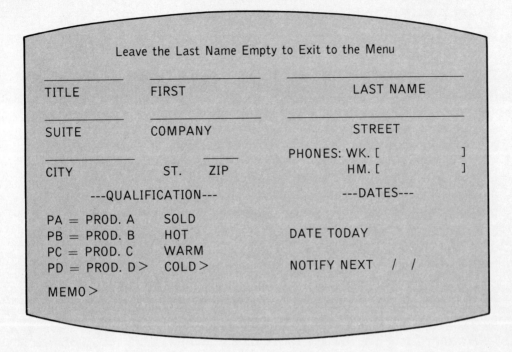

*Figure 4-2*   The Mailform Entry Screen

main menu. All client information will be saved except for this one last record.

The Qualification section requires the staff to assess which product the caller has expressed interest in and to note which one: PA, PB, PC, PD.[1] The caller's degree of interest is also gauged and noted, using the following designations:

|   |   |   |
|---|---|---|
| S | SOLD | The caller has bought the product. |
| H | HOT | A hot prospect. |
| W | WARM | Caller has expressed some interest. |
| C | COLD | Interest waned on the phone. |

The dates are displayed to the right in the YEAR/MONTH/DAY format. If the TICKLER date is not altered, the staff will be notified on the TICKLER date to contact the prospect. The operator may override the date with a unique date for this client. Use the DATE TODAY as a model for entering an alternative TICKLER date.

As many prospects can be entered at one time as desired. To exit, simply enter no information on one last record. The screen will clear and the main menu will again be displayed. Comprehensive records of each caller are retained on your computer by dBASE II and MAILFORM.

---

1. See Chapter 17 for Date and Time Mechanics.

25

# THE PRINTING OPTIONS: MENU SELECTIONS 2-7

The etiquette of business communication has undergone a rapid change in relation to technology. Good business practice formerly required that a handwritten personal note be sent by post to clients. Handwritten deliberation was replaced (with some reluctance) by typewriters and the photocopied form letter.

Electronic typewriters and then computers later allowed the placement of names and addresses into a client file. The headings and addresses were merged with a standard set of paragraphs to produce a letter. Like the shuffling and mixing of cards from both hands into one full deck, client data is merged with the boilerplate to produce the look of an individually typed letter. (see Figure 4-3)

MAILFORM produces labels and letters on all clients and prospects ever entered in the file. The standard option is to print letters and the labels (or envelopes) for the day's callers at the end of every business day.

## Option 2: Printing the Day's Form Letters

Letters will be selected and printed by MAILFORM according to the product discussed and degree of interest of each caller. You will need to compose at least one form letter for your company before using this option for the first time. (Entering Boilerplate Text is discussed in Chapter 5.)

The operator must first enter the date as it is to appear on the letters (i.e., September 30, 1983). The screen will clear and the choice of form letters must be entered.

A variety of options are available. MAILFORM looks for every prospect who called you on today's date. The product or service is first determined (PA, PB, PC, PD), then the degree of interest is determined.

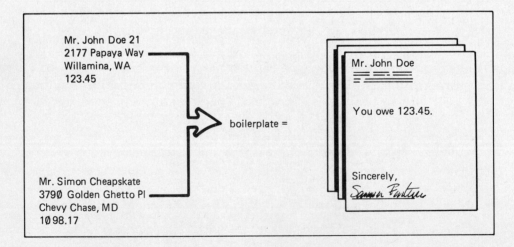

*Figure 4-3.* Shuffling Addresses and Letters: Merge-printing

As now designed, MAILFORM is structured to print a letter titled PRODUCTA.LTR if the client has been recorded as having an interest in this product (PA) and having purchased it ('S' for sold). The letter PRO-DUCTB.LTR is printed for a similar sale of that product.

Any client who does nct meet the standard of interest or degree automatically receives a catch-all letter, titled in this example as GENE-RAL.LTR on the directory. If GENERAL.LTR or any other is to be the only letter sent, simply type in its name for all three choices.

The entry of the selected letter criteria may look like Figure 4-4.

Letters may be added to the directory and the criteria to print this letter may easily be changed by changing the dBASE II code. Other people in the office may have done so. Every effort should be taken to be aware of any modifications to the program before the letters are printed.

Once the selections are established, the word WAITING will appear. Position your letterhead into the printer. Press any key to activate printing. The printer will respond after a short pause. A status message will be printed at the end of each letter.

```
Record Number XX Has Been Printed.

Ready the Printer for the Next Letter.
Press any Key to Continue.
```

Note the record number if the letter is unsatisfactory for any reason. Position the next letter in the printer and press any key to continue. The entire cycle will repeat until the last letter is printed. The main menu will then appear on the screen.

```
                    Mailform Letter Printer

        Prints form letters for unprinted Clients and Prospects.
        You will be given the choice of form letters.
        Choose your letter from the form letters below.
        Press Any Key to Continue.

   WAITING

   GENERAL.LTR          PRODUCTB.LTR          PRODUCTA.LTR

   Form letter for the GENERAL inquiry :general.ltr
   Form letter for the sale of Product A :producta.ltr
   Form letter for the sale of Product B :productb.ltr
   WAITING
```

*Figure 4-4.* Screen of Selected Letters

## Option 3: Printing a Single Letter

Problems in printing the day's form letters will be rare. Occasionally one letter will be smudged or not acceptable for some other reason. Option 2 was designed to print several letters at one time; Option 3 prints one designated letter only.

Option 3 requires entry of the record number in the client file before the proper name and address are printed. The record number was shown during the the initial printing of the record's address when Option 2 was chosen. The printing of the single letter can be done immediately if the record number of the misprinted letter was noted at that time. Otherwise, the record number must be found by LISTing the file. The operation to print one letter is otherwise the same as printing all of them (Option 2).

## Option 4: Printing the Day's Labels or Envelopes

Option 4 allows the printing of addresses on standard labels or envelopes for all of the day's callers. The order is the same as the form letters, which automates the matching of addresses and headings to envelopes, and letters.

The operator chooses to print the addresses on either envelopes or labels. Insert labels, if chosen, in the printer before proceeding. Arrange the labels so that the pattern shown in Figure 4-5 will be printed just within the boundaries of a label.

The LABELPRN routine has a test routine to print a few labels to align the print head precisely on the label and to ensure that the labels are properly positioned in the printer. Each test label should be completely filled with print, and the print head should be advanced to the first line of the next label.

The operator should print one test label, then position the labels until the printer prints a test that completely fills a label. No border should be visible. The top part of the word "TOP" should be positioned on the edge of the label, almost abutting the bottom of the word "BOTTOM" of the

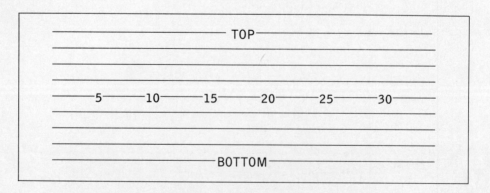

*Figure 4-5.* Label Boundaries

previous label. Once done, the labels are exactly positioned. The day's labels will be printed once the operator signals that there is no more need to print another test label.

Envelopes will be printed without a test pattern. Position the envelope in the carriage half-way down (lengthwise). The address will be indented over about 35 spaces. Once completed, the following message will be printed:

Position A New Envelope.

Press Any Key to Continue.

The program will announce that all of the addresses for the day's calls were printed. A press of any key returns to the main menu.

## Option 5: Printing a Single Label or Envelope

Option 5 operates by the same method as Option 4 and serves the same purpose for labels as Option 2 does for letters. Damaged labels can be singly replaced by positioning the labels in the printer and entering the record number of the name and address.

## Option 6: The TICKLER Letter Option

One of the most powerful features is the TICKLER option. The TICKLER option automatically notifies prospects of a pre-determined date. A TICKLE date was stored when the name of a caller was first entered. A series of form letters can be printed like the other letters, but the TICKLER option will allow letters to be printed only for the names that have the TICKLE date matching today's date; people will not be notified either before or after their time.

The operation is exactly like the printing of labels and letters. You may wish to print the TICKLER materials at the same time as the day's form letter and labels.

## Option 7: The Report Options

Reports should be generated at the end of each business day. The reports about calls can be postponed, however, until convenient. MAILFORM prints letters and labels only for records that have never before generated a listing.

Please note: Many of the reports require the printer to produce at least 130 characters per line. Most dot matrix printers can be commanded to do this, and most daisy wheel printers have a wide carriage that allows this print if wide paper is used. See Chapter 5 for the modifications if not already performed.

Option 7 of the main MAILFORM clears the screen and offers a sub-menu of the various reports as shown in Figure 4-6.

Option 0 exits the report sub-menu and returns to the main MAIL-FORM menu.

Position the paper in the printer and turn the printer on before selecting any option other than 0 or 9.

Options 1–7 prepare two client reports. One is the phone report, which lists the name of the client and any other information necessary to contact the client by telephone (see Figure 4-7). The second is the address report, which lists the phone and address (see Figure 4-8). These options differ only by the order by which the prospects are printed. The NAME report is alphabetical by last name. The COMPANY option produces the list of clients in order of the name of the company. PRODUCT and INTEREST reports order clients first by product (PA, PB, PC, PD). Within each product is the degree of interest (HOT, SOLD, WARM, etc.).

Option 7 gives the traveling salespeople the list of prospects by geographical area. Prospects within each area code for each state are printed. An itinerary can be planned from the report.

Option 8 is the QUICK LIST report. A simple report in the order that the callers phoned will be produced, without the waiting required for dBASE II to organize the prospects by names.

Option 9 totals the active prospects and clients for the day. The letters and labels that were printed are totaled as well.

Do not be alarmed if the printing does not occur immediately. The organizing of some of the files in a given order takes a short time.

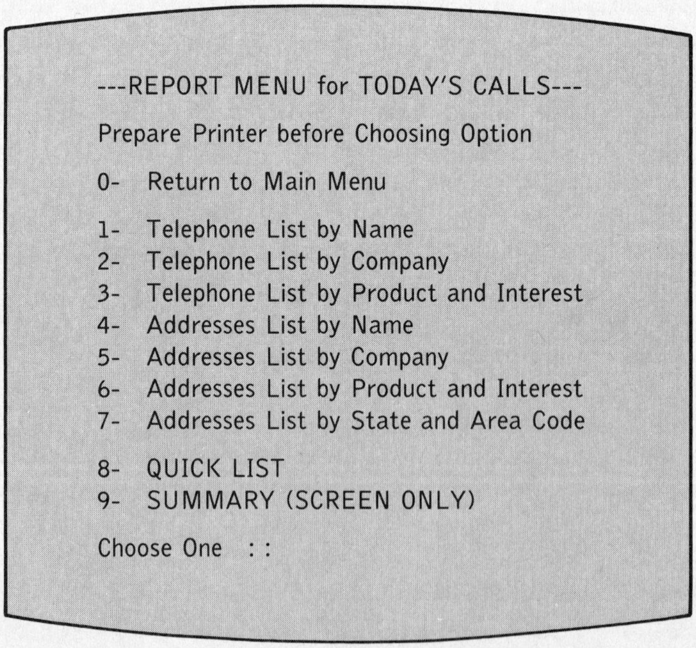

```
---REPORT MENU for TODAY'S CALLS---

Prepare Printer before Choosing Option

0-   Return to Main Menu

1-   Telephone List by Name
2-   Telephone List by Company
3-   Telephone List by Product and Interest
4-   Addresses List by Name
5-   Addresses List by Company
6-   Addresses List by Product and Interest
7-   Addresses List by State and Area Code

8-   QUICK LIST
9-   SUMMARY (SCREEN ONLY)

Choose One  : :
```

*Figure 4-6.* The Report Sub-menu Screen

## TODAY'S PHONE LISTING FOR PROSPECTS AND CLIENTS

| TITL | FIRST | LAST NAME | COMPANY | WORK PH. | HOME PH. | IN | QU | NOTES |
|---|---|---|---|---|---|---|---|---|
| Mr. | Granite | Bedrock | Tower of Power | 432-847-8273 | 404-377-5273 | PA | S | Bought a trivet |
| Mr. | Charles | Pickens | Bide-A-Wee Nursery | 512-902-0922 | 504-434-9383 | PB | H | Just bought house |
| Mr. | Charles | Jones | Federal Gov't | 435-924-9309 | 435-827-8431 | PA | H | Bid contract |
| Ms. | William | Fossil | | 607-923-8245 | | PC | S | |

*Figure 4-7.* The CLIENT Phone Report

## TODAY'S ADDRESSES OF PROSPECTS AND CLIENTS

| TITL | LAST NAME | COMPANY | STREET | CITY | ST/ZIP | WK PHONE | IN | QU |
|---|---|---|---|---|---|---|---|---|
| Mr. | Bedrock | Tower of Power | 1 Petunia Way | Bedrock | IA 30302 | 432-847-8273 | PA | S |
| Mr. | Pickens | Bide-A-Wee Nursery | 43 Longfellow | Carlsbad Caverns | NM 23546 | 512-902-0922 | PB | H |
| Mr. | Jones | Federal Gov't | 18 Tower Pl | Rock City | TN 29825 | 435-924-9309 | PA | H |
| Ms. | Fossil | | 864 Hunter L. | Muncie | IA 39232 | 607-923-8245 | PC | S |

*Figure 4-8.* The ADDRESS Report

## HOUSEKEEPING: MENU SELECTION 9

The client file requires periodic attention in the same manner that a house requires seasonal cleaning. The options in this sub-menu maintain the client records. Press Option 9 in the main MAILFORM menu to display the housekeeping options, illustrated in Figure 4-9.

Backing up the records is a major duty. Serious consequences to your business may occur if your data was damaged or altered in some manner. The first housekeeping option creates a copy of the data on another floppy disk, or on a hard disk drive if one is used.

Select Option 1 to back up the file. Prepare another disk drive for copying. The program will ask you for a filename and the drive on which the backup will be copied. Be very cautious about the choice of a filename: If a name is given that matches a file on the destination drive, the new data will erase the old file and will be written over it. Remove the backup disk once it is completed and store it in a safe place.

The other options address the problem of unwanted records. Many records that reside on the disk are no longer useful. Valuable storage space is wasted—a problem not immediately evident in daily operation. The records, however, slow down the printing or reporting of the useful records, which is noticeably irritating. Both problems are minimized by weeding out the unwanted records. Option 2 eliminates all records *except* clients. There are times when you may want all prospects to be deleted, leaving only the clients in the file. Exercise this option with care because once it is chosen, the warm and hot prospects cannot be recovered.

Option 3 retains all active prospects and clients. The records designated as COLD were "backed out" during entry.

COLD and WARM prospects are eliminated in Option 4. Prospects who were initially categorized WARM are not marked to be deleted, but they serve an increasingly limited purpose as time progresses.

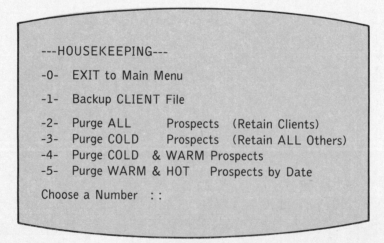

```
---HOUSEKEEPING---

-0-   EXIT to Main Menu

-1-   Backup CLIENT File

-2-   Purge ALL        Prospects  (Retain Clients)
-3-   Purge COLD       Prospects  (Retain ALL Others)
-4-   Purge COLD  & WARM Prospects
-5-   Purge WARM & HOT    Prospects by Date

Choose a Number  : :
```

*Figure 4-9.* HOUSEKEEPING Menu - Screen Presentations

The last option (Option 5), like Option 3, also allows WARM and HOT prospects to be eliminated. They can, however, be selectively deleted by the date of first calling. You will be asked for a date. Any prospects on or before that date will be deleted. All clients will be retained; all COLD prospects will be erased.

The disk drive will be busy for several moments during the use of any of the housekeeping options. The main MAILFORM menu will then be on the screen once the backup or purge is completed. Faster operation times may be noted once the unwanted records have been deleted.

## RECOMMENDED ORDER OF USE

The printer must be set up differently for labels, which require a special tractor feeder, than for letters, which do not. The easiest way to reduce setups is to print all the letters for the day, then the labels. When done, print the reports. Run the housekeeping as needed.

*Table 4-1.  Recommended Order and Frequency of MAILFORM Use*

*Letters*

| | | |
|---|---|---|
| Clients/Prospects | Daily | Mail |
| Corrections | Daily | Mail |
| Ticklers | Daily | Salesperson |

*Envelopes or Labels*

| | | |
|---|---|---|
| Clients/Prospects | Daily | Mail |
| Corrections | Daily | Mail |

*Reports*

| | | |
|---|---|---|
| Clients/Prospects | Daily | Sales Manager |
| Geographic | As needed | Salesperson |

*Housekeeping*

| | |
|---|---|
| Backup | Daily, minimum Weekly |
| Purge | Weekly, minimum Monthly |

## SUMMARY

The MAILFORM program and dBASE II will serve you well to boost communication with clients and prospects. As you become more accustomed to its operation, other uses will be apparent. The program can be easily installed and modified to serve these other purposes. Chapter 5 outlines the installation and the principles of operation.

# 5

## INSTALLING MAILFORM

Several types of dBASE files are used in the MAILFORM system. All information is stored in CLIENT.DBF, the database file. The purpose of all other files is to verify, enter, and generate reports or addresses from this file.

The system is named after the main menu, a command file that provides the operator with all of the main program options. The MAILFORM main menu calls other command files to process the information or produce the letters. The remaining other files configure the entry screen (.FMT files), or reports (.FRM files).

## CLIENT.DBF  THE ITEMS OF CLIENT INFORMATION

The heart of the MAILFORM system is the client file, appropriately titled CLIENT. Information on all clients and prospects is stored in this file. All letters, labels, and promotional reminders are generated from CLIENT. Type CREATE CLIENT at the dot prompt in dBASE II. Enter the following information after each field number (see Figure 5-1).

Exit the CREATE mode and type DISPLAY STRUCTURE. dBASE II should give you the following message:

** TOTAL ** 00204

*Table 5-1.  List of Files and Main Functions*

| File Name | Stands For | Function |
|-----------|-----------|----------|
| CLIENT.DBF | Client file | Retains client data |
| MAILFORM.CMD | Mail formulator | Main menu |
| CLIENTIN.CMD | Client input | Enters client data |
| ENTRYSCN.FMT | Entry screen | Formats entry of data |
| FORMLETR.CMD | Form letter | Prints form letters |
| SINGLTR.CMD | Single letter | Prints one letter |
| LABELPRN.CMD | Label printer | Prints all labels |
| SINGLAB.CMD | Single label | Prints one label |
| RPTMENU.CMD | Report menu | Sub-menu of reports |
| ADDRESS.FRM | Address form | Report configuration |
| PHONE.FRM | Phone # form | Report configuration |
| HOUSEKP.CMD | Housekeeping | File backup |
| TICKLETT.CMD | Tickler letter | Prints tickler letters |

*Utility Files Used (On Drive A)*
INIT.CMD
DTVERIFY.CMD

Carefully check that your database has the same total and that the fields are identical in name, type, and length.

Once completed, you have a framework that can store all essential information for client tracking. The CLIENT.DBF database can be easily modified. However, familiarity with the MAILFORM system is recom-

| FLD | NAME | TYPE | WIDTH | DEC |
|-----|------|------|-------|-----|
| 001 | MR:MS | C | 004 | |
| 002 | FIRSTNAME | C | 015 | |
| 003 | LASTNAME | C | 020 | |
| 004 | COMPANY | C | 020 | |
| 005 | SUITE:ETC | C | 015 | |
| 006 | STREET | C | 025 | |
| 007 | CITY | C | 025 | |
| 008 | ST | C | 002 | |
| 009 | ZIP | C | 005 | |
| 010 | WKPHONE | C | 012 | |
| 011 | HMPHONE | C | 012 | |
| 012 | INTEREST | C | 002 | |
| 013 | NOTE | C | 020 | |
| 014 | QUALIFIED | C | 001 | |
| 015 | TICKLER | C | 008 | |
| 016 | ORIGDATE | C | 008 | |
| 017 | LASTMAIL | C | 008 | |
| 018 | NOWMAILED | L | 001 | |

*Figure 5-1.*  Entry Information to Build Client File

mended before these changes are made. A description of each field and its use is below.

## Table 5-2. Description of the Client Database

| NAME OF FIELD | DESCRIPTION OF FIELD |
|---|---|
| MR:MS | Mr., Mrs., Ms. Four characters are allowed, including the period. |
| FIRSTNAME | First name. |
| LASTNAME | Last name. |
| COMPANY | Company name, if applicable. |
| SUITE:ETC | Suite, apartment, post office box. |
| CITY | City of residence. |
| ST | State of residence. Space is reserved for the two-letter abbreviation. |
| ZIP | The five-digit zip code. |
| WKPHONE | Area code and local work phone number, including hyphens. |
| HMPHONE | Area code and home phone number. |
| INTEREST | This field determines the prospect's interest in your business, i.e., product A as distinguished from product B. |
| NOTE | A short descriptive line of 20 characters can be entered here, to highlight to the manager special information. |
| QUALIFIED | This field categorizes the prospective client into four categories: COLD, WARM, HOT, and SOLD. |
| TICKLER | A date for subsequent follow-up. |
| ORIGDATE | The ORIGinal DATE of the client's call. |
| LASTMAILED | The last date of correspondence. |
| NOWDATE | Today's date. |
| NOWMAILED | This field indicates that a letter and label have been printed on the LASTMAILED date. |

# MAILFORM.CMD   MAIN MENU

There are three sections of the MAILFORM menu:

## Section I: The Housekeeping

The Housekeeping section documents the name of the command file. The operator determines where the program and data files are to be found. Two utilities, INIT.CMD and DTVERIFY.CMD, verify that previous files and programs are closed and that the system date is correctly entered.

## Section II: The Prompt.

The Prompt section informs the operator of the various options of the MAILFORM system. The operator is presented with lines across the page by the use of dBASE SAY statements. The entry by the operator is obtained by the GET command and is assigned to the variable called CHOICE. The PICTURE statement allows only a single character to be entered.

### Section III: The CASE.

The CASE statement executes a command chosen as an option chosen by the operator. Due to brevity, no provision has been made in the menu for editing and deleting records; these can be done directly to records in CLIENT.DBF by use of the EDIT and DELETE commands. You will find that other staff members easily become accustomed to these simple dBASE II commands.

The DO WHILE/ENDDO loop is used in MAILFORM to allow easy operation of more than one menu option without again typing DO MAIL-FORM.

CODE FOR MAILFORM.CMD

```
* MAILFORM.CMD
* module purpose: to control options for mailform system
* monitors and tracks client prospects and qualification
* controls printing of form letters and labels
* generates reports

* *********** SECTION I ****** HOUSEKEEPING

DO a:init

ERASE

SET default to &dfdefault
USE CLIENT
SET default to &pfdefault

DO a:dtverify
* Establish System Dates
* One for the file - YY/MM/DD (mfiledate)
* One for viewing - DD/MM/YY (mviewdate)
* See Chapter 17 On Dates and Durations
STORE viewdate to mviewdate
STORE filedate to mfiledate

DO WHILE t

    * ****** SECTION II **** PROMPT PROCEDURE

STORE ' ' TO choice
ERASE
@ 2,14 SAY "CLIENT PROSPECT AND QUALIFICATION MENU "
@ 5,10 SAY "0 EXIT FROM MENU "
@ 7,10 SAY "1 ADD PROSPECT TO LIST "
@ 8,10 SAY "2 PRINT FORM LETTERS -- TODAY'S PROSPECTS"
```

```
@ 9,10 SAY "3 PRINT FORM LETTER -- SINGLE PROSPECT "
@ 11,10 SAY "4 PRINT LABELS ---------- TODAY'S PROSPECTS"
@ 12,10 SAY "5 PRINT LABEL ---------- SINGLE PROSPECT "
@ 14,10 SAY "6 TICKLER LETTERS"
@ 15,10 SAY "7 REPORT OPTIONS"
@ 17,10 SAY "8 HOUSEKEEPING --------- BACKUP and PURGE "
@ 20,15 SAY "Choose an Option " GET choice PICTURE '#'
READ

* ********** SECTION III *********** CASE PROCEDURE
DO CASE
    CASE choice= '0'
        QUIT
    CASE choice= '1'
        DO clientin
    CASE choice= '2'
        DO formletr
    CASE choice= '3'
        DO singltr
    CASE choice= '4'
        DO labelprn
    CASE choice= '5'
        DO singlab
    CASE choice= '6'
        DO ticklett
    CASE choice= '7'
        DO rptmenu
    CASE choice= '8'
        DO housekp

    OTHERWISE
        @ 22,10 SAY " Invalid Choice. Press Any Key to Resume. "
        WAIT
        ERASE
    ENDCASE

ENDDO t
```

## PAINTING A SCREEN WITH THE ENTRYSCN FORMAT FILE

CLIENTIN formats the screen by calling ENTRYSCN.FMT, a format file. A format file is a series of SAY and GET statements saved as another file.

Although the MODIFY command can be used to enter EN-TRYSCN.FMT, the use of a word processor is recommended. Enter each statement exactly as detailed. The number of characters in the PICTURE clauses for each field is identical to those in CLIENT.

CODE FOR ENTRYSCN.FMT

```
* ENTRYSCN.FMT
* Paints Screen with Prompts for Easy Entry into CLIENT.DBF

@ 1,15 SAY "Leave the Last Name Empty to Exit to the Menu"
@ 3, 5 GET mr:ms PICTURE "!XXX"
@ 3,25 GET firstname PICTURE "!XXXXXXXXXXXXX"
@ 3,50 GET lastname PICTURE "!XXXXXXXXXXXXXXXXXXXXXXX"
@ 4, 5 SAY "^____^"
@ 4,25 SAY "^_____^"
@ 4,50 SAY "^_____^"
@ 5, 5 SAY "TITLE"
@ 5,25 SAY "FIRST"
@ 5,62 SAY "LAST NAME"
@ 7, 5 GET suite:etc PICTURE "!XXXXXXXXXXXXX"
@ 7,25 GET company PICTURE "!XXXXXXXXXXXXXXXXXX"
@ 7,50 GET street PICTURE "!XXXXXXXXXXXXXXXXXXXXXX"
@ 8, 5 SAY "^_____^"
@ 8,25 SAY "^_____^"
@ 8,50 SAY "^_____^"
@ 9, 5 SAY "SUITE"
@ 9,25 SAY "COMPANY"
@ 9,62 SAY "STREET"
@ 11, 5 GET city PICTURE "!XXXXXXXXXXXXXXXXXXXXXXXXX"
@ 11,35 GET st PICTURE "!!"
@ 11,40 GET zip PICTURE "#####"
@ 12, 5 SAY "^_____^"
@ 12,35 SAY "^^ ^_____^"
@ 12,50 SAY "PHONES: WK. ["
@ 12,63 GET wkphone PICTURE "###-###-####"
@ 12,75 SAY "]"
@ 13,05 SAY "CITY"
@ 13,35 SAY "ST. ZIP"
@ 13,58 SAY "HM. ["
@ 13,63 GET hmphone PICTURE "###-###-####"
@ 13,75 SAY "]"
@ 15,15 SAY "---- QUALIFICATION ----"
@ 15,55 SAY "---- DATES ----"
@ 17, 5 SAY "PA = PROD. A"
@ 18, 5 SAY "PB = PROD. B"
@ 19, 5 SAY "PC = PROD. C"
@ 20, 5 SAY "PD = PROD. D>"
@ 20,20 GET interest PICTURE "!!"
@ 17,35 SAY "SOLD"
@ 18,35 SAY "HOT"
@ 19,35 SAY "WARM"
@ 20,35 SAY "COLD>"
@ 20,40 GET qualified PICTURE "!"
@ 18,50 SAY "DATE TODAY"
@ 18,63 SAY mfiledate
@ 20,50 SAY "NOTIFY NEXT"
```

```
@ 20,63 GET tickler PICTURE "##/##/##"
@ 22, 5 SAY "MEMO>"
@ 22,10 GET NOTE
```

Save the file as ENTRYSC.FMT and verify upon completion that the file name is correct. To examine your handiwork, place this file on your program disk. At the dBASE dot-prompt, type:

```
USE CLIENT
SET COLON OFF
APPEND BLANK
SET FORMAT TO ENTRYSCN
READ
```

You should be rewarded with the screen shown in Figure 5-2.

## CLIENTIN.CMD  THE CLIENT ENTRY PROGRAM

CLIENTIN accomplishes two purposes. First, the entry of data necessary to contact the caller is monitored, and second, (and equally important) is the determination of the caller's interest in the product or service.

CLIENTIN stores in each record the information necessary for the TICKLER option in the main menu. Follow-up letters can be generated

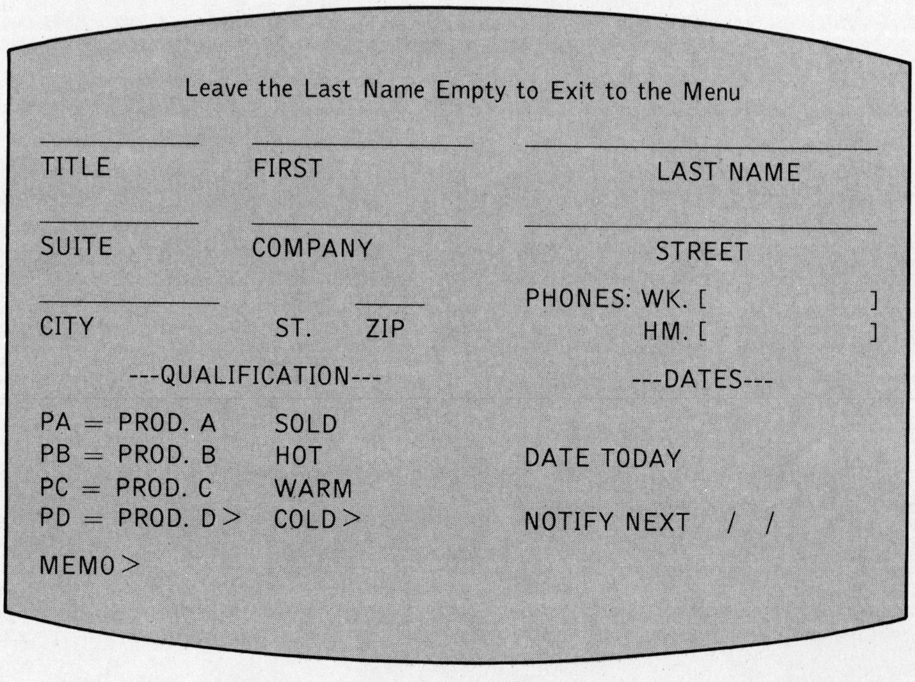

*Figure 5-2.*  ENTRYSCN.FMT  A Formatted Screen for Mailform

after any period has transpired. A report is also produced so that the sales manager can contact hot prospects and possibly close more sales.

Like the MAILFORM menu, the program CLIENTIN.CMD can be segmented into three major sections. Each has a specialized function.

### Section I: Housekeeping

Documentation and the overall characteristics of the command file are established in this section. The screen is cleared and the file is opened. The default date for the tickler field is entered into a memory variable, MTICKLER, which will be carried through each entry and displayed on the screen.

### Section II: Screen Generation and Prompting

This section prepares CLIENT for entry of a record and calls the format file. ENTRYSCN paints the screen and prompts the operator to enter the information. ERASE is used to clear the screen just before entry of a record, and an empty record is constructed by the APPEND BLANK command.

SET FORMAT TO ENTRYSCRN calls up a file that formats the screen. ENTRYSCRN contains the SAY/GET and PICTURE commands. The READ statement, when executed, inserts all the data into the corresponding fields of the temporary file.

dBASE II can format data to or from only one of three possible devices at a time: the screen, the printer, or a specialized file called a format file (see Figure 5-3). When a command SET FORMAT TO ENTRYSCRN is typed, statements from only this file can be read. Every READ statement

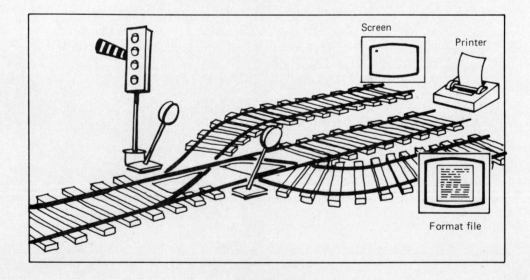

*Figure 5-3.* Switching the Screen/Printer/Format File Source

will query this ENTRYSCRN file for the SAY/GET commands and paint the entry screen. However, in Section III of our routine (CLIENTIN), the operator will be asked to respond to prompts that do not originate in the format file. These also use READ statements. The command SET FORMAT TO SCREEN toggles control from ENTRYSCRN.FMT back to our CLIENTIN command file.

## Section III: Client Qualification

The entry is verified in Section III. An empty LASTNAME field halts the processing of CLIENTIN, and clears all variables, and returns to the menu. Information has been obtained, verified, polished, and stored in the CLIENT file.

The MAILFORM system depends upon the operator's answer to the two questions at the bottom of the entry screen. These concern the type and extent of interest in the product or services. If the prospect is designated as WARM, HOT, or SOLD, the record will be added to the corresponding report at the end of the day.

Two dates are also placed into each record. The system date for the first entry of the client or prospect is put into the ORIGDATE field of the CLIENT file. The default date for the next notification can be overridden by the operator and a new tickler date entered into the TICKLER field for that particular entry. Dates are stored in the YEAR/MONTH/DAY format.

An entry that is nearly completed can be halted before the record is posted to the file. Designating the prospect as COLD aborts the entry by deleting the record.

The entire process is repeated by the use of the DO WHILE/ENDDO loop, until the operator chooses to exit by stepping through one last record with the LASTNAME field left empty. Control is returned to the MAILFORM menu.

CODE FOR CLIENTIN.CMD

```
* CLIENTIN.CMD

* ************ section I ******* housekeeping
* entry routine for mailform series
* enters records into client.dbf
* called by mailform menu
* uses entryscn.fmt format file to paint screen

* SET talk OFF
ERASE
USE client

* Establish global date for tickler file
STORE "What Is the Next Notification Date? " to prompt
DO a:dtverify
store ' ' to prompt
```

```
* SEE CHAPTER 17 FOR DESCRIPTION OF DATE ARITHMETIC
* Bring in verified date from dtverify into this routine


If filedate = mfiledate
   ERASE
   @ 10,05 SAY '#** WARNING! Cannot TICKLE on same data as first letter.
   @ 12,05 SAY ' Exit to Menu. Re-enter and Correct.'
   WAIT
ENDIF filedate = mfiledate
STORE filedate to mtickler

* ****** end of section I ******

* ******** set up DO WHILE loop ******
STORE t TO onemore
DO WHILE onemore


       * ******* section II ****************
       * screen generation and entry

       ERASE
       APPEND BLANK
       REPLACE tickler WITH mtickler

       SET colon off
       SET FORMAT TO entryscn
       READ
       SET FORMAT to screen
       SET colon on

       * ********** section III ************************
       * verification of information entered
       * prompting for additional information
       * return to menu

       IF lastname= ' '
           * main method of exiting routine
           * operator has entered null record to exit
           * first nullify this entry by deleting record

           DELETE

           * housekeeping before exiting
           RELEASE mtickler,forget,prompt,onemore
           RETURN
       ENDIF lastname

IF qualified= "C"
        ERASE
STORE f to forget
@ 10, 5 SAY " PROSPECT is NO LONGER Interested. "
@ 12, 5 SAY " Do You Wish to Mark for Deletion (T/F)? " GET forget
READ
```

```
        IF forget
              DELETE
              LOOP
        ENDIF forget
    ENDIF "C"

    IF qualified < > "C"
        * Lead is not Cold
        * Consider as a Prospect and record second mailing date
        REPLACE tickler with mtickler
    ENDIF qualified= < > "C"

    * add today's date into record
    REPLACE origdate WITH mfiledate

  ENDDO onemore
```

The MAILFORM system can now accept and store your client information. The menu, which also carries the name of the system, controls the selection of the various options. The CLIENTIN command file processes the entry of information into the CLIENT data file. Screen entry is painted (formatted) by the ENTRYSCN format file.

## MERGING OF DATA AND LETTERS

Your new storehouse of client information will be used to contact clients at a later date. The command files in the next chapter will address labels and produce attractive letters that appear individually typed. The MAILFORM system has several advantages over a word processor (such as the Wordstar with Mailmerge combination) in the generation of form letters. These, and the techniques of precision printing, will be illustrated.

Several popular word processors manage words and arrange them in a highly attractive format, with corrected spelling, hyphenation, and justification. However, they do not currently manage data such as making selections, extracting a partial list of names from a larger file under certain conditions (all who live in a certain zip code or those who did not pay their bills last month). dBASE II shines at the latter. On the other hand, dBASE II was never intended to check spelling or hyphenate words.

There are circumstances where the use of dBASE II to generate text is warranted: When the boilerplate is to be limited to two or three paragraphs and will be rarely revised, and when addresses must be selectively extracted from the file and merged with the boilerplate. Under these conditions, dBASE II is a candidate to handle the processing of both data (the addresses) and the words (the form letters).

The MAILFORM print routines illustrate the use of dBASE II to work with words, creating form letters and labels under a variety of conditions. The routines are highly automated. Depending upon the entry of the prospect or client, the appropriate form letter is chosen and the client's record is flagged indicating that the printing is to occur. The letters are printed as a group at the end of the day, along with labels for the envelopes.

dBASE II also further tracks the printing. The date of printing will be placed into the record so that checks can be run later if there is some question that a key client was not notified.

All automated letter writing works on the same principles illustrated above. The file contains the addresses. The boilerplate is the body of the letter, which is used for many letters but appears to be written individually for each recipient.

In the dBASE program FORMLETR.CMD, data is taken from fields in the CLIENT database, assembled into an address or heading, and sent to the printer by the use of common dBASE printing commands (see Figure 5-4). Several techniques are emphasized:

1. Using dBASE commands to select records to generate an address.
2. Polishing the appearance of the address once the information is found.
3. Printing the contents of the field using the WHAT IS command ( ?).
4. Using @ SAY statements as an alternative to enable printing positioned by coordinates.

## THE MAILFORM PRINT ROUTINES

### Letters and Labels

There are four command files used by MAILFORM to print the necessary letters and labels. These command files are responsible for the selection

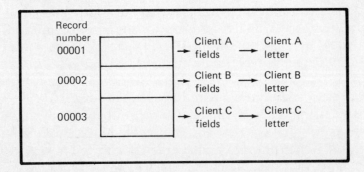

*Figure 5-4.* Printing from a dBase Client File

of the form letters and the printing of letters and labels. All work is done on the same principles outlined above, which can be used by the business person in other printing routines.

FORMLETR.CMD        Prints form letters for all prospects that called. Selects a proper letter for each client or prospect. Prints all in one batch at the close of day.

SINGLTR.CMD        Prints one form letter for one client. Used in case of error during batch print.

LABELPRN.CMD        Prints labels for all letters generated by FORMLETR.

SINGLAB.CMD        Prints label for one address in file. Used in case of error during batch print of labels.

The other files required are the form letters. Many different letters can be created. We shall use three names of letters as examples:

GENERAL.LTR        Letter for general prospects informing them of your service.

PRODUCTA.LTR        Letter welcoming a client who purchased Product or Service A to your firm.

PRODUCTB.LTR        Letter welcoming a client who purchased Product or Service B to your firm.

Note that all files end with LTR. dBASE uses several types of files and automatically places a suffix after each (.DBF, .FMT, .MEM, .FRM, .NDX, .CMD) if they are generated by dBASE. The operator or programmer, however, can name files with any suffix and can use them if the entire name is used, i.e., DO GENERAL.LTR is called by its entire name, including the .LTR extension.

# FORMLETR.CMD   THE FORM LETTER GENERATOR

*Basic Operation*

FORMLETR is the key MAILFORM print routine. The program uses all the precision printing principles to merge the names and addresses for the CLIENT file with the boilerplate. After housekeeping is accomplished, the operator is prompted to select any three letters from any form letters that are on the disk. The proper boilerplate will be extracted and printed, depending upon the input into CLIENT by the operator when the prospect first called. The letters can be remarkably different, depending upon the entry by the operator at that earlier time (see Figure 5-5).

   Like the MAILFORM main menu, the code for FORMLETR.CMD is also separated into four sections. The first and last perform the housekeeping functions, the second performs the prompting and selec-

## Entry A yields this

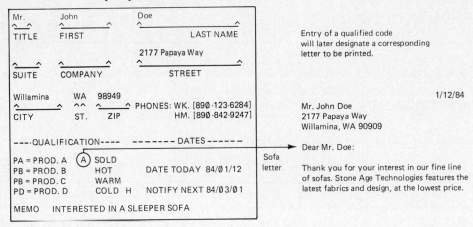

Entry of a qualified code
will later designate a corresponding
letter to be printed.

1/12/84

Mr. John Doe
2177 Papaya Way
Willamina, WA 90909

Dear Mr. Doe:

Thank you for your interest in our fine line
of sofas. Stone Age Technologies features the
latest fabrics and design, at the lowest price.

## Entry B yields this

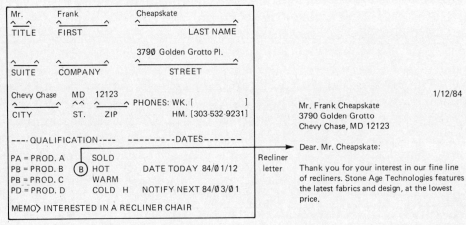

1/12/84

Mr. Frank Cheapskate
3790 Golden Grotto
Chevy Chase, MD 12123

Dear. Mr. Cheapskate:

Thank you for your interest in our fine line
of recliners. Stone Age Technologies features
the latest fabrics and design, at the lowest
price.

*Figure 5-5.* Examples of Merged Printing

48

tion of the letters, and the third arranges the information into an attractive address.

### Section I: Basic Housekeeping

Note that the last record in the file is stored to the variable called COUNTER. Since all prospects are added sequentially, this was the last record added in the batch that requires printing.

### Section II: Operator Prompting and Letter Selection

Section II prompts the operator with @ SAY statements. Three new techniques are of value. These are WAIT, SET CONSOLE ON, and SET CONSOLE OFF. To stop and wait for operator entry, the WAIT command is often used. This, however, puts the word WAITING on the screen. SET CONSOLE OFF suppresses the WAITING and any other message on the screen. SET CONSOLE ON resumes screen operation.

The command LIST FILES LIKE *.LTR will do a disk directory on the default drive and show all filenames that end in the .LTR extension.

=== TECH TIP ===

*Use of File and List File Like Commands*

*To list all files on the default disk use:*

*LIST FILES LIKE *.**

*To check for existence of a file use:*

*IF FILE (filename)*
  *[do one thing]*
*ELSE*
  *[do another]*
*ENDIF*

The FILE command also does a directory. A requested filename is entered by the operator to one of the CHOICE variables (by use of the ACCEPT) command. The FILE command within a DO WHILE loop checks the filename stored in the CHOICE variable until the operator has chosen a boilerplate file that exists on the disk.

### Section III: Operator Prompting and Letter Selection

Section III merges the data in CLIENT with the text in the boilerplate, using all the precision printing principles. The first unaddressed record in CLIENT is first found by use of the LOCATE command. Both standard statements (?) and @ SAY commands are sent to the printer with SET FORMAT TO PRINT and SET PRINT ON.

dBASE has a command to set margins to accommodate a wide variety of printer settings. You probably use your printer for a number of applications: spreadsheets, envelopes, letters of all widths. In a shared office environment, each of these usually requires different placements of the paper. The changing of the printer's margins can be time-consuming and irritating.

Make the software do the work. Always establish one margin on the printer and never change it. Tell the dBASE program what margin is desired, rather than changing the machine. SET MARGIN to 8 allows 8 columns to be added on the left, the same standard margin used by Wordstar.

The date and address are printed first. The CASE structure allows the choice of the letter depending upon the contents of the CLIENT record and the conditions for selection. In this example, the two conditions of product and interest are imposed: the Product A letter is printed if the field QUALIFIED contains 'S' (for SOLD) and the INTEREST field contains 'PA' (for product A). The Product B letter will be printed if the INTEREST field contains 'PB' and QUALIFED also contains an 'S' for each prospect record. All other letters invoke the OTHERWISE command, and GENERAL.LTR is selected.

Once selected, the form letter can be printed. Each letter is a command file which consists simply of statements to be printed. As with all other command files, the LTR files are invoked by using the DO command with the name of the file (DO GENERAL.LTR). The paragraphs and closing to the letter are printed and control is returned to FORM-LETR, which issues the EJECT command to expel the page from the printer. The record is updated with the information that the printing has been accomplished, by changing the NOWMAILED field to TRUE.

The next statements inform the operator of the printing progress. All messages to the printer are defeated (SET PRINT OFF/SET FORMAT TO SCREEN). The record number is displayed by the use of a special purpose command, # , the current record number function. The COUNTER variable, which was determined in Housekeeping, had the total number of records in the CLIENT database file. The remainder to be printed (counter − #) is displayed to the operator. The operator is prompted to insert another letter in the printer.

Section III will continue merging all the unprinted records in the CLIENT file into the proper form letter until all records are printed and the end of the file is reached.

### Section IV: Housekeeping before Exiting

The last section of FORMLETR resets the margin to the normal value and eliminates unwanted variables. Control is returned to the MAIL-FORM main menu.

CODE FOR FORMLETR.CMD

```
* formletr.cmd
* module purpose: prints day's letters
* choses proper form letters from list
* chosen by operator before execution
```

\* updates file that printing has occurred

\* SECTION I- HOUSEKEEPING
\* Go to the first record of the file
\* GO TOP

25 spaces

\* Get Spelled Out Version of date
ERASE
STORE '                              ' TO spelldate
@ 5,5 SAY "Please spell out today's date for the letter " GET spelldate
READ

\* SECTION II - Select Form Letters
\* Place prompts and directory of form letters on screen
ERASE
@ 3,30 SAY 'Mailform Letter Printer'
@ 5,10 SAY 'Prints form letters for unprinted Clients and Prospects.'
@ 6,10 SAY 'You will be given the choice of form letters.'
@ 7,10 SAY 'Choose your letter from the form letters below.'
@ 8,10 SAY 'Press Any Key to Continue.'

SET CONSOLE OFF
WAIT
SET CONSOLE ON

LIST files LIKE *.ltr

STORE ' ' TO CHOICE1,CHOICE2,CHOICE3

\* Ensure that existing form letters are selected
DO WHILE .not. FILE(choice1)
    ACCEPT 'Form letter for the GENERAL inquiry ' TO choice1
ENDDO WHILE .not. FILE(choice1)

DO WHILE .not. FILE(choice2)
    ACCEPT 'Form letter for the sale of Product A ' TO choice2
ENDDO WHILE FILE(choice2)

DO WHILE .not. FILE(choice3)
    ACCEPT 'Form letter for the sale of Product B ' TO choice3
ENDDO WHILE FILE (choice3)

WAIT

\* Other form letters for other products can be added
\* Using this construction
\* Add to above entry routine
\* Add to CASE selection below to choose additional letters
ERASE

\* SECTION III Selects and Prints A Letter
\* For Each Unprocessed Record

    \* Check the NOWMAILED field in each record
    \* Step through the entire file to the first
    \* Undeleted entry that has not been printed
    LOCATE for .not. nowmailed .and. .not. *

```
DO WHILE .not. eof

* Turn on printer and establish margin
SET FORMAT TO PRINT
SET PRINT ON
SET MARGIN TO 8

* Put the Spelled Out Date in the Letter
@ 5,60 SAY spelldate
* Position the print head down 4 more lines
* Print the first address line

@ 10,0 SAY TRIM(mr:ms) + ' ' + TRIM(firstname) + ' ' + TRIM(lastname)


* check for data in the floating fields.
* do not print if empty
IF company < > ' '
    ? company
ENDIF company < > ' '

IF suite:etc < > ' '
    ? suite:etc
ENDIF suite:etc < > ' '

* Print the remainder of the address fields
? street
? TRIM(city) + ", " + st + " " + zip

* put in line feeds to separate address and salutation of letter
?
?
?
? 'Dear ' + TRIM(mr:ms) + ' ' + TRIM(lastname) + ':'
?
?
?
* call up letter according to choice in the prospect file
* Uses Macros (&) to acquire proper file (See Chapter 2)

DO CASE

    * Pick if a client and interested in product A
    CASE qualified= 'S' .AND. interest= 'PA'
       DO &choice2

    * Pick if a client and interested in product B
    CASE qualified= 'S' .AND. interest= 'PB'
       DO &choice3

    OTHERWISE

       * Print the general letter for all other conditions
       DO &choice1

ENDCASE
```

```
* Eject this page from printer
EJECT

* Inform the operator on the screen of progress
* First switch the processing back to the screen
SET PRINT OFF
SET FORMAT TO screen
ERASE
@ 8,0 SAY 'Record Number '
* Use ?? to continue print statements on the same line
?? #
?? ' Has Been Printed '

* Take these next 6 commands out if continuous paper used
@ 13,0 SAY "Ready the Printer for the Next Letter. "
@ 14,0 SAY "Press any Key to Continue. "

SET CONSOLE OFF
    WAIT
    SET CONSOLE ON
    ERASE

    * Advance to the next undeleted record written today
    * Repeat the entire printing procedure until EOF
    CONTINUE

ENDDO WHILE .not. eof

* Section IV Housekeeping Before Exiting

SET FORMAT TO SCREEN
SET PRINT OFF
SET MARGIN TO 4
RELEASE choice1,choice2,choice3,spelldate,counter
RETURN
```

# SINGLTR.CMD   Prints One Letter

Problems in printing form letters will be rare. Occasionally, however, a form letter for one prospect will be smudged or require repeat printing for some other reason. FORMLETR was designed to print several letters at one time, then change the NOWMAILED field in client to ensure that duplicate letters could not be inadvertently printed.

SINGLTR requires the record number in the CLIENT file to determine which name and address to use. The operator may make note of this when FORMLETR announced completion of the former letter, or the CLIENT file may be listed.

The same code is used to prompt for selection one form letter and to verify that the form letter is on the default disk drive. SINGLTR uses the same printing routines to reprint the one desired letter. No restraints on repeat printing are used, but the menu option must be chosen each time for the printing of a letter.

**CODE FOR SINGLTR.CMD**

```
* singltr.cmd
* module purpose: prints one form letter
* chosen by operator before execution

* SECTION I- HOUSEKEEPING

USE CLIENT
ERASE
SET talk OFF
* Get record number in CLIENT
STORE 0000 to number
@ 10,05 SAY "What is the Record Number "
@ 11,05 SAY "Of the Letter to Be Printed? " GET number
READ
GOTO number
```

*25 spaces*

```
* Get Spelled Out Version of date
ERASE
STORE '                         ' TO spelldate
@ 5,5 SAY "Please enter today's date for the letter " GET spelldate
READ


* SECTION II - Select The Form Letter
* Place prompts and directory of form letter on screen
ERASE
@ 3,30 SAY 'Mailform Single Letter Printer'
@ 5,10 SAY 'Prints a form letter for a Client or Prospect.'
@ 6,10 SAY 'You will be given the choice of a form letter.'
@ 7,10 SAY 'Choose your letter from the form letters below.'
@ 8,10 SAY 'Press Any Key to Continue.'

SET CONSOLE OFF
WAIT
SET CONSOLE ON

LIST files LIKE *.ltr


STORE ' ' TO CHOICE1
* Ensure that an existing form letter is selected
DO WHILE .not. FILE(choice1)
    ACCEPT 'Please Enter the Form letter ' TO choice1
ENDDO WHILE .not. FILE(choice1)

WAIT
ERASE


* SECTION III Selects and Prints The Letter

* Turn on printer and establish margin
SET FORMAT TO PRINT
SET PRINT ON
SET MARGIN TO 8
```

```
* Put the Spelled Out Date in the Letter
@ 5,60 SAY spelldate
* Position the print head down 4 more lines
* Print the first line of the business address

@ 10,0 SAY TRIM(mr:ms) + ' ' + TRIM(firstname) + ' ' +  TRIM(lastname)

* check for data in the floating fields.
* do not print if empty

IF company < > ' '
    ? company
ENDIF company < > ' '

IF suite:etc < > ' '
    ? suite:etc
ENDIF suite:etc < > ' '

* Print the remainder of the address fields
? street
? TRIM(city) + ", " + st + " " + zip

* put in line feeds to separate address and salutation of letter
?
?
?
? 'Dear ' + TRIM(mr:ms) + ' ' + TRIM(lastname) + ':'
?
?
?
* call up letter according to choice in the prospect file
* Uses Macros (&) to acquire proper file (See Chapter 2)
DO &choice1
* Eject this page from printer
EJECT

* Section IV Housekeeping Before Exiting
SET FORMAT TO SCREEN
SET PRINT OFF
SET MARGIN TO 4
RELEASE choice1,number,spelldate
RETURN
```

# LABELPRN.CMD  Batch Label Printer

*Basic Operation*

LABELPRN prints addresses or the labels on envelopes for the letters generated by FORMLETR. These are generated in the same order to automate the insertion of letters in the addressed envelopes.

LABELPRN allows two options. One is printing labels on standard 1-UP (one label per row) labels. The other is printing directly on an envelope, with a pause and prompt after each.

The operator is prompted to choose the option. If the variable ENVE-LOPE is true, the margins and form feeds are established to print in the center of the envelope. The other option, whereby ENVELOPE is false, requires a special adjustment for printing labels.

## Homing in on Label Boundaries

Printing labels requires extreme precision. Each address line must placed exactly within the confines of the label. Both simple and complex addresses must be handled so that no address exceeds the lines allotted in each label.

Labels come in many sizes and types. Some allow seven lines of type, some eight, and some more. LABELPRN assumes that 1-15/16″ × 3″ labels are used. However, once the software is written to adapt to your labels, the system never needs modification, unless the label size is changed. For this reason, always buy the same size labels once your program is working.

The labels used in LABELPRN allow are nine-line labels. Only eight lines can be used; the other line is a label border shared between two labels, in the same way that two houses share one driveway (see Figure 5-6).

Borders are needed for labels as well as letters (see Figure 5-7). A liberal border can be made once precise alignment has been attained. LABELPRIN will create a top margin of two lines and a left margin of four spaces.

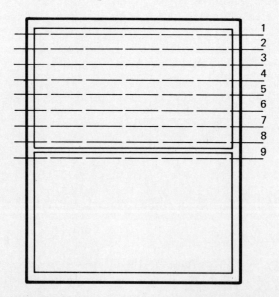

*Figure 5-6.* Label Boundaries for a 1-15/16′ × 3′ Label

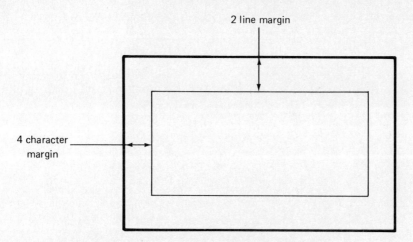

*Figure 5-7.* Labels Need Margins Too

The variety of addresses presents even more problems with labels than it does with form letters. Unwanted lines in addresses must also be eliminated as in FORMLETR to produce a polished appearance.

FORMLETR allows the bottom margin of each letter to vary, depending upon the number of empty lines in each CLIENT record. No adjustment is made because the difference in positions of a couple of lines in a letter is not noticeable. On the other hand, printing on a small label requires adjustments. The printer must advance nine lines per label. Since each address must fill one and only one label, the correct number of line feeds must be added after a simple address to bring the number of line feeds exactly to nine.

The variable SPACER does the adjustment. SPACER is increased by one each time a line is skipped due to emptiness. The number of line feeds stored in SPACER are then issued to the printer after each label by a DO WHILE loop and the ? command to increment the printer to the first line of the next label.

═══════════════════ **TECH TIP** ═══════════════════

*Precision Printing: Principles of Printing Labels*

1. *Use an alignment test routine before printing.*

2. *Once positioned, make a border for each label.*

3. *Remove empty lines and place at end of label.*

4. *Eliminate unwanted spaces on address lines.*

*Locking Out*

All efforts to promote a personalized look to your letters will be wasted if duplicates are sent. A feature at the close of printing of each label by LABELPRN ensures that a duplicate of the letter will not be printed mistakenly. Once a label is printed for a letter, any further printing is impeded. The NOWMAILED field in each record of CLIENT is updated from FALSE to TRUE with the REPLACE command.

The code for LABELPRN follows. Many of the techniques can be used in other label printing routines. Many of the margins and borders can be adjusted to suit other labels, printers, and tastes.

**CODE FOR LABELPRN.CMD**

```
* labelprn.cmd
* prints labels for unprinted clients or prospects

* determine if envelopes or labels will be printed
ERASE
GO TOP
SET TALK OFF

STORE 'T' TO labels,repeat
@ 5,10 SAY "Enter 'T' for Labels; 'F' for Envelopes. " GET labels
READ
STORE !(labels) TO labels
ERASE

* conduct test to align labels in printer
IF labels = 'T'
   * Establish standard margin
   SET MARGIN TO 8
   DO WHILE repeat = 'T'
      SET PRINT ON
      ? '=============== TOP ================='
      ? '====================================='
      ? '====================================='
      ? '====================================='
      ? '====5=====10===15===20===25===30======'
      ? '====================================='
      ? '====================================='
      ? '====================================='
      ? '=============== BOTTOM ==============='
      SET PRINT OFF
      ACCEPT "Another Test Label (T/F)? "TO repeat
      STORE !(repeat) TO repeat
   ENDDO WHILE repeat
   * Label is completely filled with test message
```

```
        * Offset slightly to right for border in each label
        SET MARGIN to 12
ENDIF labels = 'T'

ERASE

* establish margin for envelopes, if chosen
IF labels < > 'T'
        * This is the amount of tabbing over to the right
        * Change to suite your printer or envelopes
        SET MARGIN TO 35
ENDIF labels < > 'T'

* turn on printer
SET PRINT ON
* check the nowmailed field in each record
* step through the entire file to the first
* entry for which a label has not been printed
LOCATE FOR .not. nowmailed .and. .not. *

DO WHILE .not. eof

        STORE 2 TO spacer
        * spacer can be adjusted to the height of labels

        * Create 2 line border on top
        * Does not hurt printing of envelopes
        ?
        ?
        * print the contents of the address fields
        * check for data in the floating fields.
        * do not print if empty
        * make adjustments later by spacing down one more line

        ? TRIM(mr:ms) + ' ' + TRIM(firstname) + ' ' + TRIM(lastname)

        IF company < > ' '
           ? company
        ELSE
           STORE spacer + 1 TO spacer
        ENDIF company < > ' '

        IF suite:etc < > ' '
           ? suite:etc
        ELSE
           STORE spacer + 1 TO spacer
        ENDIF suite:etc < > ' '

        ? street
        ? TRIM(city) + ", " + st + " " + zip

        * put in line feeds to adjust for empty lines
        * has no ill effect in printing of envelopes
        DO WHILE spacer > 0
           ?
```

```
            STORE spacer - 1 TO spacer
            ENDDO WHILE spacer > 0

        * record that both letters and labels have been printed for prospect
        * advance to the next record written today
        * repeat the entire printing procedure until eof
        REPLACE nowmailed WITH t,lastmail with mfiledate
        CONTINUE

        * pause to reload if envelope option has been chosen
        * then issue an eject to remove printed envelope
        IF labels < > 'T'
            SET PRINT OFF
            @ 12, 0 SAY "Position A New Envelope. "
            @ 14, 0 SAY "Press Any Key to Continue. "
            SET CONSOLE OFF
            WAIT
            SET CONSOLE ON
            ERASE
            SET PRINT ON
            EJECT
        ENDIF labels < > 'T'

    ENDDO WHILE .not. eof

    SET PRINT OFF
    SET FORMAT TO SCREEN
    SET MARGIN TO 4
    ERASE
    @ 10,10 SAY " All Labels Have Been Printed in File."
    @ 12,10 SAY " Press Any Key to Continue. "
    SET CONSOLE OFF
    WAIT
    SET CONSOLE ON

    RELEASE spacer,repeat,labels
    RETURN
```

# SINGLAB.CMD  Single Label Printer

A replacement for a label damaged during printing is frequently required. SINGLAB performs the same function of printing a single label that SINGLTR did for one form letter.

CODE FOR SINGLAB.CMD

```
        * singlab.cmd
        * module purpose: prints one label as desired

        USE client
        ERASE

        * get record number in client
        STORE 0000 TO number
```

```
@ 10,05 SAY "What is the Record Number "
@ 11,05 SAY "Of the Label to Be Printed? " GET number
READ
GOTO number

* determine if an envelope or a label will be printed
ERASE
STORE 'T' TO labels
@ 5,10 SAY "Enter 'T' for a Label; 'F' for an Envelope. " GET labels
READ
STORE !(labels) TO labels
ERASE

* establish margin for either a label or an envelope
IF labels = 'T'
    SET MARGIN TO 12
ELSE
    SET MARGIN TO 35
ENDIF labels = 'T'

ERASE
* turn on printer
SET PRINT ON

STORE 2 TO spacer
* spacer can be adjusted to the height of labels
* create 2 line border on top
* does not hurt printing of envelopes
?
?
* print the contents of the address fields
* check for data in the floating fields.
* do not print if empty
* make adjustments later by spacing down one more line

? TRIM(mr:ms) + ' ' + TRIM(firstname) + ' ' + TRIM(lastname)

IF company < > ' '
    ? company
ELSE
    STORE spacer + 1 TO spacer
ENDIF company < > ' '

IF suite:etc < > ' '
    ? suite:etc
ELSE
    STORE spacer + 1 TO spacer
ENDIF suite:etc < > ' '

? street
? TRIM(city) + ", " + st + " " + zip

* put in line feeds to adjust for empty lines
* has no ill effect in printing of envelopes
DO WHILE spacer > 0
```

```
      ?
         STORE spacer - 1 TO spacer
      ENDDO WHILE spacer > 0

      * issue an eject to remove printed envelope
      * if envelope option has been chosen
      IF labels < > 'T'
         EJECT
      ENDIF labels < > 'T'

      SET PRINT OFF
      SET MARGIN TO 4
      ERASE
      @ 10,10 SAY " The Label Has Been Printed."
      @ 12,10 SAY " Press any key to continue. "
      SET CONSOLE OFF
      WAIT
      SET CONSOLE ON

      RELEASE spacer,labels,number
      RETURN
```

# TICKLETT.CMD THE TICKLER
# LETTER PRINTER

TICKLETT.CMD selects client records by tickler date, to be used to print timely form letters and labels. While the selection process is unique, the printing is not, and FORMLETR and LABELPRN can be used without modification by TICKLETT.

Several passes through an entire client file will be necessary, which may be time consuming on a large file which has few candidates to be printed on the tickler date. The speed is increased by creating *tempfile,* a TEMPorary FILE of the client records which have a tickler date which meets or exceeds the day of printing. The command *COPY ALL TO tempfile FOR mfiledate = tickler* creates a much smaller file with only the records which will be needed.

Once the printing is done, the CLIENT file is again USEd and the temporary file is deleted. A last REPLACE command ensures that duplicate tickler letters will not be printed. Control is returned to the main MAILFORM menu.

CODE FOR TICKLETT.CMD

```
      * ticklett.cmd
      * module purpose: prints letters and labels
      * based upon date in the tickler field
      * uses existing routines by copying to new file

      ERASE
      @ 10, 5 SAY "Prepare to Print Tickler Letters"
      @ 12, 5 SAY "Please Wait"
```

```
SET default to &dfdefault
COPY ALL TO tempfile FOR mfiledate = tickler
USE tempfile
SET default to &pfdefault

* print form letters using formletr
* allow formletr to work by changing tracking field
REPLACE ALL nowmailed WITH f
SET talk OFF
DO formletr

* use labelprn to print labels in tempfile
* print labels for unprinted tickler letters
DO labelprn

* open the main file again
* dispose of temporary file
* SET default to &dfdefault
USE client
DELETE FILE tempfile
SET default to &pfdefault

* record in CLIENT that tickler letters were printed
* on this date for this tickler date
REPLACE ALL lastmail WITH mfiledate,tickler WITH mfiledate ;
   FOR tickler = mfiledate
RETURN
```

## ENTERING BOILERPLATE TEXT

You have many form letter options. The limitations are on the number of letters that can be entered as command files onto your default drive. While not as easily entered as a word processor, form letters can be entered without difficulty and used repeatedly.

Word processors use invisible control characters to hyphenate words and to polish extensively the appearance of the text. dBASE does not know how to process the characters and will stop when the characters are encountered. Therefore, if a word processor is used to enter the text, be careful that it does not enter the invisible characters.

All short letters can safely be entered by the use of the MODIFY COMMAND. This is the text editor used in dBASE II. Other word processors can also be used, but always use the option reserved for non-formatted text. For Wordstar, this is the N Document mode. Other word processing packages have a comparable option.

The MODIFY COMMAND option will be used to enter the all-purpose letter GENERAL.LTR. Prepare by first creating a draft of the letter on your word processor and printing the results for use as a model. Don't use right justification, in order to create the ragged-right appearance of an individually typed letter.

Enter dBASE II and set default to the disk that will be used later for programs. Type MODIFY COMMAND GENERAL.LTR at the dot prompt. The screen will clear completely.

Never forget to document your work. Always precede a command file with remarks that inform the reader of your name and the code's features. Preface each line of the remarks with a comment character ( * ). Comments will also be used to fashion a template to guide the entry of the boilerplate. Nothing on the line will be printed, but the comments will tell you when entering text when to end a line and start on another. Enter these lines:

```
* GENERAL.LTR
* THIS IS THE ALL PURPOSE LETTER
* THIS IS THE TEMPLATE FOR CREATING THE BOILERPLATE
*              20              40              60
* - - - - - - - - - - - - - - - - - - - - - - - - - - - - - - - - - - - - -
```

The number of characters on each line is determined by your printer, letterhead, and the pitch of the print. Sixty characters per line will generally suffice. Do not exceed 66 letters per line because some versions of dBASE cut off characters past this point.

Type in each line as it appears in the draft. NOTE: You must preface each line with the WHAT IS command ( ? ) and enclose each line by single quotes or double quotes. dBASE prints the contents in the quotes without trying to do other operations. Double quotes are recommended because single quotes are often used in text. An error would result if this line was entered and later processed:

```
? ' A jolt was delivered with Mary's use of single quotes. '
```

Where did the sentence end, after Mary or at the end of the line? Double quotes eliminate any error messages:

```
? "A jolt was delivered with Mary's use of single quotes."
```

---

## ═══════════TECH TIP═══════════

### *Precision Printing: Single and Double Quotes*

*Single and double quotes must enclose text that is to be printed on the screen or at the printer. Single and double quotes must be used consistently; if a single quote is used at the beginning of a phrase, a double quote cannot be used at the end of a phrase. Avoid error messages by enclosing the phrase that uses an apostrophe with double quotes.*

---

Enter in the boilerplate text for each letter. Each paragraph must be separated by question marks to force the printer to issue line feeds. Do not worry about the vertical placement of the paragraphs at this time; this is done by FORMLETR. End each with the closing. As a sample, GENERAL.LTR may be the following:

```
* GENERAL.LTR
* THIS IS THE ALL PURPOSE LETTER
* THIS IS THE TEMPLATE FOR CREATING THE BOILERPLATE
*                  20                 40                 60
* - - - - - - - - - - - - - - - - - - - - - - - - - - - - - - - - - - - - - - *
? "Thank you for your interest in our fine line of sofas and"
? "recliners. Stone Age Technologies features the latest fabrics"
? "and design, at the lowest price."
?
?
? "Please find enclosed a brochure about our product line and"
? "do not hesitate to visit our luxurious showroom."
?
?
? "Very truly yours,"
?
?
? "Conway W. Gravel"
? "President"
```

A printed draft of boilerplate will be generated by dBASE. To print the paragraphs once they have been entered, simply type at the dot-prompt:

```
SET TALK OFF
SET PRINT ON
DO GENERAL.LTR
```

The boilerplate text will print. When done, type:

```
EJECT
SET PRINT OFF
```

The other letters for Product A and Product B are completed in the same manner.

# INSTALLATION OF THE REPORT GENERATION PROGRAMS

## RPTMENU.CMD The Report Sub-Menu Program

The report menu works like all the other MAILFORM menus—by presenting prompts to the operator and executing the corresponding program (see Figure 5-8). Two types of reports can be chosen, one for phone numbers and another for addresses. Each can list out alphabetically by last name or by another field. REPORTMENU also produces two other reports, the QUICK LIST of clients, and the summary count of the day's prospects and clients.

## Column Width: An Embarrassment of Riches

dBASE II is capable of generating a wide array of reports, and the CLIENT file has the capacity to store many items that can form several useful reports.

MAILFORM takes only the most essential information for the daily reports and positions all the data for each client or prospect entirely on one line of the page. A printer must be capable of printing at least 130 columns across a page. There are two methods of accommodating these columns on paper.

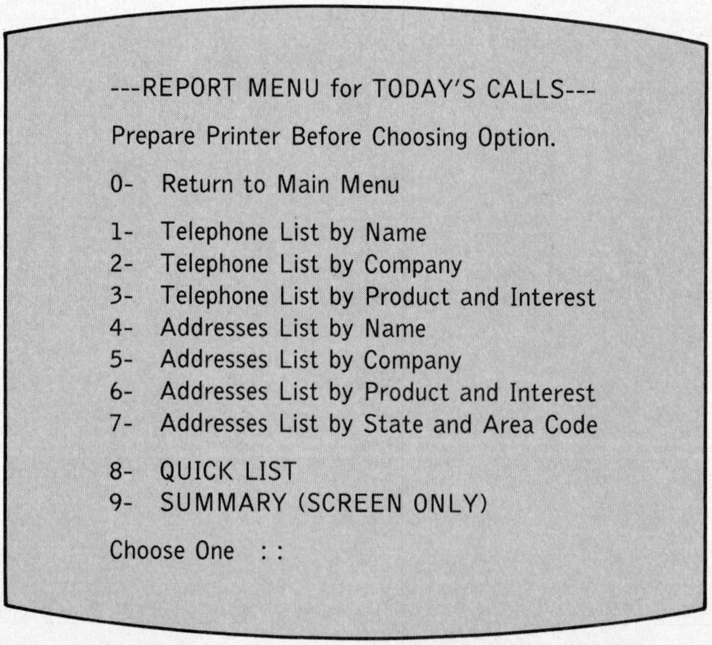

```
---REPORT MENU for TODAY'S CALLS---

Prepare Printer Before Choosing Option.

0-   Return to Main Menu

1-   Telephone List by Name
2-   Telephone List by Company
3-   Telephone List by Product and Interest
4-   Addresses List by Name
5-   Addresses List by Company
6-   Addresses List by Product and Interest
7-   Addresses List by State and Area Code

8-   QUICK LIST
9-   SUMMARY (SCREEN ONLY)

Choose One  : :
```

*Figure 5-8.* Screen for Report Sub-Menu

A change of print size will be necessary if you wish to use standard 8-½″ paper. Nearly all dot matrix printers and most daisywheel printers have the ability to change print size if the computer has given the printer a special instruction. This is done from within dBASE II by the doing the following:

```
? CHR(NN)
```

The NN is a number from 0 to 255 that the printer expects to switch pitch. The control codes can be found in the printer manual. Two codes are needed: one to switch to compressed pitch, the other to resume normal printing. A utility program used by MAILFORM and all other main programs in this text allows easy and permanent entry of these codes.

The INIT routine needs only to run once and will store the special CHR codes for your printer in a special file called CONFIG.MEM on the default disk. Four words will then alter your printer: (normprint, comprint, stdform, and altform). The codes alter normal print and compressed print pitch, as well as standard (66 lines) and alternate form feed (42 lines).

The command ? &comprint switches the printer to the smaller print. Just before exiting, ? &normprint returns the printer to the normal printing. The & symbol is a macro, which informs dBASE II not to take the comprint at face value but to consider the contents as a command to be executed, not data to be displayed.

If you have a wide carriage on your printer (about 15″), no adjustment to the code is needed. You will need to use wide paper, perhaps the 14″ data processing paper. Simply remove the normprint and comprint statements in the code.

RPTMENU has some other unique features that affect operation. Menu Option 9 uses the COUNT command. This can be slow to operate, but the use of the command is straightforward. Other COUNTS can be added to the reporter using this syntax.

RPTMENU Options 1–7 use two FORM files and otherwise differ only in the order in which the data is printed. All use the SET HEADING TO command, which prints a second heading on each page of the report to supplement the heading coded into the FORM files. All work on the same principle: Order a file by first indexing on the key field, SET HEADING TO a temporary title to indicate just how the report FORM is being used, print out records that meet the condition of being entered on this date, and close and delete the index file.[1]

Option 7 organizes the reports by state and telephone area codes, since ZIP codes are not a suitable indicator of location. The index looks for the field ST and within each state will organize by the first three numbers of the prospect's phone number. The $(wkphone,1,3) command is used to index only on three characters, starting at the first position.

---

1. See the Section's "Technical Tutorial" for details on Reporting.

═══════════════════ TECH TIP ═══════════════════

*Flexible Use of Report Command*

*1. Develop a form file.*

*2. Order a file by different fields.*

*3. Set heading to <PHRASE> depending on use.*

*4. Print under various conditions (DATE).*

*5. Close index (SET INDEX TO) and delete.*

Option 8 illustrates the simplest method of producing a written dBASE II report. Simply SET PRINT ON, and LIST the fields in the order desired with the conditions that will determine which records will be printed. SET PRINT OFF after the printing is completed.

All the reports require 130 columns. The clutter would be confusing if 130 columns were echoed to an 80-column computer screen during printing. Any changes to the screen are aborted until printing is done by typing SET CONSOLE OFF. The screen is activated just before returning to the main MAILFORM menu by the command SET CONSOLE ON.

═══════════════════ TECH TIP ═══════════════════

*Eliminating Video Clutter*

*To eliminate clutter on screen during printing, use the command before printing:*

*SET CONSOLE OFF*

*To activate the screen again, use*

*SET CONSOLE ON*

CODE FOR RPTMENU.CMD

```
* rptmenu.cmd
* module purpose: produce a variety of reports

ERASE
* suppress page eject every time a report is run
SET EJECT OFF

DO WHILE t

    ERASE
    STORE ' ' TO rptform
    @ 1,10 SAY "--- REPORT MENU for TODAY'S CALLS ----"
    @ 3,10 SAY 'Prepare Printer Before Choosing Option.'

    DO WHILE rptform < '0' .OR. rptform > '9'
```

```
     @ 6,10 SAY '0- Return to Main Menu'
     @ 8,10 SAY '1- Telephone List by Name '
     @ 9,10 SAY '2- Telephone List by Company'
     @ 10,10 SAY '3- Telephone List by Product and Interest'
     @ 11,10 SAY '4- Addresses List by Name'
     @ 12,10 SAY '5- Addresses List by Company'
     @ 13,10 SAY '6- Addresses List by Product and Interest'
     @ 14,10 SAY '7- Addresses List by State and Area Code'
     @ 16,10 SAY '8- QUICK LIST '
     @ 17,10 SAY '9- SUMMARY (SCREEN ONLY)'
     @ 20,10 SAY 'Choose One ' GET rptform PICTURE '#'
     READ


ENDDO WHILE rptform < '0' .OR. rptform > '9'

IF rptform = '9'
  ERASE
   COUNT FOR .NOT. * .AND. mfiledate = origdate to calls
   @ 10,0
   ? calls
   ?? 'CALLS were received today.'
   ?
   COUNT FOR NOWMAILED .AND. .NOT. * .AND. mfiledate= origdate to sent
   ? sent
   ?? 'Letters and labels were printed today '
   WAIT
   RELEASE calls,sent
   LOOP
ENDIF

IF rptform < > '0' .and. rptform < > '9'
      * send down control code to convert printer to 130 columns
      * code sent established by INIT
      SET PRINT ON
      ? &comprint
      SET PRINT OFF
      ERASE
      @ 10,05 SAY "PLEASE WAIT. FILE IS BEING ORDERED AND  PRINTED. "
      * SUPPRESS CLUTTER ON SCREEN WHILE REPORT IS BEING  WRITTEN
      SET CONSOLE OFF
ENDIF rptform < > '0' .OR. rptform < > '9'

DO CASE

    CASE rptform = '0'
        RELEASE rptform
        SET INDEX TO
        DELETE FILE order.ndx
        SET EJECT ON
        RETURN
```

```
CASE rptform = '1'

    INDEX ON lastname + firstname TO order
    SET HEADING TO ORDERED BY NAME
    REPORT FORM phone FOR mfiledate = origdate TO PRINT

CASE rptform = '2'

    INDEX ON company + lastname TO order
    SET HEADING TO ORDERED BY COMPANY AND LAST NAME
    REPORT FORM phone FOR mfiledate = origdate TO PRINT

CASE rptform = '3'

    INDEX ON qualified + interest TO order
    SET HEADING TO ORDERED BY QUALIFICATION AND PRODUCT
    REPORT FORM phone FOR mfiledate = origdate TO PRINT

CASE rptform = '4'

    INDEX ON lastname + firstname TO order
    SET HEADING TO ORDERED NAME
    REPORT FORM address FOR mfiledate = origdate TO PRINT

CASE rptform = '5'

    INDEX ON company + lastname TO order
    SET HEADING TO ORDERED BY COMPANY AND LAST  NAME
    REPORT FORM address FOR mfiledate = origdate TO PRINT

CASE rptform = '6'

    INDEX ON qualified + interest TO order
    SET HEADING TO ORDERED BY QUALIFICATION AND  PRODUCT
    REPORT FORM address FOR mfiledate = origdate TO PRINT

CASE rptform = '7'

    INDEX ON st + $(wkphone,1,3) TO order
    SET HEADING TO PROSPECT LIST BY AREA
    REPORT FORM address FOR mfiledate = origdate TO PRINT

CASE rptform = '8'

    SET PRINT ON
    ? 'REC # TITL FIRST LAST NAME '
    ?? ' COMPANY WORK PH. TICKLER DATE '
    ?
    LIST ALL mr:ms,firstname,lastname,company,wkphone,'        ',tickler ;
    FOR mfiledate = origdate
    SET PRINT OFF

ENDCASE


* reset printer to standard pitch
* reset code set by INIT
* also position paper to top of form
SET PRINT ON
```

8 spaces

```
? &normprint
EJECT
SET PRINT OFF
* Restore operation of screen
SET CONSOLE ON

ENDDO WHILE t
```

## The Report Form Files

Reports are generated by the use of the dBASE II report generator. The dBASE command REPORT looks for information about the shape or FORM of a report and takes information from the CLIENT database file and places it on the screen or on the printer. The FORM, which is a file on the disk, has a filename with the ending .FRM appended to it.

A FORM file is a hatrack that, like a framework for holding headwear, tells dBASE II the following (see Figure 5-9):

- The items to print from each record
- Totals and subtotals
- The width and length of pages and items
- Headings, both left and right justified

*Figure 5-9.*  Report Form is a Hatrack

The REPORT command has limitations but is nevertheless very powerful if several techniques are used. Most of these are utilized in the MAILFORM series.

## Installation of the MAILFORM Report Form

Two FORM files are needed to produce the reports generated by Options 1 to 7. ADDRESS.FRM positions the prospect and client information as an address list, and PHONE.FRM prints a phone list.

Install the FORM files directly from within dBASE II. Be sure to first USE the file (CLIENT) and set the default to the disk that has all of the other MAILFORM programs (SINGLAB .. FORMLETR). To install the PHONE form, type:

```
REPORT FORM PHONE
```

The screen will clear and dBASE II will prompt you to flesh out the FORM (see Figure 5-10).

Two techniques are used to improve the appearance of the report. The < and > left and right justifies the headings for each item. The semicolons force the underlines to wrap around underneath the titles for each item.

═══════════════════════════TECH TIP═══════════════════════

*Report Form Format Characters*

*Use in the form file format characters:*

   <   *to Left Justify Report Headings*
   >   *to Right Justify Report Headings*
   ;   *to wrap headings to the next line*

*Example:*

*WIDTH, CONTENTS*
*25,FIELD*
*ENTER HEADING:* > *A HOUSE;DIVIDED;_____*

*Becomes in the REPORT:*

                         *A HOUSE*
                         *DIVIDED*

_____

The PHONE report will flash by the screen and show all records in CLIENT. Headings and page numbers will also be shown on the screen.

```
REPORT FORM PHONE

ENTER OPTIONS, M= MARGIN, L =LINES, W =WIDTH M=2, W=130
PAGE HEADING? (Y/N) Y
ENTER PAGE HEADING? TODAY'S PHONE LISTING
DOUBLE SPACE REPORT? (Y/N) N
ARE TOTALS REQUIRED? (Y/N) N
COL     WIDTH, CONTENTS
001      5,MR:MS
ENTER HEADING: < TITL;----
002      15,FIRSTNAME
ENTER HEADING: < FIRST;----
003      20,LASTNAME
ENTER HEADING: LAST NAME;------------
004      15,WKPHONE
ENTER HEADING: WORK PH.;----------
005      15,HMPHONE
ENTER HEADING: HOME PH.;----------
006      5,INTEREST
ENTER HEADING: < IN;--
007      5,QUALIFIED
ENTER HEADING: < QU
008      20,NOTE
ENTER HEADING: < NOTES
009                          (PRESS THE CARRIAGE RETURN)
```

*Figure 5-10.* Dialog for the Phone Form

# The Unthinkable but Typical: A Mal-FORMed Report

Rarely will the FORM of the report be perfect the first try. The dBASE II manual suggests that the FORM file be deleted and the dialog attempted again. There is an easier way. Make minor changes to the FORM file by typing MODIFY COMMAND PHONE.FRM. Do not forget to type the .FRM extension because the MODIFY COMMAND looks for files that end only in .CMD unless otherwise instructed. The dialog will appear as in the left column below. Compare to the first entry, of the REPORT dialog (shown in standard type) used when the REPORT FORM command first established PHONE.FRM.

## THE FORM FILE REVEALED

M-2,W-130

Y
TODAY'S PHONE LISTING FOR PROSPECTS AND CLIENTS

N
N
5,MR:MS
<TITL;------
15,FIRSTNAME
<FIRST;------
20,LASTNAME
<LAST NAME;------
20,COMPANY
COMPANY;------
15,WKPHONE
<WORK PH.;------
15,HMPHONE
<HOME PH.;------
5,INTEREST
<IN;--
5,QUALIFIED
<QU;--
20,NOTE
<NOTES;------

## THE FULL REPORT DIALOG AT FIRST ENTRY

ENTER OPTIONS, M-LEFT MARGIN, L-LINES/PAGE, W-PAGE WIDTH
M-2,W-130
PAGE HEADING? (Y/N) Y
ENTER PAGE HEADING? TODAY'S PHONE LISTING FOR PROSPECTS AND CLIENTS
DOUBLE SPACE REPORT? (Y/N) N
ARE TOTALS REQUIRED? (Y/N) N
COL WIDTH,CONTENTS
001 5,MR:MS
ENTER HEADING: <TITL;------
002 15,FIRSTNAME
ENTER HEADING: <FIRST;------
003 20,LASTNAME
ENTER HEADING: LAST NAME;------
004 15,WKPHONE
ENTER HEADING: WORK PH.;------
005 15,HMPHONE
ENTER HEADING: HOME PH.;------
006 5,INTEREST
ENTER HEADING: <IN;--
007 5,QUALIFIED
ENTER HEADING: <QU
008 20,NOTE
ENTER HEADING: <NOTES
009 (PRESS THE CARRIAGE RETURN)

Minor changes can then be easily made and the results checked until satisfactory by typing REPORT FORM PHONE or REPORT FORM PHONE TO PRINT.

The other FORM file, ADDRESS.FRM, is completed in the same way and is outlined below. Enter in each line after typing the dBASE II command REPORT FORM ADDRESS.

REPORT FORM ADDRESS

```
M=2,W=130
Y
TODAY'S ADDRESSES OF PROSPECTS AND CLIENTS
N
N
5,MR:MS
TITL;====
20,LASTNAME
< LAST NAME;===========
20,COMPANY
COMPANY;======
25,STREET
STREET;=====
25,CITY
< CITY;======
8,ST + ' ' + ZIP
ST/ZIP;=====
12,WKPHONE
WK PHONE;=======
3,INTEREST
IN;==
3,QUALIFIED
QU;==
```

## TRACKING PRINTING BY USING LOGICALS FOR AUDITS

Several steps have been used to ensure against the embarrassment of sending the same letter to the same client. The printing of the labels for the form letters by LABELPRN locks out further printing later on of these letters as a group.

The locking out is done by placing a T in the NOWPRINT field of each of the CLIENT records printed on that date. NOWPRINT is a dBASE II logical field; it is either True or False. The code says, in effect, "The label for this letter is now printed." All the routines that print groups of letters are instructed to skip the NOWPRINT field at a later time.

There are other audit fields that can be seen by use of the LIST command. The LASTMAIL field has the LAST date on which a letter was mailed. This may or may not be the date of first contact with the prospect, ORIGDATE.

Quick reports can be developed in dBASE II using these fields in order to check the progress of communication. A sample of the commands follow.

LIST ALL FOR .NOT. NOWMAILED          Check for mail not
                                      mailed.
LIST ALL FOR LASTMAIL = '83/09/23'    Check mailings on
                                      9/23/83.
LIST ALL FOR TICKLER = '84/03/13'     Check people to be
                                      tickled.

Many other reports can be generated from the CLIENT file. dBASE II offers almost unlimited potential. Other methods for generating reports will be offered in later sections of this text.

## THE HOUSEKEEPING FILE

The operation and installation of HOUSEKP.CMD is straightforward but critical. The operator should ideally have a third disk drive to which the backup CLIENT file should be sent. A suitable alternative is the transfer of all CLIENT records from a hard disk to a floppy disk.

Many systems have two disk drives. All the CLIENT data is on drive B and the dBASE II commercial program resides with the MAILFORM program files on drive A. An awkward remedy to the backup problem is the placement of the backup files on the program disk when HOUSEKP is used. The name A:BACKUP may be given. As soon as possible, either the operator or the manager should exit MAILFORM and dBASE II and use the copy program of the computer system to copy CLIENT over to a third diskette. The interim file BACKUP can then be deleted once the CLIENT file is safely transferred to its destination backup diskette.

CODE FOR HOUSEKP.CMD

```
* housekp.cmd
* module purpose: backs up file and purges old leads

DO WHILE t

    ERASE
    STORE ' ' TO tkchoice

    @ 1,10 SAY '--- HOUSEKEEPING ---'
    @ 3,10 SAY '-0- EXIT to Main Menu'
    @ 5,10 SAY '-1- Backup CLIENT File '
    @ 7,10 SAY '-2- Purge ALL Prospects (Retain Clients)'
```

```
@ 8,10 SAY '-3- Purge COLD Prospects (Retain ALL Others)'
@ 9,10 SAY '-4- Purge COLD & WARM Prospects '
@ 10,10 SAY '-5 Purge WARM & HOT Prospects by Date'
@ 12,10 SAY 'Choose a Number ' GET tkchoice PICTURE '#'
READ

* allow viewing of run time message of copied or deleted records
* a notice of each 100 records processed will be on screen
* this message turned on by SET TALK ON
SET TALK ON

DO CASE

   CASE tkchoice = '0'
      SET TALK OFF
      RELEASE tkchoice,purgedate,back,prompt
      RETURN

   CASE tkchoice = '1'
      ERASE
      STORE '        ' TO back
      @ 2, 5 SAY "What drive and file name to copy CLIENT to? " GET back
      READ

      @ 4, 5 SAY "Prepare Backup Drive and Disk. Press to  Continue. "
      SET CONSOLE OFF
      WAIT
      SET CONSOLE ON

      * see chapter 2 for discussion on macros
      COPY ALL TO &back
   CASE tkchoice = '2'

      ERASE
      DELETE ALL FOR qualified < > 'S'
      PACK

   CASE tkchoice = '3'

      ERASE
      * these records already deleted when backing out of clientin
      PACK
   CASE tkchoice = '4'

      ERASE
      DELETE ALL FOR qualified = 'W'
      PACK

   CASE tkchoice = '5'

      ERASE
      * eliminate clutter of talk in dtverify
      SET TALK OFF
```

*(callout: 8 spaces)*

```
                    STORE 'Enter Date Before Which Records Are Purged ' TO
                      prompt
                    DO A:dtverify
                    ERASE
                    STORE filedate TO purgedate
                    SET TALK ON

                    DELETE ALL FOR (qualified = 'W' .OR. qualified = 'H' ) ;
                    .AND. purgedate > = origdate
                    PACK

               OTHERWISE

                    @ 20, 5 SAY "INVALID CHOICE. Press Any Key to Continue. "
                    SET CONSOLE OFF
                    WAIT
                    SET CONSOLE ON

          ENDCASE

          SET TALK OFF

     ENDDO WHILE t
```

# MODIFICATIONS AND EMBELLISHMENTS

## Product and Interest Codes and Criteria

The codes PA. . .PD (Product A. . .Product D) can easily be revised to reflect your products. The file for entry of data (entryscrn.fmt) must be altered to prompt for your customized entry codes. Once done, your codes will be stored in the INTEREST field for FORMLETR to use as criteria for selection of a corresponding form letter.

First alter the prompts on the entry screen. MODIFY COMMAND entryscrn.fmt and revise the following prompts:

```
@ 17, 5 SAY "PA = PROD. A"
@ 18, 5 SAY "PB = PROD. B"
@ 19, 5 SAY "PC = PROD. C"
@ 20, 5 SAY "PD = PROD. D>"
```

                         ↑_____↑  Revise the Prompts

MODIFY COMMAND formletr and change the selection prompts (FORM letter for the sale of Product A, etc.) to reflect the revised product codes. All prompts for the original Product A through D in MAILFORM will reflect your unique codes.

The FORMLETR selection criteria must also reflect the product code changes. Alter the following codes accordingly.

```
CASE qualified = 'S' .AND. interest = 'PA'
CASE qualified = 'S' .AND. interest = 'PB'
```

The first code will pick one form if qualified is equal to 'S' and interest is equal to 'PA'. Change the code to recognize not the 'PA' but your particular product code. Change the second CASE statement for another printing option. The MAILFORM client contact routine will be tailored to your unique products and services.

# WORKING WITH WORDS: A TECHNICAL TUTORIAL

The MAILFORM series illustrates the ability of dBASE II to work with words by organizing data, merging it with text, and printing the result precisely where the user wishes it to be positioned. Major techniques are used in MAILFORM that can be repeated in other office applications are:

1. The CASE structure
2. Use of @ SAY/GET commands to paint a screen
3. Methods of designing an entry screen and printing routines to produce polished reports
4. The commands to send types of dBASE II statements to the printer.

## THE CASE STRUCTURE

The CASE structure is a method of producing a variety of operations. Consider the example in Figure 6-1. Type this test routine by using the MODIFY COMMAND or another text editor and save as 3BEARS.CMD.
Once started (DO 3BEARS), the menu screen below will be presented.

```
Pick a Bear

1.     Papa Bear
2.     Mama Bear

Choose a Number     :  :
```

```
* 3BEARS.CMD
* test of the case command in menus
STORE ' ' TO selection
ERASE
@ 3,0 SAY 'Pick a Bear '
@ 5,0 SAY '1. Papa Bear '
@ 6,0 SAY '2. Mama Bear '
@ 9,0 SAY ' Choose a Number ' ;
GET selection PICTURE '#'
READ

DO CASE

  CASE selection= '1'
    ERASE
    ? ' PAPA BEAR HAS BEEN SELECTED '
  CASE selection= '2'
    ERASE
    ? ' MAMA BEAR HAS BEEN SELECTED '

  OTHERWISE
    * you chose something besides 1 or 2
    ERASE
    ? ' YOU DID NOT CHOOSE PAPA OR MAMA '
    ? ' YOU WILL BE GIVEN BABY BEAR '

ENDCASE
```

*Figure 6-1.* 3 Bears Decision Structure

The operator enters a choice from the keyboard and dBASE II assigns it the the variable called *selection.* The menu selection is started by the *DO CASE* statement. The first condition which meets the test of a CASE command will allow subsequent commands to be processed. For example, if you chose the first option (1. Papa Bear), an ERASE would be issued and the corresponding Papa Bear message would be flashed on the screen. All other CASE commands would be ignored (Mama Bear) and processing will resume after the ENDCASE statement.

If no condition is found to meet one of the CASE conditions, the optional OTHERWISE statement allows other commands to be processed. This is very useful to recover from invalid menu selections and to prompt the operator for a correct menu code. We programmed the selection of a key besides 1 or 2 to result in the BABY BEAR option.

Typing DO 3BEARS every time you wish this program becomes tiresome. The use of the DO WHILE/ENDDO construction allows the program to repeat and do your bidding. Endless cycles of 3BEARS, however, do not permit your computer to do other tasks. The option to exit 3BEARS or any other repetitive command file is essential. The revisions are added in Figure 6-2 to the original 3BEARS. These repeat execution, halting only when the operator wishes to see a message (the WAIT command at the bottom), or to exit the routine (Option 0).

Another method of accomplishing what the CASE does is by using a series of IF/ENDIF statements as shown in the next example.

Like the CASE construction, the choice of one key would allow one choice to be enacted. The IF/ENDIF arrangement, however, required an ENDIF to end each segment. More importantly, if Option '0' was chosen, it would be executed twice, once for each of the IF conditions. The DO CASE structure considers all the options and only processes the first one that meets the given condition.

```
* 3BEARS.CMD
* new and improved version
* test of the case command in menus
DO WHILE T

STORE ' ' TO selection
ERASE
@   5,0 SAY 'Pick a Bear '
@   8,0 SAY '0. No Bear-Exit from Routine '
@   9,0 SAY '1. Papa Bear '
@  10,0 SAY '2. Mama Bear '
@  11,0 SAY ' Choose a Number ' ;
GET selection PICTURE '#'
READ

DO CASE

  CASE selection= '0'
    CANCEL
  CASE selection= '1'
    ERASE
    ? ' PAPA BEAR HAS BEEN SELECTED '
  CASE selection= '2'
    ERASE
    ? ' MAMA BEAR HAS BEEN SELECTED '

  OTHERWISE
    * you chose something besides 1 or 2
    ERASE
    ? ' YOU DID NOT CHOOSE PAPA OR MAMA '
    ? ' YOU WILL BE GIVEN BABY BEAR '
    WAIT
  ENDCASE
ENDDO BEARS
```

*Figure 6-2.* Revised 3 Bears Decision Structure

```
IF selection = '0'
   do one thing
ENDIF

IF selection= '1'
   do another thing
ENDIF

IF selection= '0'
    do one thing (again)
ENDIF
```

## SCREEN FORMATTING

A clear and concise screen is essential for repetitive entry of data. The simple column of fields that dBASE lists after typing the APPEND command is suitable for a small number of entries but tiresome after several hours. Which screen appears easier to use, Screen 1 (Figure 6-3) or Screen 2 (Figure 6-4)?

Screen 1 uses the simple entry routine invoked by typing APPEND. The dBASE II user is presented with as many as 32 fields in one column that continues down the screen.

Screen 2 has the data arranged across as well as down the screen. The first name is first, the last name is to the right on the same line, and the phone number is below. The computer is told exactly the coordinates to paint the prompts (lines, arrows, and descriptions) with the SAY command. The GET command enables the computer to position the cursor precisely on the console and await the entry of data from the keyboard. Users have considered this "painting" the screen, an apt description. The commands that would paint Screen 2 are below:

```
FIRSTNAME : Thomas        :
LASTNAME  : Bigshot         :
PHONE     : 523-567-1845:
```

*Figure 6-3.* Screen 1: The APPEND Command, Unformatted Screen

84

F. NAME                    L. NAME

: Thomas        :          : Bigshot          :

PHONE                      523-567-1845

*Figure 6-4.*  Screen 2: Painting a Screen, SAY/GET Statements

```
* paint screen2
erase
@ 2, 5 SAY "F. NAME"
@ 2,25 SAY "L. NAME"
@ 4, 5 GET FIRSTNAME
@ 4,25 GET LASTNAME
@ 6, 5 SAY "PHONE"
@ 6,25 GET PHONE
READ
```

These statements accomplish exactly the same purpose as the APPEND statement. If a data file is in use with fields by the names of FIRSTNAME, LASTNAME, and PHONE, the corresponding data will be entered into the dBASE II file. The READ command enables data to be entered at positions on the screen determined by the GET commands. The first number after the @ is the vertical coordinate, the second is the horizontal. This Draw-by-the-Numbers enables virtually any form to be drawn on the screen (see Figure 6-5).

*Figure 6-5.*  Drawing a Form on the Screen

PICTURE statements can also be used with SAY/GET statements. Information will not be allowed to be entered unless it is in the proper format. We can ensure that only numbers are entered into the PHONE field by adding the following:

```
@ 6,25 GET phone PICTURE '###-###-####'
```

The # symbol ensures that only a number will be entered for that position in the PHONE field. The cursor will skip over the hyphens, which is another protection against entry errors.

Another PICTURE command converts a lower case letter to upper case. We wish to convert the first letter of each entry to upper case, the rest retain as lower case. This is to add a polished appearance to any letters or labels.

| *All Upper Case* | *Mixed Cases* |
|---|---|
| MR. THOMAS BIGSHOT | Mr. Thomas Bigshot |
| 4987 THUNDER ROAD | 4987 Thunder Road |
| NEW YORK CITY, NY 10010 | New York City, NY 10010 |

We finish our Screen 2 with this refinement:

```
*  paint screen2
*  final and revised version
erase
@ 2, 5 SAY "F. NAME"
@ 2,25 SAY "L. NAME"
@ 4, 5 GET FIRSTNAME      PICTURE "!XXXXXXXXX"
@ 4,25 GET LASTNAME       PICTURE "!XXXXXXXXXXXX"
@ 6, 5 SAY "PHONE"        PICTURE "###-###-####"
@ 6,25 GET PHONE
READ
```

The '!' within the first two PICTURE clauses forces any character entered in this position to upper case. The X allows any character to be entered.

The screen formatting commands (@, SAY, GET, READ, PICTURE) are valuable additions to any dBASE program. The screen can be readily and accurately painted with prompts and information secured and initially verified upon entry by the operator.

# PRECISION PRINTING OF ADDRESSES

With the greater flexibility of dBASE II comes the necessity to tell a program to handle the printing of the words for all conditions that may occur. Addresses may occur in the simple form:

Farmer MacDonald
R.F.D. 1
Everyplace, IA 10039


But life is rarely that simple. A few, but not all, of the addresses of
prospects are in this form:

Ms. Emily Post, Esquire
Alpha, Beta, Gamma, and Fedlock, P.C.
Attorneys at Law
1 Exchange Place
The Medlock Building
Suite 47
100082 Plaza Road
Internal Post Box 5478
Atlanta, Georgia 30098-1234


A command file must be able to adapt to any configuration of addresses and titles. To store the largest address, however, requires that all
records be structured that size. This results in empty fields for the records
with the simpler addresses and wasted space on the disk.

The following field list would print the contents of each record:

? FIRSTNAME,LASTNAME,SUFFIX
? COMPANY
? COTITLE
? ADDRESS1
? ADDRESS2
? SUITE:ETC
? STREET
? BOXNO
? CITY,ST,ZIP


Note that not all fields are used in the CLIENT database. A decision was
made to use only those that were absolutely necessary, in order to pre-
serve disk storage. If used on our two addresses, the following would be
obtained:

? FIRSTNAME,LASTNAME,SUFFIX    Farmer MacDonald
? COMPANY
? COTITLE
? ADDRESS1
? ADDRESS2
? SUITE:ETC
? STREET                       R.F.D. 1
? BOXNO
? CITY,ST,ZIP                  Everyplace, IA

```
? FIRSTNAME,LASTNAME,SUFFIX    Ms. Emily Post, Esquire
? COMPANY                      Alpha, Beta, Gamma, and  Fedlock, P.C.
? COTITLE                      Attorneys at Law
? ADDRESS1                     1 Exchange Place
? ADDRESS2                     The Medlock Building
? SUITE:ETC                    Suite 47
? STREET                       100082 Plaza Road
? BOXNO                        Internal Box 5478
? CITY,ST,ZIP                  Atlanta, Georgia 30098-1234
```

Simplicity often causes complex problems for computers. Farmer MacDonald's address had several fields that were empty. dBASE, unless instructed otherwise, will dutifully print a blank line even if there are no contents in a field.

Problems also occur with address lines with non-blank fields. dBASE II puts spaces after each field to fill it up to its stated CREATED capacity. Without adjustment, there will be unwanted spaces on each printed line as well as between lines. A partial list of addresses would show this:

```
FIRSTNAME       LASTNAME            CITY          ST     ZIP

Mary-Margaret   Smith      Seattle               WA     90099
J. P.           Jones      Hastings on Hudson    NY     10083
```

dBASE II adds blanks to the shorter items so a field will always have data of the same length for every record. Varying results are obtained, depending upon the contents of each field in a record. A simple print expression produces the following addresses:

```
? FIRSTNAME,LASTNAME    Mary-Margaret        Smith
? CITY,ST,ZIP           Seattle                       WA    90099

? FIRSTNAME,LASTNAME    J. P.                Jones
? CITY,ST,ZIP           Hastings on Hudson            NY    10083
```

The addresses are obviously computer printed, which is not what we want. The last name needs to be moved so that it is one space after the first name. A comma and a space need to be placed after the city. The zip code should be positioned two spaces after the state.

Four remedies will allow printing routines to be automated, yet tailored to produce attractive addresses irrespective of the contents of any record.

## Choose Fields that Personalize

CLIENT uses the field MR:MS for the salutations (Mr., Mrs., Ms.). The operator determines the salutation upon first contact with the prospect. The salutation will be used at print time to personalize the address with the correct information.

## Choose Multi-Purpose Fields

Another option is to use multi-purpose address or title fields. Most addresses do not require use of the SUITE:ETC and COMPANY fields. These can be used for other purposes. If another title is required, it may be added to the SUITE:ETC field if no suite address is required. Using fields for different purposes allows for greater flexibility.

## Eliminate Unwanted Empty Lines

Our notification of Farmer MacDonald left empty lines in the address. Blank lines can be eliminated by first checking fields before printing to see if they are empty. If not, they are printed without modification. Otherwise, the fields are skipped without any further action. For example, to check SUITE:ETC, use this code:

```
IF SUITE:ETC < >
  ? SUITE:ETC
ENDIF
```

The code says, IF SUITE:ETC is not empty (not equal to blanks), print this field. Otherwise, no instructions are given and no printing for this line is accomplished.

=============================== TECH TIP ===============================

*Precision Printing: Eliminating Unwanted Blank Lines*

*Check the field on the line for any non-blank characters:*

```
IF FIELD < > ' '
  ? FIELD
ENDIF
```

## Eliminate Spaces between Fields

Unwanted spaces between fields on the same line can mar the appearance of an address as well. One other technique is used with labels and addresses to eliminate the problem of trailing blanks. This is accom-

plished by the TRIM function. To alter the second record, TRIM the
FIRSTNAME field.

> ? TRIM(MR:MS),TRIM(FIRSTNAME),LASTNAME        J. P. Jones

This expression, however, relies upon the commas, which separate
the fields by only one space. Standard business practice requires two
spaces between the state and the zip code, a remedy required by both
records. The following can add any number of spaces or other characters
as desired.

> ? TRIM(CITY) + ", " + ST + " " + ZIP

The contents of the first field is trimmed, the number of blanks or
other characters enclosed by the single or double quotes is added, and the
contents of each field for each record is also added. A polished address
line for each record is created:

> Seattle, WA 90099        Hastings on Hudson, NY 10099

═══════════════════════TECH TIP═══════════════════

*Eliminating Unwanted Spaces Between Spaces on a Line
Using the Trim Function*

*? TRIM(FIELD1),TRIM(FIELD2),FIELD3*

*To add more than one space between fields:*

*? TRIM(FIELD1) + ' ' + TRIM(FIELD2) + ', ' + FIELD3*

Nearly all dBASE II routines use these four principles, including the
MAILFORM series. White space is controlled, and a polished appearance
is ensured.

## SWITCHING FROM SCREEN TO PRINTER

Distinctive commands must be issued to activate the printer, depending
upon the type of information that is to be sent. SET PRINT ON or CTRL-P
allow all statements that are not @ SAY statements to be sent to print.
SET FORMAT TO PRINT allows the @ SAY statements to be transmit-
ted. GET statements are ignored because they only apply to operator
entry at the screen.
Three statements disable the printer. SET PRINT OFF turns off general print statements. CTRL-P toggles off print as well. SET FORMAT TO

SCREEN once again switches format transmission back to the screen (see Figure 6-6).

The SET FORMAT TO PRINT command allows the data designer to position text to any coordinates on the page. The order of formatting on paper, however, is far more critical than the order of formatting on the screen.

Computers speak very quickly to the screen, painting it many times per second. At speeds of thousands of characters per second, the placement of text at any point on the screen is nearly instantaneous and the order of placement is not discernible to the eye. The screen is very forgiving of the user's order of @ SAY statements.

Printers move much more slowly and usually work in only one direction. The print head is moved from upper left to lower right. Paper is fed up over the print head from top to bottom. dBASE II processes each @ SAY coordinate as it is read from a command file, which is presented in this order to the printer. Painting the bottom of a page of print before the top requires both a special (and perhaps unavailable) printer and special adaptations to a command file. The top left corner must precede the lower right.

dBASE II incorporates procedures to ensure that information is printed if the printer format statements are not in order. The cure may be worse than the cause however because the paper will be ejected and print will commence on the next sheet at the proper coordinate. Paper will rapidly spew from the printer if the sequence of format statements is not in order. As a test, turn on your printer and boot up dBASE II. Type the following:

```
SET TALK OFF
SET FORMAT TO PRINT
@ 5,0 SAY "LINE 1 "
@ 4,0 SAY "LINE 2"
SET FORMAT TO SCREEN
```

The first line was printed at 5,0 of the page, and the next coordinate (4,0) was then processed. dBASE II, not able to back the print head up, issued a page eject to the next 4,0 coordinate on the next page.

| TURNS ON | TURNS OFF | COMMANDS AND DESTINATION |
|---|---|---|
| SET PRINT ON | SET PRINT OFF | ALL BUT @ SAY/GETS ECHOED TO PRINTER |
| CTRL-P | CTRL-P | ALL BUT @ SAY/GETS ECHOED TO PRINTER |
| SET FORMAT TO PRINT | SET FORMAT TO SCREEN | DIRECTS THE @ SAYS TO EITHER SCREEN OR PRINTER |

*Figure 6-6.* Destination Commands for the FORMAT Statement

══════════════ TECH TIP ══════════════

*Precision Printing: Order of Use of @ SAY Statements to Printer*

*To print @ SAY statements without problems, always use coordinates that go from the top left to the bottom right. The EJECT command advances another page (if continuous paper is used) and clears the coordinate counter in dBASE II.*

# TECHNIQUE FOR USING THE REPORT COMMAND

The REPORT command has been the most misunderstood in the dBASE II arsenal. REPORT has often been criticized for its shortcomings (only one file, only one line, subtotals on only one field). However, there are various means to circumvent these apparent weaknesses.

There are several ways to increase the flexibility of REPORT:

- Use several FORMS to REPORT data from one file.
- Index a file on various fields for use with one FORM.
- REPORT out records FOR different conditions.
- Use the SET HEADING TO command for each variant.

## Use Several FORMS to REPORT Data from One File

REPORT has no limitations on the number of REPORT FORMS that can be used to generate reports on a data file. MAILFORM, like many other data files, has over 200 characters of information per record. The difficulty arises in delivering only the data that is needed to be meaningful for each purpose.

MAILFORM uses two FORMS for a variety of purposes. One of them, PHONE, generates only the data necessary for daily use and to notify the manager. The other, ADDRESS, produces a report suitable for archival purposes. Each prints only the portion of CLIENT necessary for its intended purposes.

Do not hesitate to use several other FORMS if the need arises. The provision to produce an almost infinite variety of REPORTS from the data file is the greatest power of dBASE II.

## Index a File on Various Fields for Use with One FORM

The REPORT can be greatly increased in versatility by ordering the file first; otherwise, REPORT prints out each record in the order in which it was entered.

The file can be either sorted or indexed on key fields. Indexing allows the ordering to be on more than one field, i.e., all LASTNAME fields with Smith in them can also be ordered by first name. Thus Alphonse Smith will be in the report before Zacharias Smith. For this reason, indexing is greatly preferred over sorting.

A routine way to generate a report is to first index the file, REPORT the data, turn off the index, and delete the index file. The MAILFORM report menu, RPTMENU, uses this common technique.

```
INDEX ON lastname + firstname TO order    ORDERS THE FILE
REPORT FORM phone to PRINT                PRINTS ORDERED FILE
SET INDEX TO                              TURNS OFF INDEX
DELETE order.ndx                          DELETES INDEX FILE
```

## REPORT Records for Different Conditions

The most powerful feature of the REPORT command is the ability to display data only if certain conditions are met by the record that is a candidate to be reported. However, these conditions must be applied in the REPORT command.

All the reports in MAILFORM are daily reports; therefore, only records that were added on the date stored to mfiledate are slated to be in the report. Records have their date of entry stored in the file as origdate. The condition phrase is added to the REPORT command to display only these records.

```
REPORT FORM phone FOR mfiledate = origdate
```

All records in the CLIENT file are searched and printed out according to the configuration in the chosen FORM file, but each record is queried to see if mfiledate is equal to origdate. Records are displayed only if the condition or conditions are met.

## Use the SET HEADING TO Command

All the REPORT techniques allow for a wide variety of data to be presented. The reader of the report needs clarification of the type of report, the order of indexing, and the conditions that were applied. Use of one

PHONE BY NAME

```
INDEX ON lastname + firstname TO order
SET HEADING TO ORDERED BY NAME
REPORT FORM phone FOR mfiledate = origdate
SET INDEX TO
DELETE FILE order.ndx
```

## ADDRESS BY PRODUCT AND INTEREST

```
INDEX ON qualified + interest
SET HEADING TO ORDERED BY QUALIFICATION AND PRODUCT
REPORT FORM address FOR mfiledate = origdate
SET INDEX TO
DELETE FILE order.ndx
```

PHONE BY COMPANY

```
INDEX ON company + lastname TO order
SET HEADING TO ORDERED BY COMPANY AND LAST NAME
REPORT FORM phone FOR mfiledate = origdate
SET INDEX TO
DELETE FILE order.ndx
```

## ADDRESS BY STATE AND AREA CODE

```
INDEX ON st + $(wkphone,1,3) TO order
SET HEADING TO PROSPECT LIST BY AREA
REPORT FORM address FOR mfiledate = origdate
SET INDEX TO
DELETE FILE order.ndx
```

*Figure 6-7.* Method of Producing Various Reports

FORM file, however, only allows for one heading to be stored in the FORM file.

The SET HEADING TO <PHRASE> command allows for a customized heading also to be printed on the report, which can be easily changed by changing the PHRASE. Added before the REPORT command, PHRASE will be placed at the top of the REPORT as a supplement to the heading coded into the FORM when it was made. SET HEADING TO then can clarify the precise type of report that is generated by using one FORM file for many purposes. Using all these techniques is evident in RPTMENU. Four types of reports from two FORM files are illustrated in Figure 6-7.

The use of the four steps dramatically increases the flexibility of the REPORT generator. Use each as illustrated in RPTMENU to add a wide range of reporting power to your dBASE II programs.

## TECH TIP

### *Flexible Reporting Methods*

*Use several FORMS to REPORT data from one file. Index a file on various fields for use with one FORM REPORT out records for different conditions. Use the SET HEADING TO command for each variant.*

Close adherence to these methods will allow fast, efficient, and complete generation of dBASE II reports.

## SUMMARY

MAILFORM has illustrated the techniques of menu generation (CASE structure), screen painting (@ SAY/GET/READ), precision printing (labels and letters), and reporting (REPORT). Practice with each will enable quick mastery of the essentials for developing powerful dBASE II input and output procedures.

# SECTION THREE

## Money and Material Management

Management of sales, purchases, and bills can be tedious. Fortunately, the development of a custom designed dBASE II program to manage money and material is easy.

Financial software serves essentially three purposes: to pursue payment of money owed to you (accounts receivable), to prompt repayment of money you owe to others (accounts payable), and to track material assets (inventory).

Three systems are featured in Section Three. INVENT manages the inventory of your product. INVOICE is a set of dBASE II files that performs as a simple but serviceable accounts receivable that updates the inventory of your products. PAYBILLS prompts you for the bills that must be paid to others and posts the payments to a file for printing by CHKCUT. The command files do the following:

- Maintain a file of all customers, their addresses, tax codes, and the accumulated balance owed to you.
- Maintain a file of your products, costs and prices, descriptions, and the quantity in stock.
- Maintain a file of all daily sales for each inventory item and invoice. The inventory is automatically adjusted when the product is invoiced. Reports are generated on the sales activity, inventory, and accounts owed to you (accounts receivable).
- Bill up to ten separate line items on the same invoice. Taxes are automatically determined from a tax code recorded for each cus-

tomer. Key information can be overridden by the operator if necessary.

- Maintain a file of vendors who serve your company, their addresses, the discount policy for each, and the balance you owe.

- Maintain a file of checks outlining daily payments to outside vendors. Allow the operator to pay for all outstanding bills submitted by a vendor or for any part. Discounts are automatically calculated. Vendors are paid with an attractive and tamper-proof check and stub. Each payment is spelled out (i.e., ***EXACTLY ONE THOUSAND DOLLARS***). Reports are produced on check activity, vendors paid, and amounts outstanding (accounts payable).

Installation of the three dBASE II systems will provide comprehensive control over billing of purchases, monitoring of inventory, and the posting and paying of bills to vendors. The dBASE II code for each, while similar, describes opposite processes. In one, resources leave your company in exchange for cash from others (accounts receivable) while the process is reversed with accounts payable.

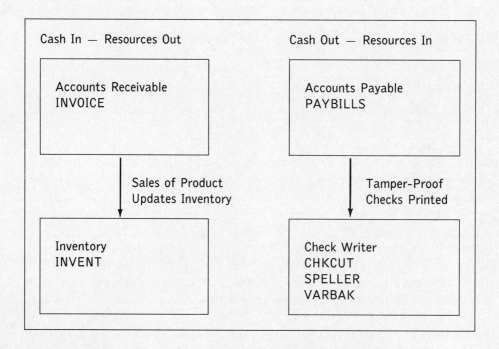

Outline of the Money and Material Management Systems

# 7

# INVENTORY CONTROL: USING INVENT

Keeping track of what is in inventory is a difficult task without an organized manner for adding items when purchases are made and withdrawing items when they are sold. Physical counts of inventory periodically update the count of stock on-hand. Valuation of inventory for financial statements is easily done if the cost of the item is obtained from the inventory file when the quantity purchased is updated. Sales can be automatically deducted from the inventory file when the invoice is prepared.

This section discusses creation and maintenance of the inventory files, adjustments after physical inventory, and valuation of inventory. The first chapter explains how to use the INVENT program and the second explains the programs and techniques.

Inventory program INVENT has three main parts:

1. Adding, editing, deleting items in inventory file.
2. Updating quantity on-hand and cost with purchase receipts.
3. Listing inventory quantities and values.

The menu as it displays on the screen is shown in Figure 7-1.

```
--INVENTORY MENU--

0-EXIT from MAIN MENU

1-ADD a PRODUCT
2-EDIT a PRODUCT
3-REPORT OPTIONS

Choose One  : :
```

*Figure 7-1.* The Screen for the Inventory Menu

## ADDING ENTRIES TO INVENTORY

Adding to the inventory file includes adding new items to inventory, correcting the description, and deleting items. A sub-menu displays the options to select. The Add option allows the addition of new inventory items including the costs, prices, and quantity onhand. Many of the other normal dBASE II functions, such as deletion, can be done manually at the dot-prompt level. Data for using this option comes from purchase orders for items not previously stocked in inventory. The inventory file contains product code, product description, purchase cost, product price, quantity on-hand, and the reorder level (see Figure 7-2).

You paid the unit cost of $15.00 and plan a resale price of $26.55 for the item to be entered into inventory. The number in stock, 125, is obtained from your records, purchase orders, or receipts. The level to reorder (100) is your estimation of the amount of stock below which you

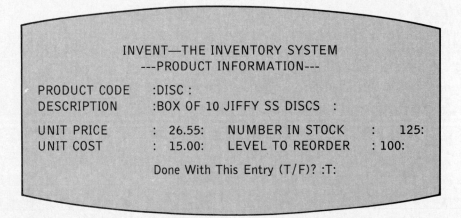

```
INVENT—THE INVENTORY SYSTEM
         ---PRODUCT INFORMATION---

PRODUCT CODE   :DISC :
DESCRIPTION    :BOX OF 10 JIFFY SS DISCS  :

UNIT PRICE     : 26.55:   NUMBER IN STOCK    :   125:
UNIT COST      : 15.00:   LEVEL TO REORDER   : 100:

               Done With This Entry (T/F)? :T:
```

*Figure 7-2.* Adding a New Product to the Inventory

```
            INVENT—THE INVENTORY SYSTEM
              ---PRODUCT INFORMATION---

PRODUCT CODE      :DISC :
DESCRIPTION       :BOX OF 10 JIFFY SS DISCS  :

UNIT PRICE        :  26.55:    NUMBER IN STOCK    :   125:
UNIT COST         :  15.00:    LEVEL TO REORDER   : 100:

                  Done With This Entry (T/F)? :T:

                  Add Another (T/F)? :T:
```

*Figure 7-3.* Adding a New Product to the Inventory—Completed Entry

should be notified for reordering. Figure 7-3 shows a completed entry for this addition to the inventory.

## EDITING INVENTORY

The Edit option allows modifications to inventory records in the file. Any field can be changed with this option, so you should be very careful, especially with the product code. The fields changed with this option are usually the stock on-hand, cost and price, or, in this case, the change of the reorder level from 100 to 125 (see Figure 7-4).

Once done with an entry, INVENT will ask if another entry is to be edited. The next entry will be displayed for editing if desired. A negative answer to the Add Another question will restore control to the main inventory menu (see Figure 7-5).

```
            INVENT—THE INVENTORY SYSTEM
              ---PRODUCT INFORMATION---

PRODUCT CODE      :DISC :
DESCRIPTION       :BOX OF 10 JIFFY SS DISCS  :

UNIT PRICE        :  26.55:    NUMBER IN STOCK    :   125:
UNIT COST         :  15.00:    LEVEL TO REORDER   : 125:

                  Done With This Entry (T/F)? :T:
```

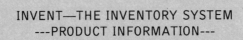

*Figure 7-4.* Editing an Entry in the Inventory File

```
         INVENT—THE INVENTORY SYSTEM
            ---PRODUCT INFORMATION---

PRODUCT CODE    :DISC :
DESCRIPTION     :BOX OF 10 JIFFY SS DISCS  :

UNIT PRICE      :  26.55:    NUMBER IN STOCK   :    125:
UNIT COST       :  15.00:    LEVEL TO REORDER  : 125:

                Done With This Entry (T/F)? :T:

                Add Another (T/F)? :T:
```

*Figure 7-5.*  Completion of Editing in the Inventory File

# REPORTING INVENTORY

Three reports are produced. The first lists all items (product code and description) in inventory with quantities on-hand and the cost and price of each item. It can be run as often as necessary although the valuation part is probably not needed any more often than once a month. The second report generates an identical report for products whose supply has fallen below the reorder level. The third report gives more detailed information about the value and potential profit from the sale of each product.

## The General Report

The first report produces basics inventory summaries and can be run as often as desired (see Figure 7-6). The most apt time is immediately after each receipt of inventory.

## The Low Stock Report

The second report uses the REORDER LEVEL for each product. The same report as the general report will be produced for only the number of items on hand that are equal to or less than the reorder level. The current REORDER LEVEL for Jiffy Discs is 125 units (see Figure 7-7).

## The Detailed Report

The third report outlines additional financial data not available in the other reports (see Figure 7-8). The GROSS VALUE for each type of prod-

```
PAGE NO. 00001      -------------- GENERAL REPORT ---------------
10/24/83
                       INVENTORY REPORT

                DESCRIPTION         COST       PRICE     # IN
TYPE              OF ITEM          OF ITEM    OF ITEM    STOCK

ACMEC   ACME RGB COLOR MONITOR     243.75     487.50       8
DISC    BOX OF 10 JIFFY SS DISCS    15.00      26.55     125
PLUGS   PHONE PLUGS                  1.14       1.75      75
SUPPR   SURGE SUPPRESSORS           21.50      39.95      36
** TOTAL **

                                                         244
```

*Figure 7-6.*  Inventory Report 1 - The General Report

```
PAGE NO. 00001      ---------- ITEMS IN SHORT SUPPLY ----------
10/24/83
                       INVENTORY REPORT

                DESCRIPTION         COST       PRICE     # IN
TYPE              OF ITEM          OF ITEM    OF ITEM    STOCK

DISC    BOX OF 10 JIFFY SS DISCS    15.00      26.55     125
** TOTAL **

                                                         125
```

*Figure 7-7.*  Inventory Report 2 - Low Stock Report

```
PAGE NO. 00001      ---------- VALUE OF INVENTORY STOCK ---------
10/24/83
                       INVENTORY REPORT

        COST     PRICE
         OF       OF      # IN     GROSS      NET     PROFIT/
TYPE    ITEM     ITEM    STOCK     VALUE     VALUE     STOCK

ACMEC   243.75   487.50     8     1950.00   3900.00   1950.00
DISC     15.00    26.55   125     1875.00   3318.75   1443.75
PLUGS     1.14     1.75    75       85.50    131.25     45.75
SUPPR    21.50    39.95    36      774.00   1438.20    664.20
** TOTAL **

                         244     4684.50   8788.20   4103.70
```

*Figure 7-8.*  Inventory Report 3 - Value of Inventory Stock

uct is generated by what you paid for each times the number on hand. The NET VALUE is the amount generated from sales. The PROFIT/-STOCK is the difference.

## SUMMARY

Operation of the simple inventory program is completed. By itself, it may serve a limited purpose as a summary of inventory data. Computerized inventory becomes truly useful when your sales automatically adjust the level of each product. Sales of your product will be linked to inventory by the INVOICE system (Chapter 10).

# INSTALLING INVENT

INVENT is a straightforward use of dBASE II. One data file is used (PRODTYPE), which is supported by two command files. Two FORM files allow a general report and a detailed inventory report.

## Table 8-1. List of Files and Main Functions

| File Name | Stands For | Function |
|---|---|---|
| PRODTYPE.DBF | Product Type File | Retains Inventory Data |
| INVENT.CMD | Inventory | Simple Inventory Menu |
| PRODSCRN.CMD | Product Screen | Screen for Add, Edit |
| PRODPRN.CMD | Product Printer | Prints Product Report |
| TYPERPT.FRM | Type Report | General Type Report |
| TYPE2RPT.FRM | Type 2 Report | Detailed Type Report |

Utility Files Used (On Drive A)
INIT.CMD
DTVERIFY.CMD

## PRODTYPE.DBF   THE PRODUCT FILE

The product file keeps an inventory of each product with the price and description of each item. The number on hand is maintained by IN-VOICE.

### Table 8-2.   Structure for File: B:PRODTYPE.DBF

NUMBER OF RECORDS: 00000
DATE OF LAST UPDATE: 12/02/83
PRIMARY USE DATABASE

| FLD | NAME | TYPE | WIDTH | DEC |
|-----|------|------|-------|-----|
| 001 | TYPE | C | 006 | |
| 002 | DESCRIPT | C | 025 | |
| 003 | PRICE | N | 007 | 002 |
| 004 | COST | N | 007 | 002 |
| 005 | STOCK | N | 007 | |
| 006 | REORDER | N | 004 | |
| ** TOTAL ** | | | 00057 | |

### Table 8-3.   Description of the Product Database

| Name of Field | Description of Field |
|---------------|----------------------|
| TYPE | The product code |
| DESCRIPT | The description of the product |
| PRICE | Price per item of the product |
| COST | Cost per item of the product |
| STOCK | The number in stock of the product |
| REORDER | Reorder level of the product |

# INVENT.CMD   THE INVENTORY OPTION

A simple inventory is maintained. There are three options: add a new record to the inventory, revise an existing record, or print one of three reports.

Like MAILFORM, there are three sections to the INVOICE menu.

### Section I: Housekeeping Section.

The Housekeeping section determines the drive location of the data and opens the file to be used. As with MAILFORM, the dBASE II utility file DTVERIFY is used to establish the system date.

### Section II: The Prompt Section.

The operator is prompted to choose the INVENT options. The menu options are presented in a loop.

### Section III: Branch to Execution.

The operator's wishes are executed after his or her selection is implemented. Each of the other command files is called depending upon the operator's choice.

A menu selection technique used by INVENT is the use of the substring search function, i.e., the @ command used to determine the position in a line of characters. INVENT uses the code:

```
STORE ' ' TO typech
DO WHILE @(typech, '012') = 0

   [prompts here for 0 to 2]
   @ 10, 5 SAY "Choose An Option" GET typech PICTURE '#'
   READ
ENDDO
```

The dBASE II @ command asks the question, "Where is the value represented by typech in the phrase '012'." If not found, a value of zero is returned to typech, and the DO WHILE loop continues asking until any input is given which is a part of the phrase '012'.

The menu construction easily allows for varied answers to be programmed into a menu command file. Consider the next:

```
STORE '      ' TO answer                           6 spaces
DO WHILE @(answer, 'YES NO MAYBE HI MOM!') = 0

   [Prompts Here for All Options]
   @ 10, 5 SAY "Choose An Option" GET answer PICTURE '!!!!!!'
   READ
ENDDO
```

The DO WHILE continues looping until the operator enters some or all of the letters in the phrase. Use of this menu technique is often a welcome variation from numbered menu options.

**CODE FOR INVENT.CMD**

```
     * invent.cmd
     * program by michael clifford
     * module purpose: maintains simple inventory

     * section I - housekeeping
     DO a:init
     ERASE
     SET DEFAULT TO &dfdefault
     USE prodtype
     SET DEFAULT TO &pfdefault
     DO a:dtverify
     SET DATE TO &viewdate

     * section II - operator prompting of options

     STORE t TO again
     DO WHILE again
         ERASE
         STORE ' ' TO typech
```

```
            DO WHILE @(typech, '0123' )=0
               @ 3,15 SAY " == INVENTORY MENU == "
               @ 6,15 SAY " 0-EXIT from MAIN MENU "
               @ 8,15 SAY " 1-ADD a PRODUCT "
               @ 9,15 SAY " 2-EDIT a PRODUCT "
               @ 10,15 SAY " 3-REPORT OPTIONS "
               @ 14,15 SAY " Choose One " GET typech PICTURE '#'
               READ

            ENDDO WHILE @(typech, '0123' )=0

            * section III - branch to execution

            IF typech= '0'
               * index the file on product code.
               * indexed file is needed by INVOICE system.
               INDEX ON type to invndx
               CLEAR
               CANCEL
            ENDIF typech= '0'

            IF typech= '1'
               * add a record
               STORE 'T' TO repeat
               DO WHILE repeat = 'T'
                  APPEND BLANK
                  DO prodscrn
                  @ 22,15 SAY "Add Another (T/F)? " GET repeat PICTURE '!'
                  READ
               ENDDO WHILE repeat = 'T'

            ENDIF typech= '1'

            IF typech= '2'
               * edit a record
               GO TOP
               STORE 'T' TO repeat
               DO WHILE .NOT. eof .AND. repeat = 'T'
                  DO prodscrn
                  @ 22,15 SAY "Edit Another (T/F)? " GET repeat PICTURE '!'
                  READ
                  SKIP
               ENDDO WHILE .NOT. eof .AND. repeat = 'T'
            ENDIF typech= '2'

            IF typech= '3'
               * report options
               DO prodprn
            ENDIF typech= '3'

         ENDDO WHILE again
```

## PRODSCRN.CMD THE ADDITION AND EDITING SCREEN

PRODSCRN serves to provide both the addition and editing options with a display of all fields for an inventory record. PRODSCRN will present the current record, looping until desired. Once done, control is returned to the main menu.

### CODE FOR PRODSCRN.CMD

```
* prodscrn.cmd
* module purpose: permits additions and edits
* to inventory file, prodtype
STORE t TO done
DO WHILE done
    STORE 'T' TO decision
    ERASE
    @ 3,20 SAY "INVENT - THE INVENTORY SYSTEM"
    @ 4,20 SAY "---- PRODUCT INFORMATION -----"
    @ 7, 0 SAY "PRODUCT CODE"
    @ 7,15 GET type PICTURE '!!!!!!'
    @ 8, 0 SAY "DESCRIPTION"
    @ 8,15 GET descript PICTURE '!!!!!!!!!!!!!!!!!!!!!!!!!!!'
    @ 11, 0 SAY "UNIT PRICE"
    @ 11,15 GET price
    @ 12, 0 SAY "UNIT COST"
    @ 12,15 GET cost
    @ 11,30 SAY "NUMBER IN STOCK"
    @ 11,50 GET stock
    @ 12,30 SAY "LEVEL TO REORDER"
    @ 12,50 GET reorder
    @ 20,15 SAY "Done With This Entry (T/F)? " GET decision PICTURE '!'
    READ
    IF decision = 'T'
        STORE f TO done
    ENDIF decision = 'T'
ENDDO WHILE done
RELEASE done,decision
RETURN
```

## PRODPRN.CMD THE PRODUCT REPORTER

PRODPRN is the last command file used by INVENT to generate one of three reports by using FORM files. After a choice is made by the operator (with the use of the '@' function), a general report FORM (TYPERPT) is used unconditionally in the first menu option. The second option uses the same FORM to report only records which have indicated that the present stock is equal to or lower than a predetermined stock level. The last option uses the TYPE2RPT FORM file to provide more detailed inventory information.

CODE FOR PRODPRN.CMD

```
* prodprn.cmd
* module purpose: reports on inventory
DO WHILE t
    ERASE
    STORE ' ' TO rptpr
    DO WHILE @(rptpr, '0123' )=0
        @ 3,15 SAY '==== INVENTORY REPORTS ===='
        @ 5,15 SAY '- 0. Return to Main Menu'
        @ 7,15 SAY '- 1. General Report'
        @ 8,15 SAY '- 2. Items in Short Supply'
        @ 9,15 SAY '- 3. Value of Inventory'
        @ 12,15 SAY "Select a Report " GET rptpr PICTURE '#'
        READ
    ENDDO WHILE @(rptpr, '0123' )=0

    IF rptpr = '0'
        RELEASE rptpr
        RETURN
    ENDIF rptpr = '0'

    SET PRINT ON
    SET EJECT OFF
    SET CONSOLE OFF

    IF rptpr = '1'
        SET HEADING TO ---------- GENERAL REPORT -------------
        REPORT FORM typerpt
    ENDIF rptpr = '1'

    IF rptpr = '2'
        SET HEADING TO ------ ITEMS IN SHORT SUPPLY ------
        REPORT FORM typerpt FOR stock <= reorder
    ENDIF rptpr = '2'

    IF rptpr = '3'
        SET HEADING TO ------ VALUE OF INVENTORY STOCK ------
        REPORT FORM TYPE2rpt
    ENDIF rptpr = '3'

    EJECT
    SET HEADING TO
    SET CONSOLE ON
    SET PRINT OFF
ENDDO WHILE t
```

## TYPERPT.FRM THE INVENTORY FORM

The TYPERPT FORM file generates a report of inventory from the PRODTYPE data file. Use PRODTYPE and REPORT FORM TYPERPT. Answer the dialog as illustrated in Figure 8-1.

## TYPE2RPT.FRM THE DETAILED INVENTORY FORM

TYPE2RPT generates the configuration for the more detailed inventory report and is entered in the same manner (see Figure 8-2).

## MODIFICATION AND EMBELLISHMENTS

dBASE II allows many modifications that can be completed. In addition, many other reports can be easily generated with very little additional effort.

Additional fields may be added to the inventory file (PRODTYPE). One field (ONORDER) may track back orders. The field may be updated by use of the Edit menu option. A FORM file would then be revised to allow reporting of the articles on order.

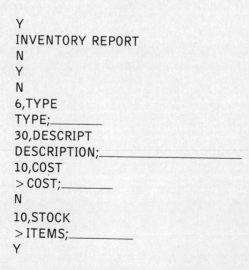

```
Y
INVENTORY REPORT
N
Y
N
6,TYPE
TYPE;_____
30,DESCRIPT
DESCRIPTION;_____
10,COST
>COST;_____
N
10,STOCK
>ITEMS;_____
Y
```

*Figure 8-1*  Dialog for TYPERPRT Form File.

```
Y
INVENTORY REPORT
N
Y
N
6,TYPE
;TYPE;====
9,COST
>COST;OF ITEM;=======
N
9,PRICE
>PRICE;OF ITEM;=======
N
6,STOCK
# IN;STOCK;======
Y
9,STOCK * COST
>GROSS;VALUE;=====
Y
9,STOCK * PRICE
>NET;VALUE;=====
Y
9,STOCK * (PRICE - COST)
PROFIT/;STOCK;=======
Y
```

*Figure 8–2.* Dialog for TYPE2PRT Form File.

## SUMMARY

INVENT by itself serves the useful but limited purpose of tracking the products on hand. Updating the addition of inventory is easy—just record the products as they are received by using the Add or Edit options of the menu.

Recording the depletion of inventory as it is being used is another matter. A time-consuming task, adjusting inventory will likely be neglected unless the updating is somehow automated. A useful remedy is to register depletion of inventory when a sales invoice is being written for the products in the inventory. Effort is saved by tying the purchase directly to the inventory.

The next two chapters will first outline the operation, then installation, of INVOICE. INVOICE runs with the inventory file to produce a listing of products that are current and reflect the sales of inventory. Once INVENT is installed, tracking your resources out of your enterprise is complete.

# INVOICING AND SALES REPORTING USING INVOICE

Collecting money owed to you or your company and keeping track of what is in stock are very important functions. This chapter discusses the features of invoicing and accounts receivable and how they relate to sales analysis and inventory control.

## THE BASICS OF SALES INVOICING AND REPORTING

### Invoicing

Invoicing is the process of billing, or sending an invoice, to a customer to show the amount due. Payment may be at the time of purchase or credit may be extended to the customer. An invoice contains information that is important to keeping track of sales and how much is owed by each customer. By storing the invoice data in a dBASE II file, we can summarize various kinds of information needed by management.

The invoice is the cornerstone to accounts receivable, sales analysis, and inventory management. The primary use is to track the amount owed by each customer, although other useful reports are created.

- A summary of invoices and payments gives an accounts receivable list by customer or invoice.
- The inventory can be updated by subtracting each line item of product sold from the inventory.

- The most profitable products can be quickly identified by summarizing invoices by product code to give a daily sales analysis.

The INVOICE system can also operate as a point-of-sales program for enterprises that have small-to-medium volume. The inventory system can be used not only with products, but also in other applications for which there are finite assets. Examples of these include the number of slots available in a classroom for instruction, or the number of hours available on certain dates for consulting time.

## Accounts Receivable

Accounts receivable is the process of keeping tabs on money owed to you. Cash flow headaches can be minimized by tracking the bills and the customers who are slow to pay their obligations. The customer file contains a balance forward amount, which is the summary of all customer payment activity. Reports can be quickly printed that summarize the total outstanding owed by each customer without adding up the line items for each invoice every time the statements are requested.

## Sales Analysis

What are the hot items? Which products are selling the fastest? Sales analysis summarizes the daily invoices and sorts by product to give the total sales each day by these products. The reports are easily generated by indexing the invoice file by certain key fields and employing the REPORT FORM command.

## Inventory Updating

How much product do I have on hand and how much should I order? These are the two key questions in handling products in your enterprise. The current status of each item can be reported by maintaining a current inventory based on sales. INVOICE supplements INVENT to produce a complete stock list and low stock warnings.

## Sales Commissions

Sales commissions reports can be calculated for each salesperson by including a sales ID on the invoice sales commissions reports. INVOICE does not include this provision, but it can be easily added. Commissions can be calculated by multiplying the total of the invoice before sales tax by a given percentage for each salesperson.

# OPERATION

INVOICE is started by entering dBASE II from your computer's operating system. Type DO X:INVOICE where X is the drive upon which the program resides. The computer will ask for the location of the data and the date. Once entered, the screen appears, as illustrated in Figure 9-1.

- Option 0 exits from dBASE II and restores the user to the operating system.
- Option 1 allows the operator to post an invoice to customer.
- Option 2 allows editing or revision of the customer data.
- Option 3 offers a sub-menu of report options.

## Option 1: Print an Invoice

The customer code is the foundation for the invoicing. INVOICE has tests that ensure that the proper code is entered. INVOICE will not allow continuation until a code is entered. You will be asked:

What is the NAME Code? : :

The NAME code will represent the customer code in INVOICE and the vendor code in PAYOUT. Once entered, the customer database is searched to determine if the code matches one stored for an existing customer. If the customer code is already in the dBASE II customer file, the customer screen will be displayed (see Figure 9-2).

The address items used in INVOICE are identical to those used in the MAILFORM client screen. The last two items are new: the TAX CODE is a one-digit number that classifies the adjustment to the money that exchanges hands. For INVOICE, this is a tax on goods purchased by the customer. The TERMS entry outlines the payment terms.

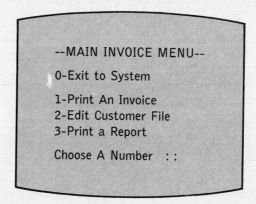

```
--MAIN INVOICE MENU--

0-Exit to System

1-Print An Invoice
2-Edit Customer File
3-Print a Report

Choose A Number  : :
```

*Figure 9-1.* Operator's View of Invoice Menu

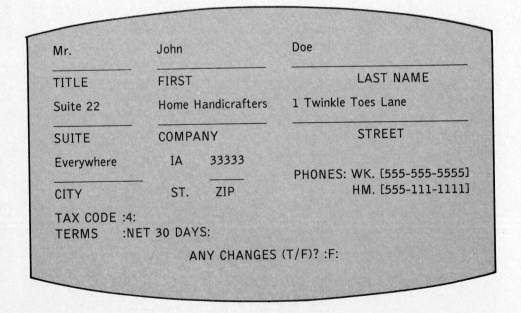

Figure 9-2.  The Invoice Customer Screen

Press RETURN or T if the correct customer has been identified by the code you entered. Enter F if you typed in the wrong code. The CORRECT NAME question will be replaced by another: ANY CHANGES (see Figure 9-3). Enter F if no changes are required. Entering T will allow for one revision of the screen.

Figure 9-3.  The INVOICE Customer Screen

If the code is not found, a message will appear on the blank screen:

Not Recorded. Enter as New Code (T/F)?

You should answer F if the code entered was mistyped and then the correct code should be entered. A T answer displays the entry screen and allows you to enter the data on the new client. INVOICE will again ask if any changes are required to your new entry.

The customer information has now been found by dBASE II. All address data and the billing information necessary for writing the invoice are available. The outlining of the invoice on the screen can then proceed. Only the data necessary for outlining the invoice is presented, all other data will be printed upon completion (see Figure 9-4).

The cursor will park between the colons under the QTY item. A sale of one item is assumed, but you may enter up to 999 items in this category.

The product code is entered in the TYPE field. INVOICE needs the product code to determine the item cost and description and to adjust the inventory. If the code is not found, N/A will be printed in the Description column and the default charge will be zero. You may enter a new or revised change for the item. See Figure 9-5 as an illustration of one item entered.

If a code corresponds to a product recorded in the product file, then the description, the cost per unit, and the total net cost will be displayed (see Figure 9-6). Enter More Items will be displayed at the bottom. Pressing RETURN, or T will allow the entry of up to nine more invoice items.

Once completed, the net charges are displayed and the total to be paid is displayed. The operator is requested to enter the amount to be paid between the colons on the PAYMENT RECEIVED line. INVOICE assumes that the purchaser will pay in full, but partial payment may be entered (see Figure 9-7). Be sure to have the printer ready.

The invoicing is completed once the payment is entered. The balance is calculated, shown on the screen, and added to the total balance outstanding for that customer (see Figure 9-8).

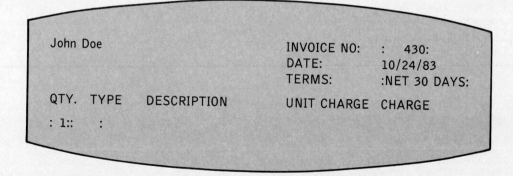

*Figure 9-4.* INVOICE Screen - Partial Display—Default Data

```
John Doe                              INVOICE NO:    :  430:
                                      DATE:          10/24/83
                                      TERMS:         :NET 30 DAYS:

QTY.  TYPE   DESCRIPTION              UNIT CHARGE  CHARGE

 1    DISC
```

Figure 9-5.  Invoice Screen—Partial Display - Inventory Search

```
John Doe                              INVOICE NO:    :  430:
                                      DATE:          10/24/83
                                      TERMS:         :NET 30 DAYS:

QTY.  TYPE   DESCRIPTION              UNIT CHARGE  CHARGE

 1    DISC   BOX OF 10 DISCS          26.55        26.55


Enter More Items? :T:
```

Figure 9-6.  INVOICE Screen - Partial Display - First Line Item

```
John Doe                              INVOICE NO:    :  430:
                                      DATE:          10/24/83
                                      TERMS:         :NET 30 DAYS:

QTY.  TYPE   DESCRIPTION              UNIT CHARGE  CHARGE

 1    DISC   BOX OF 10 DISCS          26.55         26.55

 5    SUPPR  SURGE SUPPRESSOR         39.95         199.75
 8    PLUGS  PHONE PLUG                1.75          14.00
 2    ACMEC  ACME RGB MONITOR        487.50         975.00


                 NET TOTAL CHARGES        1215.30
                 TAX RATE .05 TAX           60.76
                 TOTAL THIS INVOICE       1276.06
                 PAYMENT RECEIVED        :1276.06:
```

Figure 9-7.  INVOICE Screen - Partial Display - Entry of Amount Invoiced

118

```
John Doe                          INVOICE NO:    :   430:
                                  DATE:          10/24/83
                                  TERMS:         :NET 30 DAYS:

QTY.  TYPE   DESCRIPTION          UNIT CHARGE  CHARGE

  1   DISC   BOX OF 10 DISCS      26.55          26.55

  5   SUPPR  SURGE SUPPRESSOR     39.95         199.75
  8   PLUGS  PHONE PLUG            1.75          14.00
  2   AMEC   ACME RGB MONITOR    487.50         975.00


                        NET TOTAL CHARGES     1215.30
                        TAX RATE .05 TAX        60.76
                        TOTAL THIS INVOICE    1276.06
                        PAYMENT RECEIVED      :1276.06:
                        INVOICE BALANCE = >      0.00
```

*Figure 9-8.* INVOICE Screen - Completed Invoice

Two copies of the invoice are printed (which can easily be modified). Date and address information are added and more spaces are added on the paper. Records are made of every line item purchase, and the inventory is adjusted. Your invoice is complete (see Figure 9-9).

## Option 2: Edit Customer File

Editing of an existing customer record operates exactly as in the entry of a new customer. Enter the customer code. The customer screen will be displayed once the correct record is found. Move the cursor to the correct item and key in the change. You will be allowed one change before returning to the main menu.

## Option 3: Print a Report

The last INVOICE option allows the operator to select reports about the customers, outstanding balances, and sales (see Figure 9-10). Prepare the printer before selecting an option.

### Report Option 1: Daily Sales Report

Sales for the given date of all items are totalled by each product, the dollar volume is sub-totalled for each product, and the total dollars are presented on the last page of the report. Note in Figure 9-11 that the sales do not include tax, just the proceeds from the sale of the inventory.

```
                          YOUR COMPANY
                        YOUR STREET HERE
                       YOUR CITY STATE ZIP

Mr. John Doe                          INVOICE: 430
Home Handicrafters                    DATE :10/24/83
1 Twinkle Toes Lane Suite 22          TERMS :NET 30 DAYS
Everywhere, IA 33333
WK. 555-555-5555
      555-111-1111

QTY.          DESCRIPTION                 LINE ITEM CHARGES

  1           BOX OF 10 DISCS                       26.55
  5           SURGE SUPPRESSOR                     199.75
  8           PHONE PLUG                            14.00
  2           ACME RGB MONITOR                     975.00

              NET TOTAL CHARGES                  1,215.30

              5 % TAX                                60.76

              TOTAL FOR INVOICE --->            1,276.06

              TOTAL PAID                         1,276.06

              BALANCE                                0.00
```

*Figure 9-9.* The Completed Printed Invoice

```
---REPORT SUB-MENU---

0-Exit to MAIN MENU

1-DAILY SALES SUMMARY
2-CUSTOMER PHONE LIST and BALANCE

Prepare Printer and Choose An Option  : :
```

*Figure 9-10.* The Screen for the Report Sub-Menu

```
PAGE NO. 00001              DAILY SALES SUMMARY
10/24/83
                    ACCOUNTS PAYABLE AND RECEIVABLE

                                              SALES PER
                                              LINE ITEM
                                    QTY       (LESS TAX)

* PRODUCT: ACME RGB MONITOR
** SUBTOTAL **
                                     2          975.00

* PRODUCT: BOX OF 10 DISCS
** SUBTOTAL **
                                     1           26.55

* PRODUCT: PHONE PLUGS
** SUBTOTAL **
                                     8           14.00

* PRODUCT: SURGE SUPPRESSORS
** SUBTOTAL **
                                     5          199.75
** TOTAL **

                                    16         1215.30
```

*Figure 9-11.* Invoice Report Option 1

PHONE LIST - ALL CLIENTS

ACCOUNTS PAYABLE AND RECEIVABLE

| TITL | FIRST | LAST NAME | COMPANY | WORK PH. | HOME PH. | TAX | TERMS | BALANCE |
|---|---|---|---|---|---|---|---|---|
| Mr. | Diamond Jim | Brady | International Widget | 211-323-9876 | 211-333-9393 | 5 | NET 30 DAYS | 10000.98 |
| Ms. | Marilyn | Dearborn | Cottage Industries | 987-636-2123 | 987-283-9268 | 4 | NET 10 DAYS | 134.15 |
| Mr. | John | Doe | Home Handicrafters | 555-555-5555 | 555-111-1111 | 5 | NET 30 DAYS | 0.00 |
| Mr. | James | Zappa | Electronic Wizards | 915-838-3925 | 915-294-8104 | 4 | CASH | 0.00 |

*Figure 9-12.* Invoice Report Option 2

PHONE LIST - CLIENTS with BALANCES

ACCOUNTS PAYABLE AND RECEIVABLE

| TITL | FIRST | LAST NAME | COMPANY | WORK PH. | HOME PH. | TAX | TERMS | BALANCE |
|---|---|---|---|---|---|---|---|---|
| Mr. | Diamond Jim | Brady | International Widget | 211-323-9876 | 211-333-9393 | 5 | NET 30 DAYS | 10000.98 |
| Ms. | Marilyn | Dearborn | Cottage Industries | 987-636-2123 | 987-283-9268 | 4 | NET 10 DAYS | 134.15 |

*Figure 9-13.* Invoice Report Option 2 - Outstanding Balances

## Report Option 2: Customer Phone List and Balance

Like the MAILFORM program, a customer phone list for all customers is produced by this option. At least 132 columns will be needed for this report. The total outstanding balance owed by each customer will be listed on the right (see Figure 9-12). Option 2 will also produce a second report, highlighting customers who have outstanding balances (see Figure 9-13).

The invoicing program is completed. INVOICE will function as a simple accounts receivable for your enterprise and will allow for detailed analysis of sales.

# 10

## INSTALLING INVOICE

dBASE II accounting procedures usually use at least two data files. One file contains the names and addresses of the customers to be billed or the vendors to be paid. The other, the sales transaction file, contains the description of every change in accounts with every customer. Each record in the transaction file outlines one exchange, and the entire dBASE II data file constitutes a blow-by-blow description of every cash payment over time (see Figure 10-1).

Three files are used in the INVOICE system. One, PRODTYPE, is the inventory file discussed earlier. Another, CUST, stores all customer information. The last file, INVDBF, retains information on all money exchanged. The command files and other files manipulate the data, generate the invoices, and print the reports. The three data files (customer, inventory and sales transaction) are listed below with the other files used in the INVOICE system.

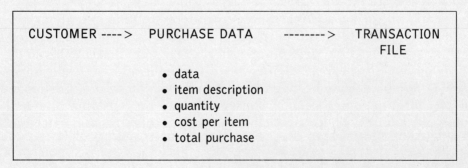

*Figure 10-1.* Transaction File: Describes Exchange of Money and Goods

## Table 10-1.  List of Files and Main Functions

| File Name | Stands For | Function |
|---|---|---|
| CUST.DBF | Customer File | Retains Customer Data |
| INVDBF.DBF | Transaction File | Retains Invoice Data |
| PRODTYPE.DBF | Product Type | Inventory File (Chapter 8) |
| INVOICE.CMD | Invoice Menu | Main Menu |
| CUSTSEAR.CMD | Customer Search | Searches for Customer |
| CUSTEDIT.CMD | Customer Edit | Edits Customer File |
| INVFMT.CMD | Invoice Formatting | Formats Customer Screen |
| INPRINT.CMD | Print INVOICE | Prints Invoice on Screen |
| TAXCODES.CMD | Tax Codes | Converts Code to Rate |
| INVPR.CMD | Prints Invoice | Prints Invoice on Paper |
| REPORTME.CMD | Report Menu | Report Menu Options |
| CUSTOMER.FRM | Customer Form | Customer Report |
| TRANACT.FRM | Transaction Form | Sales Transactions |

| Utility Files Used (On Drive A) | Other Systems Used |
|---|---|
| INIT.CMD | INVENT |
| DTVERIFY.CMD | |

What is the product price and full description? The operator can examine the PRODTYPE file and obtain this information, but the data is needed for each line item on the invoice while it is being developed on the screen. INVDBF, the invoice transaction file, is open to post the sales, but closing INVDBF and opening PRODTYPE to obtain product data is very time-consuming and disrupts the continuity of operation.

Nearly simultaneous action is needed to work these and any two of the three files. Vital data in the customer file needs to be posted to the transaction file; the transaction file needs product information from the inventory file; and the balance of each invoice for a customer needs to be posted back to the customer file to maintain an outstanding total balance. The swapping is due to the dBASE II command SELECT. Like supervising two boys to rake your yard, one in the back and one in the front, dBASE II command files shuttle between activity in a *primary* work area and in a *secondary* work area.

Nearly all the accounting procedures use more than one file at the same time. One of the main purposes for this is to save storing data for each record every time. The purchaser of every item needs to be identified for later reporting, but the entire customer address and phone number doesn't need to be stored in each transaction record. Customer address information needs to be stored only once in a customer file and not stored with every purchase. All purchases for this customer can later be associated by linking a customer code to the matching code in the sales file (see Figure 10-2). The customer code establishes a *relationship* between the customer address data and each purchase by this customer.

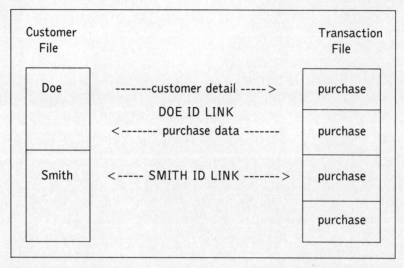

*Figure 10-2.* Files are Linked to Share Customer and Purchase Data

## DATA FILES FOR THE INVOICE SYSTEM

### CUST.DBF   The Customer File for INVOICE

Like MAILFORM, the customer file maintains all address information of the customers. The customer code is changed to NAMECODE for reasons that will be apparent later in the PAYOUT chapter.

Three other items are stored as well: BALANCE, ADJUST, and IN-VOICE. BALANCE is the total outstanding owed to you by a customer, which represents the accounts receivable. TERMS retains all data about the payment agreement (CASH, NET 10 DAYS, NET 30 DAYS). ADJUST is a single digit used in INVOICE to refer to the tax that must be charged to the purchaser. This provision is particularly useful for multi-county areas that must charge depending upon the residence of the customer.

CREATE this file or COPY the STRUCTURE of CLIENT from the MAILFORM system and MODIFY STRUCTURE. Carefully check that your structure matches the figure. See Chapter 4 for a description of the address fields.

### INVDBF.DBF   The Transaction File

The transaction file maintains one record for each product purchased; more than one of the products may be sold. The record shows the product quantity, total amount, and description of the purchase. Tax is not stored in the file but shows on the invoice.

*Table 10-2.   Structure for File: B:CUST .DBF*

NUMBER OF RECORDS: 00000
DATE OF LAST UPDATE: 00/00/00
PRIMARY USE DATABASE

| FLD | NAME | TYPE | WIDTH | DEC |
|-----|------|------|-------|-----|
| 001 | NAMECODE | C | 004 | |
| 002 | MR:MS | C | 004 | |
| 003 | FIRSTNAME | C | 015 | |
| 004 | LASTNAME | C | 020 | |
| 005 | COMPANY | C | 020 | |
| 006 | SUITE:ETC | C | 015 | |
| 007 | STREET | C | 025 | |
| 008 | CITY | C | 025 | |
| 009 | ST | C | 002 | |
| 010 | ZIP | C | 005 | |
| 011 | WKPHONE | C | 012 | |
| 012 | HMPHONE | C | 012 | |
| 013 | ADJUST | C | 003 | |
| 014 | TERMS | C | 012 | |
| 015 | BALANCE | N | 011 | 002 |
| ** TOTAL ** | | | 00186 | |

*Table 10-3.   Structure for File: B:INVDBF .DBF*

NUMBER OF RECORDS: 00000
DATE OF LAST UPDATE: 00/00/00
PRIMARY USE DATABASE

| FLD | NAME | TYPE | WIDTH | DEC |
|-----|------|------|-------|-----|
| 001 | NAMECODE | C | 004 | |
| 002 | DATE | C | 008 | |
| 003 | INVNUM | N | 006 | |
| 004 | TOTCHARGE | N | 008 | 002 |
| 005 | TYPE | C | 006 | |
| 006 | DESCRIPT | C | 025 | |
| 007 | QTY | N | 003 | |
| ** TOTAL ** | | | 00061 | |

*Table 10-4.   Name of Field Description of Field*

| | |
|---|---|
| NAMECODE | Customer code of the purchaser. Relates record to customer file. |
| DATE | Date of purchase (YY/MM/DD). |
| INVNUM | Invoice number. Identifies the form that was printed. |
| TOTCHARGE | Price for the product times the quantity. |
| TYPE | Product code. |
| DESCRIPT | The description of the product. |
| QTY | The quantity purchased of this item. |

# PROGRAM FILES FOR THE INVOICE SYSTEM

## INVOICE.CMD   Main Menu

There are three sections to the INVOICE menu: Housekeeping, Prompt, and CASE.

### Housekeeping Section

The Housekeeping section determines the drive location of the data and opens the first two of three files to be used. The last used invoice number, if stored on the disk in a separate memory file, is RESTORED to the INVOICE system. The operator is otherwise prompted to enter this number.

The dBASE II utility file DTVERIFY is used to establish the two system dates—one date for viewing and one date for placement into each record.

### The Prompt Section

The operator is prompted to choose the INVOICE options. The menu options are presented in a loop. A new technique with @ statements is used by storing SAY to the variable MODESAY (description follows for INVFMT.CMD).

### The CASE Section

The operator's wishes are executed after his or her selection is implemented. Each of the other command files are called depending upon the operator's choice. In some cases, several are called.

CODE FOR INVOICE.CMD

```
* invoice.cmd
* program by michael clifford
* module purpose: display an invoice on the screen
* print the invoice on paper
* maintain a customer file, simple inventory, and a daily
* record of sales

* section I - housekeeping
DO a:init

* test for existence of last invoice number.
* ask operator for invoice number if not saved to config.mem

IF 0=TEST(innum)
    ERASE
    STORE 0 TO innum
    @ 5,20 SAY "Please Enter LAST Used Invoice Number " ;
```

129

```
        GET innum
        READ
ENDIF TEST(innum) = 0

ERASE
SET DEFAULT TO &dfdefault
USE cust
SELECT secondary
USE invdbf
SELECT PRIMARY
SET DEFAULT TO &dfdefault

* establish system dates: one for viewing, one for file
DO a:dtverify
* set up date for reporting
* store to the dbase II system date for reporting
SET DATE TO &viewdate

DO WHILE t

    * section II - operator prompting
    * set up customer entry screen for viewing.
    * modesay variable does double duty for screen.
    STORE 'SAY' TO modesay
    STORE ' ' TO selection
    DO WHILE selection= ' '
        ERASE
        @ 3,15 SAY '== MAIN INVOICE MENU =='
        @ 5,15 SAY '0-Exit to System '
        @ 7,15 SAY '1-Print An Invoice '
        @ 8,15 SAY '2-Edit Customer File '
        @ 9,15 SAY '3-Print a Report'
        @ 12,15 SAY 'Choose A Number ' GET selection PICTURE '#'
        READ
    ENDDO WHILE selection= ' '

    * section III - execution of options
    IF selection= '0'
        * exit program.
        * save last used invoice number to memory file.
        RELEASE selection,filedate,viewdate,modesay
        SAVE TO a:config
        QUIT
    ENDIF selection= '0'

    IF selection= '1'
        * find the customer and develop invoice.
        DO custsear
        DO inprint
    ENDIF selection= '1'

    IF selection= '2'
        * edit existing customer.
```

```
        DO custedit
    ENDIF selection= '2'

    IF selection= '3'
        * display invoice report options.
        DO reportme
    ENDIF selection= '3'

    STORE ' ' TO selection
ENDDO WHILE t
```

## INVFMT.CMD    The INVOICE Screen

A new technique is employed in the INVOICE system—the use of a macro to switch a screen between saying and GETting variables. Use the word GET with the @ to obtain operator entry and assign it to a variable or a field. Sometimes, however, the SAY word needs to be employed instead of GET, to display the contents of a field without altering the code.

One way to do this has been to have two format files, one that has SAY commands to allow only display, and one that has GET commands to allow both revision and display.

However, two screens are wasteful of disk space. Another method is to "fool" dBASE II by using one screen of format statements, but the SAY or GET commands are not used. The variable MODESAY is used and is changed to SAY or GET by the use of a macro command. For example:

```
STORE 'SAY' to modesay
DO invfmt
(invfmt is called and these statements are processed)
@ 5,5 &modesay NAMECODE
@ 6,5 &modesay DATE
```

Once the macro is used, dBASE II sees the commands as:

```
@ 5,5 SAY NAMECODE
@ 6,5 SAY DATE
```

The code would allow these fields to be displayed without requiring the operator to alter the program. To allow revision, simply do the following:

```
STORE 'GET' to modesay
DO invfmt
```

dBASE II sees these statements as:

```
@ 5,5 GET NAMECODE
@ 6,5 GET DATE
```

A simple READ statement allows each of the @ statements to be altered. Only one screen formatting file is needed, which saves diskette space.

dBASE II requires that the formatting file be a .CMD file instead of a .FMT file for this technique to work reliably. The file that performs this function in the INVOICE system is called INVFMT.CMD, which refers to an INVoice command file functioning as the FMT file.

Thus, one of the first commands of the Prompt section of the INVOICE main menu is the command STORE 'SAY' to modesay, which establishes the SAY default for INVFMT to display customer information. The valuable customer data cannot be changed unless a dBASE II command specifically changes the modesay variable to the word GET, which will change the operation of INVFMT from SAYing to GETting customer data.

CODE FOR INVFMT.CMD

```
* INVFMT.CMD
SET colon OFF
@ 3, 5 &MODESAY mr:ms PICTURE "!XXX"
@ 3,25 &MODESAY firstname PICTURE "!XXXXXXXXXXXXX"
@ 3,50 &MODESAY lastname PICTURE "!XXXXXXXXXXXXXXXXXXXXXXX"
@ 4, 5 SAY "^____^"
@ 4,25 SAY "^_____^"
@ 4,50 SAY "^_____^"
@ 5, 5 SAY "TITLE"
@ 5,25 SAY "FIRST"
@ 5,62 SAY "LAST NAME"
@ 7, 5 &MODESAY suite:etc PICTURE "!XXXXXXXXXXXXX"
@ 7,25 &MODESAY company PICTURE "!XXXXXXXXXXXXXXXXX"
@ 7,50 &MODESAY street PICTURE "!XXXXXXXXXXXXXXXXXXXXXXXX"
@ 8, 5 SAY "^_____^"
@ 8,25 SAY "^_____^"
@ 8,50 SAY "^_____^"
@ 9, 5 SAY "SUITE"
@ 9,25 SAY "COMPANY"
@ 9,62 SAY "STREET"
@ 11, 5 &MODESAY city PICTURE "!XXXXXXXXXXXXXXXXXXXXXXX"
@ 11,35 &MODESAY st PICTURE "!!"
@ 11,40 &MODESAY zip PICTURE "#####"
@ 12, 5 SAY "^_____^"
@ 12,35 SAY "^^    ^_____^"
@ 12,50 SAY "PHONES: WK. ["
@ 12,63 &MODESAY wkphone PICTURE "###-###-####"
@ 12,75 SAY "]"
@ 13,05 SAY "CITY"
```

```
@ 13,35 SAY "ST. ZIP"
@ 13,58 SAY "HM. ["
@ 13,63 &MODESAY hmphone PICTURE "###-###-####"
@ 13,75 SAY "]"
@ 16, 5 say 'ADJ CODE '
@ 16,15 &MODESAY ADJUST PICTURE '#'
@ 17, 5 say 'TERMS '
@ 17,15 &MODESAY TERMS
SET colon ON
RETURN
```

Save the file as INVFMT.CMD, verifying that the file name is correct. Test by doing the following:

```
USE CUST
SET COLON OFF
APPEND BLANK
DO INVFMT
READ
```

The INVOICE screen shown in Figure 10-3 will be generated by dBASE II.

## CUSTSEAR.CMD  The Customer Entry Program

CUSTSEAR is called each time the operator wishes to post an invoice. The operator is offered the option of entering a revised code. Options are offered to revise or return and reenter.

LOCATE searches the data record by record, which is adequate for files of a few hundred records but too slow for larger files. The operator

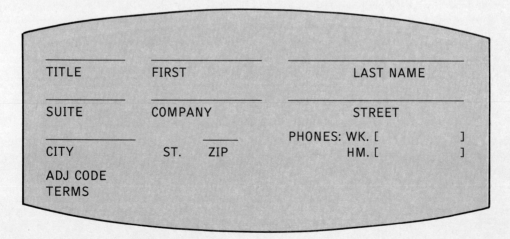

*Figure 10-3.* The Customer Entry Screen

is allowed to determine if the match is correct once a client is found and if any revisions are needed.

If the entry is for a new customer, the routine opens a new record in the file and enters the default TERMS and tax code, as well as the operator's customer code. The BALANCE field is assumed to be zero.

### CODE FOR CUSTSEAR.CMD

```
* custsear.cmd
* module purpose: search for vendor or customer code
* prompt and allow entry of new code
STORE t TO repeat

DO WHILE repeat

    ERASE
    STORE '    ' TO mcust
    @ 5,0 SAY 'What is the NAME Code?' GET mcust PICTURE '!!!!'
    READ
    STORE TRIM (mcust) TO mcust

    IF mcust = '  '
        LOOP
    ENDIF mcust = '  '

    LOCATE FOR namecode = mcust

    STORE 'T' TO enter, found
    IF eof
        STORE 'F' TO found
        @ 10, 0 SAY 'Not Recorded. Enter as New Code (T/F)? '!
        GET enter PICTURE '!'
        READ
    ENDIF eof

    IF found = 'F' .AND. enter < > 'T'
        * probably mistyped code for existing customer
        * allow another chance to correct
        LOOP
    ENDIF found = 'F' .AND. enter < > 'T'

    IF found = 'F' .AND. enter = 'T'
        * enter new code. establish default information in record.
        APPEND BLANK
        REPLACE namecode WITH mcust
        REPLACE adjust WITH '0'
        REPLACE terms WITH 'NET 30 DAYS'
        STORE 'GET' TO modesay
        ERASE
        DO invfmt
        READ
    ENDIF found = 'F' .AND. enter = 'T'
```

```
        IF  found = 'T'
            ERASE
            STORE 'SAY' TO modesay
            DO invfmt
            READ

            STORE f TO change
            STORE 'T' TO correct
            @ 22,25 SAY "CORRECT NAME? (T/F)" GET correct PICTURE '!'
            READ

            IF  correct < > 'T'
                LOOP
            ENDIF correct < > 'T'

            @ 22,0
            @ 22,25 SAY "ANY CHANGES (T/F)?" GET CHANGE
            READ

            IF  change
                ERASE
                STORE 'GET' TO modesay
                DO invfmt
                READ
            ENDIF change
        ENDIF found

        STORE f TO repeat
    ENDDO WHILE repeat

    RELEASE correct,enter,mcust,repeat,found,change
    RETURN
```

## CUSTEDIT.CMD   The Customer Edit Routine

The second main menu option invokes the routine to edit any record already recorded in the dBASE II customer file. A code needs to be entered, and the proper record will be searched by the use of the LOCATE command. Once found, the screen will be displayed. If not found, the routine returns to the main menu.

CODE FOR CUSTEDIT.CMD

```
    * custedit.cmd
    * module purpose: allow editing of an existing customer.

    STORE t TO repeat

    DO WHILE repeat
        ERASE
        STORE '      ' TO mcust
        @ 5,0 SAY 'What is the NAME Code? ' GET mcust PICTURE '!!!!'
        READ
```

135

```
            STORE TRIM(mcust) TO mcust

            * enter again if nothing entered
            IF mcust = ' '
                LOOP
            ENDIF mcust = ' '

            LOCATE FOR namecode = mcust
            STORE f TO repeat
       ENDDO WHILE repeat

       IF eof
           ERASE
           @ 10,15 SAY "NOT FOUND. PRESS ANY KEY TO CONTINUE "
           WAIT
       ENDIF eof

       IF .NOT. eof
           * the record is found.
           * allow entry of data on screen.
           STORE 'GET' TO modesay
           ERASE
           DO invfmt
           READ
       ENDIF .NOT. eof

       RELEASE repeat,mcust
       RETURN
```

# INPRINT.CMD The Invoice Generator on the Screen

INPRINT prompts the operator for each product purchased and the quantity of each. The cost, description, and amounts are obtained from the product file and merged with the operator entry to build the invoice. The purchase of each product is stored in the transaction file as a line item. (see Figure 10-4). The tax and total paid are computed and entered for the total invoice once each of the line items is completed. The outstanding balance is stored in the customer file for that particular customer.

INPRINT is the most complex command file of the INVOICE system. Many dBASE II accounting techniques are emphasized: the use of line counters with GET statements to enter an indeterminate number of lines in a precision form, posting results to sales transaction files, performing subtotals and totals on data, and the use of the SAY USING command to align numbers.

## Section I

Housekeeping is established in Section I of INPRINT. Substitute the desired company listings in the STORE statements for the first few lines

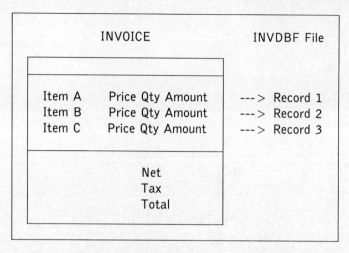

*Figure 10-4.* A Record in IVDBF and its Relation to an Invoice

of INPRINT. Your company information will be printed later at the top center of the invoice.

First, the screen is cleared and the customer code (NAMECODE) is stored to MCUST, a memory variable. TAXCODES is called to convert the ADJUST field tax code in CUST, the customer file, to a tax rate for calculations.

Each invoice will be comprised of from one to ten records, with each record outlining one line of the invoice. The record for the first invoice transaction is found by going to the bottom of the file (GO BOTTOM), finding the last record for the last transaction, and incrementing by one. Similarly, one is also added to the last invoice number to determine the current invoice number, INNUM.

## Section II

dBASE II code in Section II paints the top of the invoice on the screen with a summary of the working customer data. The line item prompt (QTY/TYPE/DESCRIPTION/UNIT CHARGE/CHARGE) is also displayed.

## Section III

Section III opens the product file. INPRINT will need to use product data with the transaction file, yet the customer record will be needed later. Since dBASE II currently can only use two files at once, the position in the customer file needs to be remembered. The current record number is determined from the # function and STORED to the memory variable CUSTPOINT, the CUSTomer POINTer to the proper record.

The product file (PRODTYPE) can be USED once the position in the customer record has been noted. The operator will be offered the opportunity to enter a product code and dBASE II will search for the corresponding cost and description. A file indexed by the TYPE field is re-

137

quired because the FIND command, unlike the relatively slow LOCATE command, is used for nearly instant determination of the proper record.

The FILE command is used in a simple procedure to recover from the attempt to open an index file that has been inadvertantly omitted or deleted. PRODTYPE will be indexed once again if the index file is not on the default disk. In either case, the index file is implemented with the SET INDEX TO command.

=============== TECH TIP ===============

*Check for an Index File before Using It*

*Recovery Procedure if an Index File Is Omitted:*

*USE prodtype*
*IF .NOT. FILE("invdx.ndx")*
    *INDEX ON KEY TO invndx*
*ENDIF*
*SET INDEX TO*

## Section IV

Section IV assembles the transaction for one item of the invoice and allows up to ten line items to be entered on the invoice. A special technique must be used, however, because of the need to position numbers, prompts, and GET commands flexibly at any coordinates on the screen.

The technique involves a loop that allows adjustments for the posting of up to ten lines of purchases on the screen (see Figure 10-5). Up to 17 lines from the top can be used for the purchases, with the variable LINE marking the row position from top to bottom. The first line is marked by the variable LINE and starts 7 lines down the page. Once done, LINE is increased by one and another invoice line is placed below it if the operator wishes.

The record in INVDBF that will store the transaction is first prepared by the APPEND BLANK command. The customer code, date, and invoice

| CODE IN INPRINT | FIRST PASS | SECOND PASS |
|---|---|---|
| STORE 7 TO line | *(moves to line 7 on page)* | |
| DO WHILE line < 17 | *(continue while line < 17)* | (continue while line < 17) |
|   APPEND BLANK | *(first invoice record)* | *(second invoice record)* |
|   @ LINE,01 GET quantity | *@ 7,1 GET quantity* | *@ 8,1 GET quantity* |
|   @ LINE,7 GET mtype | *@ 8,1 GET mtype* | *@ 8,7 GET mtype* |
|   READ | | |
|   *(REPLACE into INVDBF)* | *(fields filled)* | *(fields filled)* |
|   STORE line + 1 to line | | |
|   CLEAR GETS | *Clears the GET buffer* | *Clears the GET buffer* |
| ENDDO | | |

*Figure 10-5* Logic Used to Precision Print Indeterminate lines on Page

number are REPLACED into the record. Once done, INPRINT prompts the operator for the only two items requiring entry—the quantity and the product code. The quantity is assumed to be one, unless overridden.

The product code is any six-letter code that is needed to search the product file and return the full description and cost. The FIND command searches the indexed file and if not found, N/A will be placed at the current line of the invoice as the product description and the cost will be zero. The operator may wish to override both and type in a temporary description and cost.

Several steps occur if the product code is found. The proper description and unit cost are displayed on the current invoice line. The product code and cost are copied from PRODTYPE to the current record in INVDBF, to transfer the required sales information to the daily sales transaction file. The cost of a single item is STORED to the memory variable UNITPRICE, in order to maintain a running tabulation of the total balance for the invoice owed by the customer.

Inventory is maintained by subtracting the quantity purchased by the customer from the current number in the STOCK field in the PROD-TYPE file. The difference is the estimation of the number of items (meeting with the product code) that are on hand.

The accounting is determined for each line by multiplying the unit cost from the product file by the quantity purchased, and assigning it to linecharge. This is in turn added to the cumulative purchased amount for line items for this invoice and STORED to itemcharge.

The operator is then given the opportunity to add another item. The loop continues through ten times before exiting the DO WHILE loop.

The CLEAR GETS is often necessary when the looping technique is used. Each GET for each variable is remembered by dBASE II for each loop unless otherwise instructed, up to a limit of 64. Normal operation will not be impeded unless 64 pending GETS are exceeded, whereupon cursor chaos can result.

The ERASE command always clears all screen activity, including GETS, and INPRINT issues an ERASE before the 64 GETS are exceeded. However, placed at the bottom of the loop just before the ENDDO, the CLEAR GETS command is cursor insurance for this or any other similar dBASE II routine that uses a DO WHILE loop and multiple GETS.

The last current record of the invoice is stored to endrec, the END RECord of this invoice. This will be the last record printed in the invoice.

Section IV now has accomplished the posting of the purchases into the transaction file. The invoice gross purchases have been posted, and each purchase has updated the inventory.

## Section V

Section V subtotals, taxes, receives partial payment, and keeps tabs on the customer's total outstanding balance. The following variables are displayed in columns:

| | |
|---|---|
| mtax | tax rate to apply to purchase |
| itemcharge | gross purchase for total invoice |
| totltax | amount of tax for total invoice |
| total | total tax + gross purchase |

Once the total to be paid by the customer has been calculated, IN-PRINT allows partial payment. The variable paid is obtained by the operator (paid in full is assumed) and applied to the total. The invoice balance is then calculated.

Once the balance for this invoice is determined, the customer file is accessed at the location saved by custpoint. The unpaid balance for the invoice is applied to the field BALANCE in the customer file, which is the accounts receivable for that customer.

## *Section VI*

Section VI processes the screen oriented invoice and prints the paper version. INPRINT calls INVPR to PRint the INVoice. The command DO invpr will print an invoice as many times as it is repeated in INVOICE. INPRINT subsequently RETURNS to the main menu after final housekeeping.

CODE FOR INPRINT.CMD

```
* inprint.cmd
* module purpose: build invoice on screen
*
* Section I - Housekeeping
ERASE
STORE namecode TO mcust
STORE "Your COMPANY Here " TO yourco
STORE "Your STREET Here " TO yourst
STORE "CITY/ST/ZIP Here " TO cystzp

* establish tax rate from tax code
DO taxcodes

* get prior invoice number from transaction file
* add 1 to last invoice number
* store beginning record of transaction for invoice
SELECT secondary
* Now in INVDBF
GO BOTTOM
STORE # + 1 TO begrec
STORE innum + 1 TO innum
SELECT PRIMARY

* Section II - build invoice on screen
* preliminaries
@ 1, 2 SAY TRIM(firstname)+ ' ' + lastname
@ 1,50 SAY "INVOICE NO: "
```

```
@ 1,65 SAY innum
@ 2,50 SAY "DATE: "
@ 2,68 SAY viewdate
@ 3,50 SAY "TERMS:"
@ 3,63 SAY terms
@ 5,05 SAY "QTY. "
@ 5,10 SAY "TYPE "
@ 5,20 SAY " DESCRIPTION"
@ 5,50 SAY " UNIT CHARGE"
@ 5,65 SAY "   CHARGE"


* Section III - continue invoicing
* establish line items to be invoiced
* continue to add lines up to 10 entries
* save position in customer file
* use the product file to get price, description
STORE # TO custpoint
SET DEFAULT TO &dfdefault
USE prodtype
SET DEFAULT TO &pfdefault
* test for existence of indexed file.
* note that index file will be
* on the same disk with programs
IF .not. FILE( "invdx.ndx" )
    INDEX ON TYPE TO invndx
ENDIF .not. FILE( "invndx.ndx" )
SET INDEX TO invndx

STORE 'T' TO entermore


* Section IV - Place default data on each line of invoice
* and in each transaction record.
* Count all lines and use @ line,Y technique to
* handle any number of line items up to 10 on screen.

STORE 7 TO line
STORE 000000.00 TO itemcharge

DO WHILE line <17 .AND. entermore = 'T'
    SELECT secondary
    * Now in INVDBF
    STORE '      ' TO mtype
    STORE 0000.00 TO unitprice
    STORE 001 TO quantity
    APPEND BLANK
    REPLACE namecode WITH mcust
    REPLACE DATE WITH filedate
    REPLACE invnum WITH innum
    @ line,01 GET quantity PICTURE '# # #'
    @ line,7 GET mtype PICTURE '!!!!!!'
    READ
    REPLACE qty WITH quantity
```

*6 spaces*

141

```
* get description and price of item and return.
SELECT PRIMARY
* Now in prodtype
FIND &mtype
IF # = 0
    * Item not found. No data on record.
    * Indicate so on invoice.
    STORE '      N/A ' TO mdescript
    STORE 0.00 TO unitprice
ELSE
    * Item and data found in product file.
    STORE p.descript TO mdescript
    REPLACE s.TYPE WITH p.TYPE
    STORE price TO unitprice
    * update inventory by subtracting number sold
    REPLACE stock WITH stock - quantity
ENDIF # = 0

SELECT secondary
* return to INVDBF file.
* calculate unit price and total price per line.
* write the sale of product as a record in invdbf file.
REPLACE s.descript WITH mdescript
* The 's' is used before descript to tell dBASE II
* which DESCRIPT field in the two work areas to REPLACE.
@ line,20 GET descript
@ line,50 GET unitprice
READ
STORE quantity * unitprice TO linecharge
@ line,65 SAY linecharge
* place total sale of line item in file
    REPLACE totcharge WITH linecharge

    * add to cumulative invoice charge
    STORE itemcharge + linecharge TO itemcharge
    STORE line+1 TO line

    @ 22,10 SAY " Enter More Items? " GET entermore PICTURE '!'
    READ
    @ 22,10
    STORE # TO endrec

    * Ensure that dBASE II of 64 gets not exceeded
    CLEAR GETS
ENDDO WHILE line < 17 .AND. entermore = 'T'


* Section V - Accounting of all items
* calculate tax for all taxable items
* calculate and display gross and net.
STORE mtax * itemcharge TO totltax
@ line+1,40 SAY "NET TOTAL CHARGES "
@ line+1,65 SAY itemcharge USING '#######.##'
@ line+2,40 SAY "TAX RATE"
```

```
@ line+2,50 SAY mtax USING '.##'
@ line+2,55 SAY 'TAX'
@ line+2,65 SAY totltax USING '#######.##'
STORE itemcharge + totltax TO TOTAL
@ line+3,40 SAY "TOTAL THIS INVOICE"
@ line+3,65 SAY TOTAL USING '#######.##'

* get amount paid of bill.
* assume total is paid unless overridden by operator
* balance is balance outstanding owed by customer
STORE TOTAL TO paid
@ line + 4,40 SAY "PAYMENT RECEIVED"
@ line + 4,64 GET paid PICTURE '#######.##'
READ
@ line + 5,40 SAY "INVOICE BALANCE =>"
@ line + 5,65 SAY TOTAL - paid USING '#######.##'

* return to record in name file
* update balance field in this field with the grand total
SELECT PRIMARY
SET DEFAULT TO &dfdefault
USE cust
SET DEFAULT TO &pfdefault
GOTO custpoint

REPLACE balance WITH balance + (TOTAL - paid)

* Section VI - Printing and Exiting
* print the invoice twice
DO invpr
DO invpr

RELEASE mcust,yourco,yourst,cystzp,mtax,begrec,line
RELEASE mtype,linecost,unitprice,quantity,mdescript
RELEASE endrec,totltax,paid,custpoint
RELEASE itemcharge,entermore,total,linecharge

SELECT PRIMARY
RETURN
```

## TAXCODES.CMD  Convert Tax Codes to Rates

Many areas have different sales tax rates that apply to customers depending upon their county of residence. TAXCODES performs as a lookup table. The ADJUST field used in INVOICE is used as a tax code that is converted by TAXCODES to a corresponding tax rate.

The CASE structure is used to match codes with rates. If no code is recorded in the customer file, the OTHERWISE option is executed to warn the operator and a tax rate of 0 is assumed.

CODE FOR TAXCODES.CMD

```
* taxcodes
* module purpose: convert ADJUST field to a adjust rate
* warn operator if code not in customer file
* defaults to zero adjust rate if not specified
ERASE
DO CASE
   CASE val(adjust)= 1
      STORE 0 TO mtax
   CASE val(adjust)= 2
      STORE 0 TO mtax
   CASE val(adjust)= 3
      STORE .03 TO mtax
   CASE val(adjust)= 4
      STORE .04 TO mtax
   CASE val(adjust)= 5
      STORE .05 TO mtax
   OTHERWISE
      ERASE
      @ 10,20 SAY " WARNING-NO ADJUST CODE IS ENTERED "
      @ 12,20 SAY ' PRESS ANY KEY TO CONTINUE '
      WAIT
      STORE .00 TO mtax
ENDCASE
ERASE
RETURN
```

# INVPR.CMD   The Invoice Printer

INVPR takes the information generated on the screen by INPRINT and adds the other customer information, the name and address. The layout is more open than on the screen because more room (66 lines versus 24 lines) is available.

Your company name and address will be automatically centered on the top of each invoice. The code:

```
@ 2,(80-LEN(yourco))/2 say yourco
```

will always take the contents of yourco and center it near the top of a screen or printer, which has a width of 80 columns.

======= TECH TIP =======

*Centering Data or Prompts on 80-Column Screen*

*To center the variable mvar at line X:*

*@ X,(80-LEN(mvar)/2 SAY mvar*

The invoice heading is printed first. Your company name and address are centered at the top of the invoice. The customer information, date, invoice number, and terms follow.

All records associated with the transaction file are linked by having the same invoice number. These are searched by going to the record number of begrec, the BEGinning RECord number that was STORED in the INPRINT routine. A DO WHILE loop prints each line item, one to a line, until all the transactions with the invoice number are exhausted.

The accounting summary is printed below the transactions, once the INVDBF records are printed. Generous use of the SAY USING statements are used to align decimal points. Commas are inserted between the thousands digits to illustrate another use of the SAY USING command. Refer to the Technical Tutorial for operation of SAY USING. Control is returned to INPRINT once the printing of the invoice is accomplished.

### CODE FOR INVPR.CMD

```
* invpr.cmd
* module purpose: prints the invoice

SET PRINT ON
SET EJECT OFF
SET FORMAT TO PRINT
SET CONSOLE OFF
SET SCREEN OFF

@ 2,(80-LEN(yourco))/2 SAY yourco
@ 3,(80-LEN(yourst))/2 SAY yourst
@ 4,(80-LEN(cystzp))/2 SAY cystzp
@ 5,30 SAY "=================="
@ 8,02 SAY TRIM(mr:ms) + ' ' + TRIM(firstname) + ' ' +
   TRIM(lastname)
@ 8,55 SAY "INVOICE:"
@ 8,65 SAY innum USING '######'
@ 9,02 SAY TRIM(company)
@ 9,55 SAY "DATE  :"
@ 9,65 SAY viewdate
@ 10,02 SAY TRIM(street) + '       ' + TRIM(suite:etc)
@ 10,55 SAY "TERMS  :"
@ 10,65 SAY terms
@ 11,02 SAY TRIM(city) + ", " + st + ' ' + zip
@ 12,02 SAY 'WK. ' + wkphone
@ 13,02 SAY '    ' + hmphone
@ 14,02 SAY "*************************************************"
@ 14,50 SAY "****************************"
@ 16,02 SAY "QTY."
@ 16,31 SAY "DESCRIPTION"
@ 16,60 SAY "LINE ITEM CHARGES"

* go to beginning record number of the transaction
* write every line item in invoice
```

```
    SELECT secondary
    GOTO begrec

    STORE 18 TO line

    DO WHILE .not. eof .AND. innum=invnum
        @ line,1 SAY qty
        @ line,25 SAY descript
        @ line,70 SAY totcharge USING '# # # # # # #.# #'
        STORE line + 1 TO line
        SKIP
    ENDDO WHILE .not. eof .AND. innum=invnum

    @ line + 3,40 SAY "NET TOTAL CHARGES"
    @ line + 3,70 SAY itemcharge USING '# # # # # # #.# #'
    @ line + 5,40 SAY mtax * 100 USING '# #'
    @ line + 5,43 SAY "% TAX "
    @ line + 5,70 SAY mtax * itemcharge USING '# # # # # # #.# #'
    @ line + 11,40 SAY "TOTAL FOR INVOICE = = = = >"
    @ line + 11,66 SAY total USING '# # #,# # #,# # #.# #'
    @ line + 13,40 SAY "TOTAL PAID"
    @ line + 13,66 SAY paid USING '# # #,# # #,# # #.# #'
    @ line + 15,40 SAY "BALANCE "
    @ line + 15,66 SAY total - paid USING '# # #,# # #,# # #.# #'


    EJECT
    SET PRINT OFF
    SET FORMAT TO screen
    SET screen ON
    SET CONSOLE ON
    SELECT primary
    RETURN
```

## REPORTME.CMD  The Report Menu Options

REPORTME offers the operator two options. The first option is the Daily Sales Summary, which is produced of all sales for date logged into the system. The second option produces a phone list of customers and then a summary list of customers who owe you money.

CODE FOR REPORTME.CMD

```
    * reportme.cmd
    * module purpose: allow report options to be printed
    * close all files before proceeding
    SELECT secondary
    USE
    SELECT PRIMARY
    USE
    SET EJECT OFF
```

```
DO WHILE t

  STORE ' ' TO selection1

  DO WHILE @(selection1, '0123' )=0
     ERASE
     @ 2,15 SAY ' ------ REPORT SUB-MENU --------'
     @ 4,15 SAY ' 0-Exit to MAIN MENU'
     @ 6,15 SAY ' 1-DAILY TRANSACTION SUMMARY '
     @ 7,15 SAY ' 2-CUSTOMER PHONE LIST and BALANCE'
     @ 8,15 SAY ' 3-PRODUCT LIST and COSTS'
     @ 10,15 SAY ''Prepare Printer and Choose An Option '' ;
     GET selection1 PICTURE '#'
     READ
  ENDDO WHILE @(selection1, '0123' )=0

  * turn off clutter on screen
  SET CONSOLE OFF

  DO CASE

     CASE selection1= '0'

          RELEASE selection1
          SET EJECT ON
          SET CONSOLE ON
          USE
          SELECT secondary
          USE invdbf
          SELECT PRIMARY
          USE cust

          RETURN

     CASE selection1= '1'

          USE invdbf
          INDEX ON descript TO TYPE
          SET PRINT ON
          SET HEADING TO DAILY SALES SUMMARY
          REPORT FORM tranact FOR DATE=filedate
          * turn off index
          SET INDEX TO
          DELETE FILE TYPE.ndx

     CASE selection1= '2'

          USE cust
          INDEX ON lastname + firstname TO name
          SET PRINT ON
          * print general report
          * use compressed print code from INIT
          ? &comprint
          SET HEADING TO PHONE LIST -- ALL CLIENTS
          REPORT FORM customer
          EJECT
```

```
                            *  print summary list of clients who owe money
                            SET HEADING TO PHONE LIST—CLIENTS with BALANCES
                            REPORT FORM customer FOR balance > 0
                            *  return to normal print pitch
                            ? &normprint
                            SET INDEX TO
                            DELETE FILE name.ndx

                    CASE selection1 = '3'

                            USE prodtype
                            SET HEADING TO GENERAL REPORT—ALL INVENTORY ITEMS
                            SET PRINT ON
                            REPORT FORM typerpt
                            EJECT
                            SET HEADING TO ITEMS in SHORT SUPPLY (5 or LESS)
                            REPORT FORM typerpt FOR stock <=5
                    END CASE

                        EJECT
                        SET PRINT OFF
                        SET HEADING TO
                        SET CONSOLE ON

                ENDDO t
```

## FORM Files for Invoice

The two FORM files for the INVOICE report system are entered exactly
as they were for the INVENT system. Consult Section Two for details.

## CUSTOMER.FRM   Report on Customer Phone List and Balance

Enter dBASE II and SET DEFAULT to your program disk. Type USE
CUST and then REPORT FORM CUSTOMER. dBASE II will engage you
in a dialog to configure the report (see Figure 10-6).

The customer report will be finished once the dialog is complete. The
FORM can be abbreviated if your printer can not print 132 columns per
line.

## TRANACT.FRM   Daily Sales Summary

The daily sales report summarizes the total products sold by the number
of items for each product purchased on the given day. The report is
subtotalled by date and the product:

```
M=2,W=132
Y
ACCOUNTS PAYABLE AND RECEIVABLE
N
N
5,MR:MS
<TITL;====
15,FIRSTNAME
<FIRST;=====
20,LASTNAME
< LAST NAME;============
20,COMPANY
COMPANY;=======
12,WKPHONE
< WORK PH.;==========
12,HMPHONE
< HOME PH.;==========
5,ADJUST
<ADJ;===
12,TERMS
< TERMS;=======
11,BALANCE
>BALANCE;=======
```

*Figure 10-6.* Dialog for the Customer Form File

An important use of the REPORT command is used—the subtotal option. Contrary to the official dBASE manual, subtotals may be generated by character fields if the file is first indexed on that field. Since we wish to have a subtotal by product, the REPORTME program indexes the file by DESCRIPT first. The FORM file contains a Y (for YES), which was the response to the question SUBTOTALS IN REPORT? (Y/N), as well as the field (DESCRIPT) upon which subtotals would be accumulated.

═══════════════ **TECH TIP** ═══════════════

*Subtotalling and Reporting on a Character Field*

*To report on a character field, establish the report dialog to subtotal on the character field and* always *ensure that the file is indexed on that field before using the report command.*

---

First USE INVDBF and then type REPORT FORM TRANSACT. Enter the dialog as outlined in Figure 10-7.

The report is spaced out between columns by entering a dummy column. A WIDTH of 35 is entered in the dialog with the CONTENTS of ' ', that is, 35 spaces. No heading is required.

ENTER OPTIONS, M-LEFT MARGIN, L-LINES/PAGE, W-PAGE WIDTH
PAGE HEADING? (Y/N) Y
ENTER PAGE HEADING? *ACCOUNTS PAYABLE AND RECEIVABLE*
DOUBLE SPACE REPORT? (Y/N) *N*
ARE TOTALS REQUIRED? (Y/N) *Y*
SUBTOTALS IN REPORT? (Y/N) *Y*
ENTER SUBTOTALS FIELD: *DESCRIPT*
SUMMARY REPORT ONLY? (Y/N) *N*
EJECT PAGE AFTER SUBTOTALS? (Y/N) *Y*
ENTER SUBTOTAL HEADING: *PRODUCT:*
COL WIDTH,CONTENTS
D01 *35,' '*
ENTER HEADING:
002 *5,QTY*
ENTER HEADING:  *>;;QTY;—*
ARE TOTALS REQUIRED? (Y/N) *Y*
003 *15,TOTCHARGE*
ENTER HEADING:  *> SALES PER;LINE ITEM;(LESS TAX);—*
ARE TOTALS REQUIRED? (Y/N) *Y*
004 (PRESS THE CARRIAGE RETURN)

*ACCOUNTS PAYABLE AND RECEIVABLE*
*Y*
*N*
*Y*
*Y*
*DESCRIPT*
*Y*
*N*
*PRODUCT:*

*35,' '*

*5,QTY*
*>;;QTY;—*
*Y*

*15,TOTCHARGE*
*> SALES PER;LINE ITEM;(LESS TAX);—*
*Y*

*Figure 10-7* Dialog for TRANSACT.FRM

The long title required in the last column, SALES PER LINE ITEM; (LESS TAX), requires wrapping of three lines. This is accomplished as it was in INVENT by adding semicolons at the points we wish to force wrapping. The two semicolons before the QTY heading brings that heading and its underscore down to the same bottom line with (LESS TAX) (see Figure 10-8).

The FORM files are now completed, all the INVOICE files are now entered, and INVOICE is now ready to be used.

## EMBELLISHMENTS AND MODIFICATIONS

### Audit Trail

An audit trail that records the printing of an invoice can be accomplished by using a logical field. The technique was used in the MAILFORM series. A new field in INVDBF can be added, called printed. One line of code can be added to INVPR which will flag printed as TRUE for each of the purchased items that comprise each invoice. Add the underlined modification to the existing code as shown.

```
DO WHILE .NOT. EOF .AND. innum=invnum
    @ line, 1 SAY qty
    @ line,25 SAY descript
    @ line,70 SAY totcharge USING '#######.##'
    REPLACE printed WITH t
    STORE line + 1 TO line
ENDDO WHILE .NOT. EOF .AND. innum=invnum
```

Every purchase that was printed will be marked in the sales transaction file.

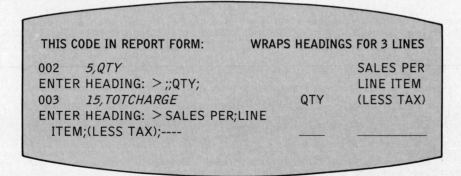

*Figure 10-8.* Wrapping Headings for 3 Lines

## Sales Analysis

The dBASE II file can be queried to produce comprehensive data about sales trends. The COUNT command can be used to determine at the dot-prompt the sales of a given item or group of items per date or range of dates. The SUM command can determine revenue from the sales under the same conditions. A REPORT FORM can be used to standardize the analysis.

TRANACT, the FORM used to display daily sales of each item, can be adapted to report over a range of days. The dBASE II code

```
REPORT FORM tranact FOR DATE > = '83/12/01' .AND. DATE < '84/01/01'
```

will produce a sales summary by product for the month of December 1983, by product. Be sure to have the file indexed on the descript field before using the REPORT command.

## Sales Commissions

Sales commissions can be generated at the time of sales by creating two more fields in INVDBF. One is the salesperson identifier code, which could be called SALESNAME. The other is COMMRATE, the commission rate applied to the salesperson.

Entry of data into the two fields may be accomplished by @ SAY/GET commands placed in the banner of default information produced at the top of the screen by INPRINT. The commission for each invoice can be calculated by multiplying the total invoice amount (less tax) by COMMRATE and assigning the result to SALESNAME. A REPORT FORM can be developed to subtotal on the COMMRATE field for the salesperson for each day. Index on SALESNAME before conducting the report.

## Maintain Tax Records

Sales tax is not stored in the INVOICE system. A tax amount field can be added, again to INVDBF. The tax amount can be taken as it is calculated and displayed at the bottom of INPRINT and REPLACEd into the tax amount field. The REPORT FORM can be changed accordingly, to display the tax.

## SUMMARY

The INVOICE system is now complete. If linked with inventory, a complete and current record of sales and current resources is maintained.

The update of inventory depletion is automated and trends in sales may be analyzed using the powerful dBASE II REPORT command.

The next two chapters focus on the opposite process: monitoring the resources and services you purchased from others. PAYBILLS, an accounts payable program, will assist in the tracking and management of payments.

# 11

# PAYING YOUR DEBTS: USING PAYBILLS

How much do I owe and when do I pay? An accounts payable program processes your bills and prompts you to pay on time to ensure that both your reputation and the water are maintained.

Just as the INVOICE system linked invoicing to inventory, accounts payable ties bills to payments. As bills are received, the vendor's name and address, total amount of the bill, and the date and terms of purchase are entered into the computer. The computer then is used to prepare checks, report cash disbursements, age payments due, and summarize amounts due by vendor so that payments may be grouped into one check.

PAYBILLS, like INVOICE, uses three files. One file, VENDOR, registers the name and address information about the vendors. The second transaction file, IOUS, registers every payment activity per bill and account. The third, CHECKFIL, records the result of these exchanges as a file of the checks that were written to the vendors.

The steps that enable a computer to pay a bill are the same as for manually paying a bill:

- Record the bills as they arrive and the date due.
- Prepare periodically a payables list in date due and vendor code sequence.
- Select vendors to be paid and vendor invoices.
- Prepare checks and report the payments.

The data necessary for the accounts payable are vendor number, vendor name and address (if you put it on the check), date payment due, terms of purchase, and the gross amount of purchase.

A report showing the payments due by data and vendor number is printed periodically so that you can select the bills that should be paid. The payments selected are summarized by vendor, and the check amounts are displayed on the screen for review before printing. When the check is printed, the check date should be updated in the accounts payable file as well as a flag marked showing that the check has been printed.

A major feature of an accounts payable is the cash disbursements journal. The disbursements journal is a list of all the checks printed each time in check number sequence and includes the vendor code, vendor name, amount of check and date paid. A third file is kept of all of these checks.

## OPERATION

Start PAYBILLS by typing the dBASE II command DO X:PAYBILLS, where X is the drive for PAYBILLS. The program will initialize. Once completed, the menu appears as shown in Figure 11-1.

- Option 0 exits from dBASE II and restores the user to the operating system.
- Option 1 allows the operator to post a bill as it is received into the computer.
- Option 2 allows editing or revision of the vendor data.
- Option 3 allows the operator to review each posted bill and pay all or part. The due date will be displayed, as well as the terms and discount rate, if any, for early payment. Once paid, the check will be posted to a check file for printing.
- Option 4 prints the current checks, which were posted but not printed.
- Option 5 offers a sub-menu of report options. Reports may be printed from the three files.

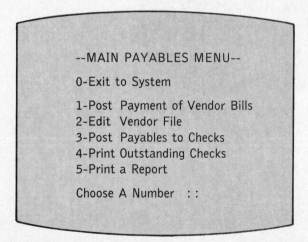

```
--MAIN PAYABLES MENU--

0-Exit to System

1-Post Payment of Vendor Bills
2-Edit  Vendor File
3-Post  Payables to Checks
4-Print Outstanding Checks
5-Print a Report

Choose A Number  : :
```

*Figure 11-1.* Operator's View of Payables Menu

# OPTION 1: POSTING A BILL

A code for a vendor is as essential to the operation of accounts payables as it is for receivables. Operation is identical for this option as it is for the first INVOICE option. You will be asked:

What is the NAME Code? :DOE:

The vendor file will be searched to determine if the code matches an existing vendor. If so, the vendor screen will be displayed as shown in Figure 11-2.

The screen is identical to the one used in INVOICE but two items are used differently. ADJ CODE reflects the discount that many vendors offer if bills are paid early. TERMS outlines the requirements necessary to receive this discount. TERMS may also be used to display other notes.

As with INVOICE, you may press RETURN or T if the correct customer has been identified by the code you entered. Enter F if you typed in the wrong code.

The CORRECT NAME question will be replaced by another: ANY CHANGES. Enter F if no changes are required. Entering T will allow for one revision of the screen (see Figure 11-3).

If the code is not found, a message will appear on the screen.

Not Recorded. Enter as New Code (T/F)?

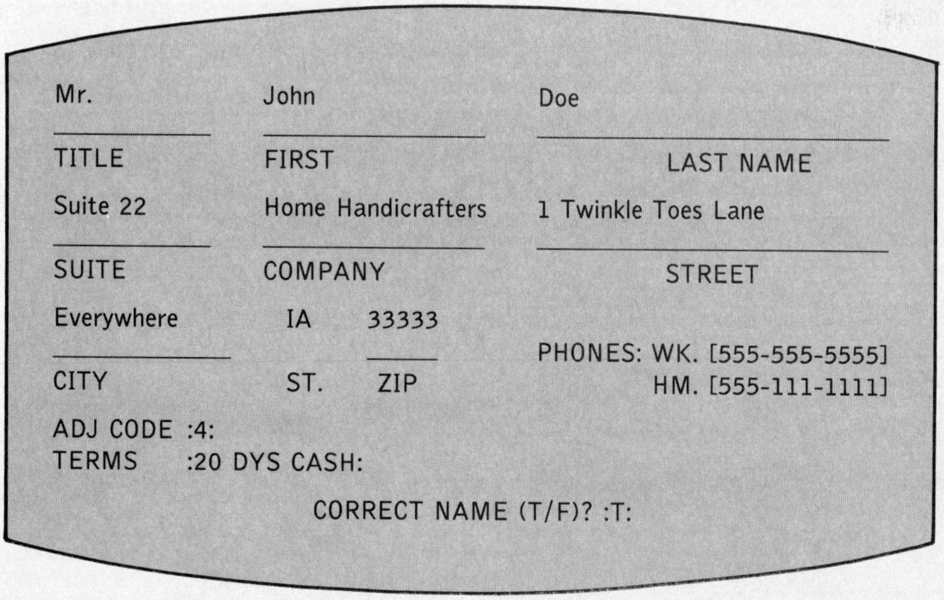

```
Mr.             John            Doe
_____         _____         _____
TITLE           FIRST               LAST NAME
Suite 22        Home Handicrafters   1 Twinkle Toes Lane
_____         _____     _____
SUITE           COMPANY                STREET
Everywhere      IA    33333
                                PHONES: WK. [555-555-5555]
_____         ____  _____           HM. [555-111-1111]
CITY            ST.   ZIP
ADJ CODE :4:
TERMS    :20 DYS CASH:
             CORRECT NAME (T/F)? :T:
```

*Figure 11-2.* The Vendor Screen

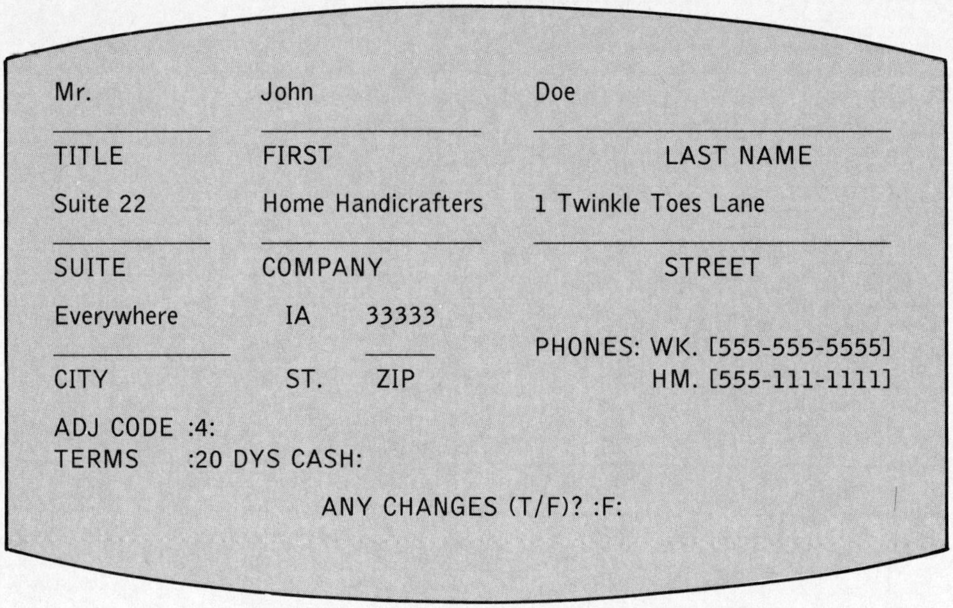

```
┌─────────────────────────────────────────────────────────┐
│                                                           │
│   Mr.              John               Doe                 │
│   ──────────       ──────────         ─────────────────   │
│   TITLE            FIRST                  LAST NAME        │
│                                                           │
│   Suite 22         Home Handicrafters  1 Twinkle Toes Lane│
│   ──────────       ──────────         ─────────────────   │
│   SUITE            COMPANY                 STREET         │
│                                                           │
│   Everywhere       IA    33333                           │
│   ──────────       ──── ─────          PHONES: WK. [555-555-5555]│
│   CITY             ST.   ZIP                   HM. [555-111-1111]│
│                                                           │
│   ADJ CODE  :4:                                          │
│   TERMS     :20 DYS CASH:                                │
│                   ANY CHANGES (T/F)? :F:                 │
│                                                           │
└─────────────────────────────────────────────────────────┘
```

*Figure 11-3.* The Vendor Screen

Answer F for another opportunity to post to an existing vendor. A T answer displays a new vendor to be entered into the dBASE II file. Make corrections if necessary.

## Posting the Bill to Be Paid

Bills are seldom paid the moment they arrive but are posted for later payment, either manually to a compartment or electronically to a file. PAYBILLS posts each bill to the IOUS file once the vendor has been identified.

The screen will clear and the request for the date will appear. Enter the due date. Payment data will subsequently be displayed as illustrated in Figure 11-4.

Three items of data should be entered. The BILL NUMBER is the identifying number on the vendor's bill or purchase order. This may not be necessary for a simple bill, i.e., an electric bill. The DESCRIPTION may be up to 20 characters and is optional. The notation will be of help, however, if a payment discrepancy arises several months later. The PAYMENT AMOUNT is required. This is the full amount to be paid to the vendor, excluding any discount. The posting is completed once the amount has been entered.

PAYBILLS will allow the option to post another bill to the same creditor. The screen will clear and the default information is displayed at the top of the screen for that creditor (see Figure 11-5).

You are allowed to enter as many bills for one creditor as are received. As with INPRINT, however, there will later be an effective limit

158

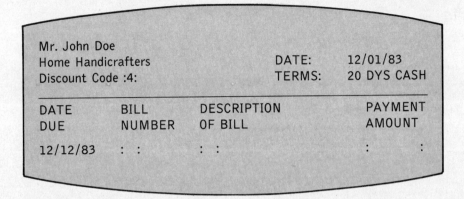

```
Mr. John Doe
Home Handicrafters                    DATE:      12/01/83
Discount Code :4:                     TERMS:     20 DYS CASH

DATE          BILL       DESCRIPTION                PAYMENT
DUE           NUMBER     OF BILL                    AMOUNT

12/12/83      :  :          :  :                      :        :
```

*Figure 11-4.* The Bill Posting Screen - Partial Display

of ten that can be shown on the screen. Owing more than ten bills to one creditor is not recommended, from both a programming and a business perspective.

Once all bills to the same creditor have been posted, PAYBILLS will request entry of bills from other vendors (see Figure 11-6). The operator is returned to the main PAYBILLS menu if the option is declined.

## OPTION 2: EDIT THE VENDOR FILE

Editing of the vendor file is identical to editing of the INVOICE customer file. The entry of a name code for the vendor allows editing and updating of vendor data. One change is allowed before returning to the main menu.

```
Mr. John Doe
Home Handicrafters                    DATE:      12/01/83
Discount Code :4:                     TERMS:     20 DYS CASH

DATE          BILL       DESCRIPTION                PAYMENT
DUE           NUMBER     OF BILL                    AMOUNT

12/12/83      :1121 :    :45 SKEINS OF YARN  :    :  102.75:

              Post Another Bill for Creditor (T/F) ? :F:
```

*Figure 11-5.* The Completed Bill Posting Screen - One Creditor

```
Mr. John Doe
Home Handicrafters                    DATE:     12/01/83
Discount Code :4:                     TERMS:    20 DYS CASH
_____
DATE          BILL        DESCRIPTION              PAYMENT
DUE           NUMBER      OF BILL                  AMOUNT

12/12/83      :1121 :     :45 SKEINS OF YARN  :  : 102.75:

              Post A Bill for NEW Creditor (T/F) ? :F:
```

*Figure 11-6.* The Completed Bill Posting Screen - All Creditors

## OPTION 3: POST PAYABLES TO CHECKS

Bills are both displayed and paid in the same manner that products were purchased in the INVOICE system; each line of the screen represents one transaction for the same company. Payments are calculated for each and carried across to a subtotal and down for the total. An adjustment is applied, in this case, an applicable discount. Once accomplished, the grand total is posted to a check file.

The screen first clears and the payment screen is displayed (see Figure 11-7).

Each bill that is not completely paid will be displayed, one to a line, in order of the vendor code (alphabetical), the date due (chronological), and the bill number (numerical). The payment of the entire outstanding

```
Home Handicrafters
                                          DATE :    11/10/83
Discount Info :4:                         TERMS:    20 DYS CASH
_____
DATE       BILL      AMOUNT    GROSS AMT   DISC.   NET PAY   BALANCE
DUE        NUMBER    DUE       TO PAY      ADJ %   FOR BILL  TO OWE

12/12/83   1121        102.75 : 102.75:    :0:
           45 SKEINS OF YARN
```

*Figure 11-7.* Payment Screen - Partial Display - Default Data and First Bill

160

```
Home Handicrafters
                                              DATE:      11/10/83
Discount Info :4:                             TERMS:     20 DYS CASH
─────────────────────────────────────────────────────────────────────
DATE        BILL       AMOUNT   GROSS AMT    DISC.    NET PAY    BALANCE
DUE         NUMBER     DUE      TO PAY       ADJ %    FOR BILL   TO OWE

12/12/83    1121         102.75 :  102.75:    :4:       98.64      0.00

            45 SKEINS OF YARN

Press Any Key to Continue Posting Bills.
```

*Figure 11-8.*   Payment Screen - First Bill - Entry of Payment Amount

bill is assumed and can be registered by pressing the RETURN key. Once done, a percentage discount is allowed. If entered, the discounted payment necessary to close the account will be calculated. A remaining balance will be displayed on the right.

Pressing any key will allow the next bill to be displayed (see Figure 11-8). Another bill for the same vendor will appear on the next line. If all bills have been paid for one vendor, then the screen will clear and bills for another vendor will be listed. The main menu will be displayed after all possible outstanding bills have been inspected and possibly paid.

The option to pay only a part of a bill for one account may often be desired (see Figures 11-9, 11-10). Enter the partial amount at the GROSS AMT column. There will rarely be a discount for such payment and a non-zero amount should not be entered.

```
Home Handicrafters
                                              DATE:      11/10/83
Discount Info :4:                             TERMS:     20 DYS CASH
─────────────────────────────────────────────────────────────────────
DATE        BILL       AMOUNT   GROSS AMT    DISC.    NET PAY    BALANCE
DUE         NUMBER     DUE      TO PAY       ADJ %    FOR BILL   TO OWE

12/12/83    1121         102.75 :  102.75:    :4:       98.64      0.00
12/15/83    1145        3000.00 : 2000.00:    :0:     2000.00   1000.00

            MODEL 27 HAND LOOM

Press Any Key to Continue Posting Bills.
```

*Figure 11-9.*   Bill Payment Screen - One Vendor - Two Bills - Partial Payment

```
Home Handicrafters
                                              DATE:      11/10/83
Discount Terms:4:                             TERMS:     20 DYS CASH
─────────────────────────────────────────────────────────────────
DATE        BILL        AMOUNT     GROSS AMT    DISC.   NET PAY   BALANCE
DUE         NUMBER      DUE        TO PAY       ADJ %   FOR BILL  TO OWE

12/12/83    1121        1234.56 :  1234.56:     :4:     1185.17      0.00
12/15/83    1145        3000.00 :  2000.00:     :0:     2000.00   1000.00
12/22/83    2018        1745.00 :   800.00:     :0:      800.00    945.00

Press Any Key to Continue Posting Bills.
```

*Figure 11-10.*  Bill Payment Screen - One Vendor - Three Bills - Partial Payment

The payment total will be written to the check file. The total represents the total amount to be applied to the outstanding bills for the vendor and is stored in the check file. The BALANCE TO OWE offers an accounting of the payment applied to each bill and also is stored, in the IOUS file. Reports on each may be requested at the operator's option.

All outstanding bills for all vendors are viewed and payments are allotted to each. Control is returned to the main menu once the inspection and payments are completed (see Figure 11-11).

```
Home Handicrafters
                                              DATE:      11/10/83
Discount Terms:4:                             TERMS:     20 DYS CASH
─────────────────────────────────────────────────────────────────
DATE        BILL        AMOUNT     GROSS AMT    DISC.   NET PAY   BALANCE
DUE         NUMBER      DUE        TO PAY       ADJ %   FOR BILL  TO OWE

12/12/83    1121         102.75 :   102.75:     :4:       98.64      0.00
12/15/83    1145        3000.00 :  2000.00:     :0:     2000.00   1000.00
12/22/83    2018        1745.00 :   800.00:     :0:      800.00    945.00

            TOTAL TO BE PAID                            2898.64

Press Any Key to Continue Posting Bills.
```

*Figure 11-11.*  Bill Payment Screen - One Vendor - Completed Payment

162

## OPTION 4: PRINTING CHECKS

All outstanding checks will be printed with this option. Checks may be printed on the day of payment or delayed until a later time. However, the date of printing of check, not the date of payment to the check file, will be printed on the check and stub.

The standard PAYBILLS will print a check stub with the check and the address on the check for display in an envelope with a window. Modification of the PAYBILLS system may be required before proceeding because the shape of check stock varies widely. You will need to ensure that PAYBILLS has been adapted to fit your needs. Alterations are suggested in Chapter 10.

Align the check stock with the print head and enter the first check number. Once done, the screen will clear and display the following message for the entire printing engagement:

```
**** CHECK PRINTING IN PROGRESS ****
```

Each stub will be printed. The check will be printed after a pause (see Figure 11-12). Once completed, each of the accounts will be updated so that the check cannot be paid twice.

## Re-Issuing a Damaged Check

A check may be damaged during printing. PAYBILLS locks out duplicate printing of checks, but this may be overridden. First, allow the printing of the other checks to finish. Then enter dBASE II, USE CHECKFIL, locate the record that corresponds to the check payment, and type:

```
REPLACE unprinted WITH t
```

Enter the PAYBILLS system again and use the check printing option. A new check will be issued to replace the damaged check.

## OPTION 5: PRINT A REPORT

The last PAYBILLS option will produce reports about the vendors, the balances for each vendor by bill, and checks printed on a given date. Detailed options are also provided about the daily transactions—the amounts paid for each balance and the bills received.

As with most complete accounts payable systems, PAYBILLS also allows each bill to be aged. All bills that are due within 30 days are printed on one report, 30–60 days for another, 60–90 days for a third, and all bills due in more than 90 days are printed on a fourth.

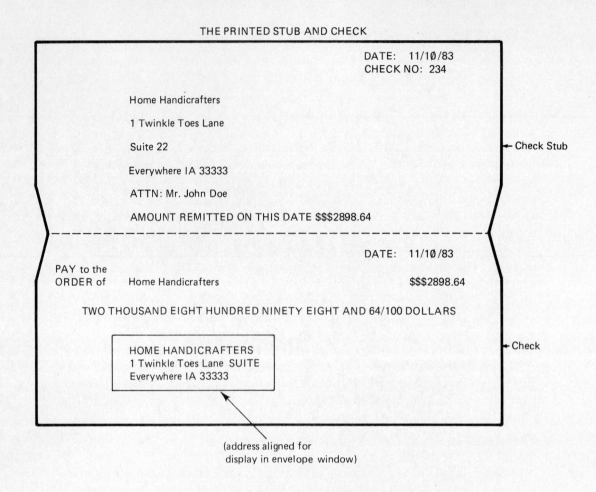

*Figure 11-12.* The Printed Stub and Check


Prepare the printer before selecting an option (see Figure 11-13). Select the last option in the PAYBILLS main menu.

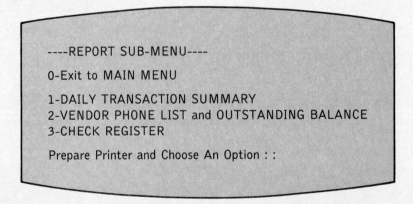

*Figure 11-13.* The Screen for the Report Sub-menu

Selection of the report option displays the first message:

Do You Wish to View (V) only or Print (P)? :V:

Viewing will scroll the report on the screen and is suitable for quick queries. The Print option cancels screen operation while the report is being sent to the printer.

## Report Option 1: The Daily Transaction Summary

The Daily Transaction Summary is a composite of several reports:

- The bills paid on this date.
- The unpaid bills received and posted on this date.
- Aged account for bills due in 30, 60, 90, and 90+ days.

The DAILY PAYMENT SUMMARY is first produced (see Figure 11-14). All payments that were made on the logged date will be displayed. The report is subtotalled by vendor ID; all payments are clumped in alphabetical order of the NAMECODE. The LAST PAYMENT column reflects the most recent payment and is most useful when the report option is used just after paying bills.

```
PAGE NO. 00001              -- DAILY PAYMENT SUMMARY--
11/10/83
                    ACCOUNTS PAYABLE TRANSACTION LIST

BILL    DATE      DATE      BILL     LAST     DATE OF
NUM.    DUE       REC.      BAL.     PAYMENT  PAYMENT   DESCRIPTION
*-------------VENDOR------------->DOE
1121   12/12/83  11/10/83     0.00    98.64  11/10/83  45 SKEINS OF YARN
1145   12/15/83  11/10/83  1000.00  2000.00  11/10/83  MODEL 4 AUTO LOOM
2018   12/22/83  11/10/83   945.00   800.00  11/10/83  MODEL 27 HAND LOOM
** SUBTOTAL **
                           1945.00  2898.64

*-------------VENDOR------------->ZAPP
321    01/18/83  11/10/84  1250.00  1000.00  11/10/83  INDUSTRIAL MONITORS
456    02/22/84  11/10/84  3500.00   500.00  11/10/83  INDUST CONTROLLER
** SUBTOTAL **
                           4750.00  1500.00
* TOTAL **
                           6695.00  4398.64
```

*Figure 11-14.* Daily Transactions - Payment Summary

Once completed, the page will be ejected and the second report will automatically be printed. All bills that were received on this date and posted to PAYBILLS will be printed, regardless of payment (see Figure 11-15).

### Aged Payments

One of the most useful reports in an accounts payable system is the aging report. Decisions about repayment may hinge on the duration that a bill has remained outstanding.

The aged reports are optional. The screen will clear and you will be asked:

Do You Wish to Age Accounts (T/F)? :F:

Pressing the RETURN key or answering F will return you to the report menu. Answering T will start the aging process.

Calendar dates for the durations of 30, 60, and 90 days from the logged date are calculated by using these useful routines. Reports for all accounts that have been due for each period will be listed for due periods of 1–30 days, 31–60 days, 61–90 days, and greater than 90 days (see Figure 11-16).

At least one page will be produced for each aged account, even if there are no accounts due within a period. A report fragment is produced even if no records meet the conditions to be REPORTed (see Figure 11-17).

```
PAGE NO. 00001                -- RECEIPT of BILLS on this DATE --
11/10/83
                    ACCOUNTS PAYABLE TRANSACTION LIST
  BILL     DATE      DATE      BILL      LAST     DATE OF
  NUM.     DUE       REC.      BAL.    PAYMENT    PAYMENT     DESCRIPTION
 *-------------VENDOR------------->DOE
 1121    12/12/83  11/10/83     0.00     98.64    11/10/83   45 SKEINS OF YARN
 1145    12/15/83  11/10/83  1000.00   2000.00    11/10/83   MODEL 4 AUTO LOOM
 2018    12/22/83  11/10/83   945.00    800.00    11/10/83   MODEL 27 HAND LOOM
 ** SUBTOTAL **
                             1945.00   2898.64
 ** TOTAL **
                             1945.00   2898.64
```

*Figure 11-15.* Daily Transactions - Receipt of Bills

```
PAGE NO. 00001              -- Payments Due between 30 to 60 days --
11/10/83
                    ACCOUNTS PAYABLE TRANSACTION LIST
BILL    DATE     DATE     BILL     LAST      DATE OF
NUM.    DUE      REC.     BAL.     PAYMENT   PAYMENT   DESCRIPTION
*-------------VENDOR-------------> DOE
1145   12/15/83  11/10/83  1000.00  2000.00  11/10/83  MODEL 4 AUTO LOOM
2018   12/22/83  11/10/83   945.00   800.00  11/10/83  MODEL 27 HAND LOOM
** SUBTOTAL **
                           1945.00  2800.00
** TOTAL **
                           1945.00  2800.00
```

*Figure 11-16.* Aged Report with Bills Due within Range

## Report Option 2: Vendor Phone List and Outstanding Balance

A phone list and other vendor data is produced by this option. The FORM (configuration) is identical to the customer report in the INVOICE system. At least 132 columns will be needed. The total outstanding balance you owe to each vendor for all unpaid bills will be on the right (see Figures 11-18, 11-19). Note that negative signs precede the balances you owe; positive balances indicate that you have overpaid the vendor and have a surplus recorded. A second summary report will also be produced that lists all vendors with which you have a current non-zero balance (both overpayments and debits).

## Report Option 3: Checks Printed on Logged Date

The third option prints a check report (see Figure 11-20). You will be asked:

```
        Enter Beginning Check Number for Report. :   0:
   Enter Last Number or Press [RETURN] for End. : 555:
```

```
** SUBTOTAL **
                       0.00      0.00
** TOTAL **
                       0.00      0.00
```

*Figure 11-17.* Remnant Printed for No Bills Due within Range

PAGE NO. 00001
11/10/83

PHONE LIST - ALL VENDORS

ACCOUNTS PAYABLE AND RECEIVABLE

| TITL | FIRST | LAST NAME | COMPANY | WORK PH. | HOME PH. | ADJ | TERMS | BALANCE |
|------|-------|-----------|---------|----------|----------|-----|-------|---------|
| Mr. | John | Doe | Home Handicrafters | 555-555-5555 | 555-111-1111 | 4 | 20 DYS CASH | −1945.00 |
| Mr. | James | Zappa | Electronic Wizards | 915-838-3925 | 915-294-8104 | 3 | early pmt | −4750.00 |
| Ms. | Sharon | Marion | Acme Office Supplies | 404-356-9087 | 404-348-9017 | 4 | 31 DYS CASH | 0.00 |

*Figure 11-18.* Vendor Report - All Vendors - Phone Numbers and Balance Owed

PAGE NO. 00001
11/10/83

PHONE LIST - VENDORS with BALANCES

ACCOUNTS PAYABLE AND RECEIVABLE

| TITL | FIRST | LAST NAME | COMPANY | WORK PH. | HOME PH. | ADJ | TERMS | BALANCE |
|------|-------|-----------|---------|----------|----------|-----|-------|---------|
| Mr. | John | Doe | Home Handicrafters | 555-555-5555 | 555-111-1111 | 4 | 20 DYS CASH | −1945.00 |
| Mr. | James | Zappa | Electronic Wizards | 915-838-3925 | 915-294-8104 | 3 | early pmt | −4750.00 |

*Figure 11-19.* Vendor Report - Vendors with Outstanding Balances (+ Is Overpayment)

Enter the first number that you wish to be printed. The last possible check number (illustrated as 555) will be displayed. Press the RETURN key to enter it into the dBASE II routine. All checks with check numbers within the given range will be printed.

Please note that all checks are assumed to be printed and numbered as an unbroken series. The report will not function correctly if groups of checks are renumbered in a different sequence.

| PAGE NO. 00001 | | CHECK REGISTER REPORT | |
|---|---|---|---|
| 11/10/83 | | | |
| ACCOUNTS PAYABLE CHECK PAYMENT REGISTER | | | |
| CHECK NUMBER | DATE PAID | VENDOR ID | CHECK AMOUNT |
| 234 | 11/10/83 | DOE | 2898.64 |
| 235 | 11/10/83 | ZAPP | 1500.00 |
| ** TOTAL ** | | | |
| | | | 4398.64 |

*Figure 11-20.* Check Register Report - Checks Printed

## SUMMARY

Operation of the PAYBILLS system is now complete. The tedious drudgery of calculating, paying, and monitoring your bills is now automated by the POSTBILLS system and dBASE II.

*Table 12-2.  List of Files and Main Functions*

| Filename | Stands For | Function |
|---|---|---|
| VENDOR.DBF | Vendor File | Retains Vendor Data |
| IOUS.DBF | Transaction File | Retains Payables Data |
| CHECKFIL.DBF | Check File | Check Payment File |
| PAYBILLS.CMD | Payables Menu | Main Menu |
| CUSTSEAR.CMD | Customer Search | Searches for Vendor (Chap. 10) |
| CUSTEDIT | Customer Edit | Edits Vendor File (Chap. 10) |
| INVFMT.FMT | Invoice Formatting | Formats Vendor Screen (Chap. 10) |
| BILLPOST.CMD | Bill Posting | Post Bills to File |
| CKPRINT.CMD | Print Check Data | Prints Bills on Screen |
| PAYFOR1.CMD | Pay One Bill | Pays Vendor Bill |
| CHKCUT.CMD | Check Cut | Cuts Check |
| SPELLER.CMD | Spells Amounts | Spells Out Amounts |
| VARBAK.CMD | Variable Backing | Works with Speller |
| PAYRPTME.CMD | Payment Report Menu | Report Sub-Menu |
| TRANSRPT.CMD | Transaction Report | Ages Payments |
| CUSTOMER.FRM | Customer Form | Customer Report |
| BILLTRAM.FRM | Bill Transaction | Transaction Report |
| CALINT.CMD | Calendar to Integer | Converts to Integer |
| INTCAL.CMD | Integer to Calendar | Converts to Calendar |
| CHECKS.FRM | Check Form | Check Form File |

Utility Files Used (On the A Drive)
INIT.CMD
DTVERIFY.CMD

Two fields acquire a different use in the PAYBILLS system. ADJUST was used to represent a tax code in INVOICE, but doubles in PAYBILLS as the amount of discount that can be used for early payment of a bill. TERMS allows further explanation about the payment and the amount of the discount.

## IOUS.DBF  The Transaction File

IOUS maintains one record for each bill submitted by the vendor and the cumulative payments towards discharging this bill. The NAMECODE is used to link this file with the other two. Data is retained on the bill number (BILLNUM) placed on your bill by the vendor, the bill's due date (DATEDUE), and the date you received the bill (DATEIN). Also stored are the amount of the last payment (LASTPAY), the date it was posted to the check file (DATEPAID), the current balance on the bill (BILLBAL), a marker for Paid In Full (PIF), and a description (DESCRIPT) (see Figure 12-1).

```
NUMBER OF RECORDS: 00000
DATE OF LAST UPDATE: 00/00/00
PRIMARY USE DATABASE
FLD            NAME       TYPE    WIDTH    DEC
001            NAMECODE    C       004
002            BILLNUM     N       005
003            DATEDUE     C       008
004            DATEIN      C       008
005            DATEPAID    C       008
006            BILLBAL     N       008      002
007            LASTPAY     N       008      002
008            PIF         L       001
009            DESCRIPT    C       020
** TOTAL **                       00071
```

*Figure 12-1.* Sturcture for File: B:IOUS .DBF

*Table 12-3.   Name of Field*
*Description of Field*

| | |
|---|---|
| NAMECODE | The Vendor ID |
| BILLNUM | Bill Number Given by Vendor |
| DATEDUE | Due Date |
| DATEIN | Date Received |
| DATEPAID | Date Posted to Check File |
| BILLBAL | Current Balance on Bill |
| PIF | Paid In Full Marker |
| DESCRIPT | Description |

## CHECKFIL.DBF  The Check File

The check file retains all key information about each check printed. The date paid, check number, and amount are stored. Also stored is a marker that the check has not been printed (unprinted), and the NAMECODE to link the check back to the vendor and transaction files (see Figure 12-2).

```
NUMBER OF RECORDS: 00004
DATE OF LAST UPDATE: 00/00/00
PRIMARY USE DATABASE
FLD            NAME       TYPE    WIDTH    DEC
001            NAMECODE    C       004
002            DATEPAID    C       008
003            CHECKNUM    N       005
004            CURRCHK     N       008      002
005            UNPRINTED   L       001
** TOTAL **                       00027
```

*Figure 12-2.*   Structure for File: B:CHECKFIL.DBF

*Table 12-4.  Name of Field*
*Description of Field*

| | |
|---|---|
| NAMECODE | The Vendor ID |
| DATEPAID | The Date Paid |
| CHECKNUM | Check Number |
| CURRCHK | Current Check Amount |
| UNPRINTED | Marker for Unprinted Checks |

# PROGRAM FILES FOR THE PAYBILLS SYSTEM

## PAYBILLS.CMD   Main Menu

The now-familiar menu arrangement is used for PAYBILLS. Options are presented and the corresponding choice is executed.

**CODE FOR PAYBILLS.CMD**

```
* paybills.cmd
* program by michael clifford
* module purpose: pay outstanding bills to vendors (creditors)
* print the checks
* maintain a vendor file and a record of payments and balances

* section I - housekeeping

DO A:init
SET default to &dfdefault
USE vendor
SELECT secondary
USE ious
SELECT PRIMARY
SET default to &pfdefault

* set up date for reporting
* establish system dates
* one for file - yy/mm/dd (mfiledate)
* one for viewing - dd/mm/yy (mviewdate)
DO a:dtverify
STORE viewdate TO mviewdate
STORE filedate TO mfiledate

DO WHILE t

   * section II - operator prompting
   * set up vendor entry screen for viewing.
   * modesay variable does double duty for screen.
   STORE 'SAY' TO modesay
   STORE ' ' TO selection
   DO WHILE selection = ' '
      ERASE
```

```
            @ 3,15 SAY '== MAIN PAYABLES MENU =='
            @ 5,15 SAY '0-Exit to System '
            @ 7,15 SAY '1-Post Payment of Vendor Bills '
            @ 8,15 SAY '2-Edit Vendor File '
            @ 9,15 SAY '3-Post Payables to Checks'
            @ 10,15 SAY '4-Print Outstanding Checks '
            @ 11,15 SAY '5-Print a Report'
            @ 14,15 SAY 'Choose A Number ' GET selection PICTURE '#'
            READ
ENDDO WHILE selection= ' '

* section III - execution of options
IF selection= '0'
      * exit program.
      RELEASE postagain,mfiledate,mviewdate,default
      RELEASE modesay,selection,filedate,viewdate
      * *** quit
      CANCEL
ENDIF selection= '0'

IF selection= '1'

      STORE 'T' TO postagain
      DO WHILE postagain = 'T'
         * find the vendor and post bill for payment.
         * the customer search routine in invoice
         * can be used to service vendor file.
         DO custsear
         DO billpost
         @ 22,0
         @ 22,10 SAY "Post a Bill for NEW Creditor? (T/F) " ;
            GET postagain PICT '!'
         READ
      ENDDO WHILE postagain = 'T'
      RELEASE postagain

ENDIF selection= '1'

IF selection= '2'
      * edit existing customer.
      * invoice edit routine can similarly be used.
      DO custedit
ENDIF selection= '2'

IF selection= '3'
      * post checks to checkfil
      DO ckprint
      * see inprint
      * allow to post and print checks later
ENDIF selection= '3'

IF selection='4'
      * print outstanding checks in checkfil
```

```
      DO chkcut
  ENDIF

  IF selection= '5'
      DO payrptme
  ENDIF selection = '5'

ENDDO t
```

## *Entering and Updating the Vendor File*

Three files are borrowed directly from INVOICE: The CUSTSEAR, CUSTEDIT, and INVFMT command files. The operation and code are detailed in Chapter 8.

# BILLPOST.CMD   The Posting Routine

BILLPOST allows the operator to enter the essential data about each bill, which is stored in the transaction file.

The screen will clear each time that the date due is requested. DTVERIFY is used to verify the date. The clearing of the screen is undesirable but so is the alternative—typing in the code for another date verification routine. Remember: Never reinvent the wheel. Use the existing and familiar dBASE II routines.

BILLPOST repeats, painting each screen, calling DTVERIFY, APPENDING BLANK, and allowing entry of the bill number, description, and amount owed. The total balance that you owe to the vendor for all bills is updated afterwards. The operator is asked if another bill exists for the vendor.

Control is passed back to the main menu once posting is completed. A DO WHILE/ENDDO loop has been placed there instead of within the BILLPOST routine. Good programming would normally require that the loop for repeating the posting be actually within the posting routine. The program CUSTSEAR, however, will only search for one vendor. Billing another vendor requires using CUSTSEAR again, which requires a loop in the main menu. The continuation messages are then split between PAYBILLS (Post A Bill for a NEW Creditor?) and BILLPOST (Post Another Bill for Creditor?). The technique is not elegant, but CUSTSEAR can be used without modification. Entry of more dBASE II code and additional effort are saved.

CODE FOR BILLPOST.CMD

```
* billpost.cmd
* module purpose: post unpaid bills to file.
*. bills will be paid later at operator's wishes.

STORE 'T' TO repeat

DO WHILE repeat = 'T'
```

```
SELECT secondary
* now in the transaction file - ious
APPEND BLANK
* use dtverify to obtain and verify date.
* dtverify unfortunately erases every time, but use of
* this existing date routine saves coding a new date routine.
* never re-invent the wheel.

STORE '= = = = = = = = = Enter Date Due of Bill = = = = = = = = ;
= = = =' TO prompt
DO a:dtverify
RELEASE prompt

* place existing data from vendor and the system
* dates into the record.
REPLACE datedue WITH filedate
REPLACE datein WITH mfiledate
REPLACE s.namecode WITH p.namecode

ERASE

* put in working information at the screen top.
* vendor, vendor id, date, and terms
@ 1, 2 SAY TRIM(firstname) + ' ' + lastname
@ 2, 2 SAY company
@ 2,50 SAY "DATE:"
@ 2,65 SAY mviewdate
@ 3, 2 SAY "Discount Code:"
@ 3,17 SAY adjust
@ 3,50 SAY "TERMS:"
@ 3,65 SAY terms
@ 5, 5 SAY "DATE"
@ 5,15 SAY "BILL"
@ 5,25 SAY "DESCRIPTION"
@ 5,55 SAY "PAYMENT"
@ 6, 5 SAY "DUE"
@ 6,15 SAY "NUMBER"
@ 6,25 SAY "OF BILL"
@ 6,55 SAY "AMOUNT"
@ 8, 5 SAY viewdate

* obtain accounts payable data from operator.
@ 8,15 GET billnum
@ 8,25 GET descript
@ 8,55 GET billbal
READ
* add balance to total outstanding balance in vendor file.
REPLACE balance with balance - billbal

@ 22,15 SAY 'Post Another Bill for Creditor (T/F)? ' ;
GET repeat PICTURE '!'
READ
SELECT PRIMARY
ENDDO WHILE repeat = 'T'
```

```
RELEASE repeat,newbucks
RETURN
```

## CKPRINT  The Generator of Balances and Payments

CKPRINT works exactly like INPRINT in the INVOICE system, except that the operator incurs payments rather than issues payments. Up to ten vendor bills are each presented on subsequent lines.

The transaction file, IOUS, is first indexed on the following expression:

```
namecode + datedue + STR(billnum,5)
```

The vendors will be in the order of the vendor ID. Each vendor's records will further be in the order of the date due. All bills with the same vendor and due date will also be listed in the order of the bill numbers. The STR command is used to allow the index expression to contain both character fields (namecode and datedue) and the numeric bill number.

Many of the bills for each vendor may have already been paid. Only the bills not totally paid need to be processed. A new technique is used, the use of DO WHILE and SKIP to walk through each record of a file to find unpaid bills.

Three techniques may be used to find one record that meets a very limited set of circumstances:

*1.* LOCATE through a file whether or not it has been indexed.

*2.* INDEX a file and use the FIND command.

*3.* use the SKIP command.

SKIP allows movement to each record until the end of the file is reached. Once found, the identified record can be processed. Following is a versatile use of the SKIP command.

```
DO WHILE .NOT. EOF
  IF pif [Paid In Full]
    SKIP
  ENDIF
ENDDO
```

The structure walks through, record by record, until either a record that meets the condition is found or end of the file is reached. Once reached, a record can then be processed.

The first unpaid bill is matched with the full vendor data in the vendor file by issuing the SELECT PRIMARY and LOCATE commands to search the VENDOR data file for the name code that matches the name code in IOUS. All the necessary data to allow operator inspection and payment is then available from the two data files.

The top portion of the screen is painted with the banner, prompts, and default information (the day's date, company, discount, and terms). A horizontal line counter, LINE, is set up to put the first bill on the eighth line.

Unlike INPRINT, each line is built in another routine, PAYFOR1, which is the routine that builds all PAYments FOR 1 vendor. The subtotals (payment for one bill and the balance remaining) and the total payment and balance for all the vendor's outstanding bills are obtained, calculated, and displayed. CKPRINT takes the grand total after returning from PAYFOR1, opens up the check file, CHECKFIL, and inserts the check data for the vendor. A loop continues the process until all bills for all vendors have been inspected and perhaps paid. Control is returned to the main menu.

CODE FOR CKPRINT.CMD

```
* ckprint.cmd
* module purpose: pays off unpaid bills

ERASE
SELECT secondary
* now in the tranasaction file - ious

STORE t TO repeat
* order all bills by vendor id, the due date, and then bill number.
INDEX ON namecode + datedue + STR(billnum,5) TO order
SET INDEX TO order

DO WHILE .NOT. eof
    * skip through all posted bills for an id with unpaid bills.
    IF pif
        SKIP
        LOOP
    ENDIF pif

    * now stopped at first unpaid bill.
    * match up with vendor in primary work area
    STORE s.namecode TO forthisguy
    SELECT PRIMARY
    LOCATE FOR p.namecode = forthisguy

    SELECT secondary

    STORE 000000.00 TO totlpay
    ERASE
    * put in banner information like the top of inprint
    * vendor, vendor id, date, and terms
    * have it like the invoice screen in inprint
    * each line is another bill for a vendor
    * up to ten lines
```

```
@ 1, 2 SAY company
@ 2,50 SAY "DATE:"
@ 2,65 SAY mviewdate
@ 3, 2 SAY "Discount Info:"
@ 3,17 SAY adjust
@ 3,50 SAY "TERMS:"
@ 3,65 SAY terms
@ 5, 0 SAY "DATE"
@ 5,10 SAY "BILL"
@ 5,20 SAY "AMOUNT"
@ 5,30 SAY "GROSS AMT"
@ 5,41 SAY "DISC."
@ 5,50 SAY "NET PAY"
@ 5,65 SAY "BALANCE"
@ 6, 0 SAY "DUE"
@ 6,10 SAY "NUMBER"
@ 6,20 SAY "DUE"
@ 6,30 SAY "TO PAY"
@ 6,41 SAY "ADJ %"
@ 6,50 SAY "FOR BILL"
@ 6,65 SAY "TO OWE"

* put first line of bill payment on line 8
* continue to pay bills for id up to ten lines
* works on same principle as invoice system.

STORE 8 TO line

* Build up total payment for one vendor.
* Display all outstading bills, like
* INVOICE did with purchases
DO payfor1

* place outstanding check in check file
SELECT PRIMARY
SET default to &dfdefault
USE checkfil
APPEND BLANK
REPLACE currchk WITH totlpay
REPLACE p.namecode WITH forthisguy
REPLACE p.datepaid WITH mfiledate
REPLACE unprinted WITH t

* open up vendor file again
USE vendor
SET default to &pfdefault

* prepare for new vendor id
SELECT secondary
STORE s.namecode TO forthisguy
STORE 8 TO line
@ 22,0 SAY "Press Any Key to Continue Posting Bills. "
SET CONSOLE OFF
WAIT
```

```
        SET CONSOLE ON
        @ 22,0
    ENDDO WHILE .NOT. eof

    SELECT PRIMARY
    RELEASE repeat,forthisguy,totlpay
    RELEASE line,mdisc,trial,linepay,linebal

    RETURN
```

# PAYFOR1  Displays and Pays for One Vendor

PAYFOR1 is the most complex routine in PAYBILLS. Each unpaid bill is displayed with a trial payment, the remaining to be paid. The payment may be the total payment, in which case a discount may be warranted. If a discount is taken, the trial payment needs to be adjusted for the discount, to yield the final payment that will close out the bill.

Once paid, the running total vendor balance in VENDOR needs to be adjusted, along with the influence of any discount. The total for each payment must be accumulated to yield the total check payment which will be issued to the printer.

A loop is first built with three conditions:

```
DO WHILE .NOT. eof .AND. s.namecode = forthisguy;
   .AND. line < 18
```

The condition is saying, "Do until the end of the file only if the vendor ID in the current record of IOUS is equal to the first record's ID for this vendor" (STORED to forthisguy in CKPRINT). The line counter, LINE, must also be less than 18, but in effect there should never be more than nine bills outstanding to one vendor and therefore never a value of LINE more than 17.

The SKIP/DO WHILE technique is again used to walk down to each record that meets the conditions of not being totally paid.

```
IF pif
   SKIP
   LOOP
ENDIF
```

The SKIP moves down to the next record of IOUS and the LOOP returns to the three condition DO WHILE, allowing the searching to continue to an unpaid bill that meets the conditions.

A bill is displayed once found. The description, date due, and bill number are displayed on the current line. The net payment, trial, is assumed to be the remaining payment on the bill (billbal) and is displayed. Both trial and the working discount (mdisc) are then obtained from the operator using the GET and READ statements.

The remainder of PAYFOR1 is the calculation of subtotals, adjustment for discounts, and updates of files. Several memory variables are used for the purpose of sub-totaling and adjusting:

trial      the trial payment of one bill
mdisc      the discount entered by operator
linepay    the payment for this one bill (one line)
linebal    the remaining balance to close this bill

Most of the complexity is due to discounting. The discount reduces the payment necessary to close out a bill, yet the full amount was entered in VENDOR as part of the total outstanding balance. XYZ Enterprises may bill you for a $100 purchase of widgets, with a 2 percent discount for early payment.

POSTBILLS entered the $100 as the total and added it to any other outstanding debts you may have for XYZ. Prompt payment, however, requires only $98 to discharge the obligation for this bill. The total outstanding balance must be adjusted to reflect the benefit of any discounts applied to any subordinate bills.

The trial balance is obtained by the operator, and a discount is applied to calculate the required payment after discount. The result is STORED to linepay with the dBASE II code:

```
STORE (trial — (trial * mdisc)) to linepay
```

The linepay variable is the amount paid for this bill after discount. The total balance owed for all bills is in the vendor file and reflects the balance before a discount is taken. The total reduction to the outstanding balance must adjust for the influence of the discount by converting the linepay variable and using the code:

```
REPLACE balance with balance + linepay + (trial * mdisc)
```

The balance is reduced not only by the total paid per bill, but also by the discount applied to the net payment as well. Negative balances can be obtained, which reflect surpluses or cash forwards. Overpayments will register as positive balances.

The balance on the bill (linebal) is calculated and displayed in the same manner. If the balance is negative or zero, a field in the IOUS record, pif, is set to TRUE, to indicate Paid In Full. The marker will be of assistance in later generating reports. The original balance for the bill is REPLACEd with the new balance (linebal). Once done, the amount to be paid for this balance is REPLACEd into IOUS as the last paid amount for this bill (lastpay).

The current line balances for the vendor are accumulated to the final payment for one vendor, totlpay. The amount will be returned to CKPRINT and placed in the check file.

Another SKIP starts the walk through the vendor's bills for the location of another unpaid bill. The line counter is increased by one to move another bill below the others. The CLEAR GETS ensures no cursor confusion will occur with an accumulation of 64 GETS.

The total payment for this vendor is displayed once the last unpaid vendor's record is processed. Control is returned to CKPRINT for processing of bills for another vendor.

### CODE FOR PAYFOR1.CMD

```
* payfor1.cmd
* module purpose: displays each outstanding bill for a vendor.
* allow partial payment and discounts.
* keeps running total for check.

DO WHILE .NOT. eof .AND. ;
    s.namecode = forthisguy .AND. line < 18

    * skip through this id for unpaid bills.
    IF pif
        SKIP
        LOOP
    ENDIF pif

    * initialize mdisc - the percentage discount
    STORE 0. TO mdisc
    * initialize trial - the trial payment
    STORE 000000.00 TO trial

    * display description of bill below finance line
    * obtain payment information from operator.
    @ line + 2,15 SAY descript
    @ line, 0 SAY $(datedue,4,5) + '/' + $(datedue,1,2)
    @ line,10 SAY billnum USING '# # # # #'
    @ line,20 SAY billbal USING '# # # # #.# #'
    STORE billbal TO trial
    @ line,30 GET trial PICTURE '# # # # #.# #'
    @ line,42 GET mdisc PICTURE '#'
    READ

    * convert single-digit percentage to hundredths
    STORE mdisc * .01 TO mdisc
    * take trial payment and adjust for discount (if any)
    * to yield payment for this bill
    STORE (trial - (trial * mdisc)) TO linepay
    @ line,50 SAY linepay USING '# # # # #.# #'

    * Update running balance owed to vendor
    * In vendor file. Adjust for discounts to reduce balance
    * by adding them to the trial payment for each line.
```

```
SELECT PRIMARY
REPLACE balance with balance + linepay + (trial * mdisc)
SELECT SECONDARY
* place date upon which payment has been made.
REPLACE datepaid WITH mfiledate
STORE billbal - linepay - (trial * mdisc) TO linebal

* indicate full payment of bill if partial
* payment plus discount reduces obligation to zero.
* also show negative balance, i.e., advance payment.
IF linebal < =0
    REPLACE pif WITH t
ENDIF linebal < = 0

@ line,65 SAY linebal USING '#####.##'
* Update balance for this bill
* Accumulate for total payment of check
REPLACE billbal WITH linebal
* update lastpay field in ious
REPLACE lastpay with linepay
STORE linepay + totlpay TO totlpay

* prepare for next line
* clear out description for new description
@ line+2,15
STORE line + 1 TO line
SKIP

* clear out pending gets in a loop
    CLEAR GETS
ENDDO WHILE .NOT. eof

* calculate and display totals for one vendor
@ line + 1,20 SAY "TOTAL TO BE PAID "
@ line + 1,50 SAY totlpay USING '#####.##'
* Return back to pay bills for other vendors

RETURN
```

## CHKCUT.CMD   Print Checks

All checks are stored in a file, CHECKFIL. The check amounts could have
been calculated from IOUS and printed, but no record of the total amount
and date would have been available for later inspection.

The REPORT command cannot be used to generate the checks. RE-
PORT prints only data from one file and places it all on one line. Checks
and stubs require that data from the vendor file be used with the check
file and that the data be painted in precise coordinates on each check and
stub, as did MAILFORM with the mailing labels.

There are several major methods to print checks and check stubs.
One is the tedious use of the ? command to express the value of a field.

Blanks are used to crudely position the data onto the check form, as shown below.

```
*  date in upper right
*  check number below
*
?
?  [position down the page with ? commands]
?  ' [position over with 50–70 blanks]              ' + mfiledate
?
?
?  '                         ' + STR(mchecknum,5)
*  must convert numeric check number to string to use with blanks
```

This method is tedious and the results cannot be formatted with the use of the SAY USING commands.

A second technique is the straightforward use of @ line,Y SAY [expression]. LINE is incremented after the printing of each check and stub, which have 42 lines. Thus, printing the date on the tenth check would result in the expression:

```
@ 425,52 say date
```

The variable, LINE, would be incremented within the loop until printing is accomplished. Ideally the routine would work well, and it is often used with other languages. However, dBASE II limits the value of the X and Y coordinates each to 255. An EJECT must be used to clear print coordinates in the same manner that an ERASE or CLEAR GETS must be used to clear screen coordinates.

A third method of printing remedies printing problems. The SAY USING commands are available, and precision printing can be accomplished without using the ? command and blanks. Each check and stub are one page, which is printed by @ line,Y coordinates. All coordinates are cleared after the printing of one check and stub by use of the EJECT command.

The EJECT command, if not altered on your printer, will usually issue a form feed of 66 lines, the length of a standard sheet of paper. The result would be chaos for the recipient of your checks. A method must be found to alter the form feed to 42 lines, or the length of your check stock.

Form feeds are altered by the use of the CHR(XX), the same type of commands that altered the print pitch in the MAILFORM print routines. INIT, the initial utility that you placed on the A drive, asked for the control codes to alter the form feed at the same time the print pitch codes were requested. These were stored in CONFIG.MEM, the memory file on the A drive. If properly installed, INIT would issue the following control codes for an the EPSON MX-80 printer:

```
? &stdform      ? CHR(27) + CHR(67) + CHR(66)      66 lines
? &altform      ? CHR(27) + CHR(67) + CHR(42)      42 lines
```

Every issuance of the EJECT will move the print head precisely to the top of the next check form. A simple DO WHILE .NOT. EOF will continue the printing until all unprinted records are exhausted.

More information is desired than is available from CHECKFIL. Any detailed data on the vendor must be acquired from the VENDOR file. CHKCUT illustrates the use of a command file to print out information from more than one file.

Each check to be printed in CHECKFIL is the driver, so named because it drives the search for the data in the VENDOR file. The vendor ID (namecode) in CHECKFIL is used to locate the corresponding ID in VENDOR. The full name and address are then accessible for printing on the check.

## Sequence for Check Printing

After obtaining a check number, CHKCUT opens checkfil and examines each record. Another search technique, the LOCATE and the CONTINUE, is used to find the first record that has a TRUE for the unprinted field.

A candidate for printing is located in the check file. Once accomplished, the matching address data is found in the vendor file by the code:

```
SELECT PRIMARY
LOCATE FOR p.namecode = s.namecode
SELECT SECONDARY
```

The check can be printed once the files are linked. The stub is printed first, with the amount at coordinates 20,50. Once done, the check amount is passed to SPELLER. SPELLER takes the numeric amount (1000) and converts it to its spelled out equivalent (EXACTLY ONE THOUSAND DOLLARS).

Once done, the rest of the check is printed. An EJECT brings the printer to the next check form. The record is prevented from repeatedly printing by REPLACing the unprinted marker with FALSE.

The check number is incremented by one and SKIP moves to the next record in CHECKFIL to be printed. Housekeeping commands restore the screen and the standard form feed to normal. Control is returned to the main menu.

CODE FOR CHKCUT.CMD

```
* chkcut.cmd
* module purpose: takes check amount and cuts checks
* close files and open vendor and check files
* save all prior memory variables to holding bin
```

```
SAVE TO holding
SELECT primary
SET default to &dfdefault
USE vendor
SELECT secondary
USE checkfil
SET default to &pfdefault

* determine vendors with checks to be written
* first, have operator align material in printer
ERASE
STORE 0000 TO mcheckno
@ 5,0 SAY "Align Checks in Printer. "
@ 8,0 SAY "Enter the First Check Number. " GET mcheckno PICT '# # # #'
READ
ERASE
@ 12,10 SAY "**** CHECK PRINTING IN PROGRESS ***"

SET EJECT OFF
SET CONSOLE OFF
SET PRINT ON
* shift to a form feed of 42 lines for checks.
* prconfig.cmd set the alternate form characters.
?? &altform
SET PRINT OFF

LOCATE FOR unprinted

DO WHILE .NOT. eof

    STORE 2 TO x
    SELECT PRIMARY
    LOCATE FOR p.namecode = s.namecode
    SELECT secondary
    SET FORMAT TO PRINT
    * BEGIN CHECK STUB
    * If eliminated, change form feed length
    @ 5,40 SAY "DATE:"
    @ 5,50 SAY mviewdate
    @ 6,40 SAY "CHECK NO."
    @ 6,50 SAY mcheckno USING '# # # #'
    @ 10,20 SAY company
    @ 12,20 SAY street
    @ 14,20 SAY TRIM(suite:etc)
    @ 16,20 SAY TRIM(city) + ' ' + st + ' ' + zip
    @ 18,20 SAY 'ATTN:   ' + TRIM(mr:ms) + '  ' + TRIM(firstname) + ;
      ' ' + lastname
    @ 20,20 SAY "AMOUNT REMITTED ON THIS DATE "
    @ 20,50 SAY currchk USING '$$$$$$$.# #'
    * END OF CHECK STUB
    *
    * BEGIN CHECK
    STORE STR(currchk,11,2) TO numr
```

```
DO speller
* pass amount to sd, convert to spelled out amt
@ 28,50 SAY viewdate
@ 30,20 SAY company
@ 30,50 SAY currchk USING '$$$$$$$$.# #'
@ 32,12 SAY sd
* PRINT ADDRESS AT BOTTOM OF CHECK FOR ENVELOPE  WINDOW
@ 35,12 say !(company)
@ 36,12 SAY TRIM(street) + '      ' + TRIM(suite:etc)
@ 37,12 SAY TRIM(city) + ' ' + st + ' ' + zip
* END OF ADDRESS IN WINDOW
* END OF PRINTING OF CHECK
* END OF PRINTING FOR BOTH CHECK AND STUB
* Advance to next check form with custom-length EJECT
* Form length was set by INIT utility on DRIVE A
EJECT
* lock out further printing of this check
REPLACE unprinted WITH f
REPLACE checknum WITH mcheckno

* move to next vendor upon which to print check
STORE mcheckno + 1 TO mcheckno
SKIP
ENDDO WHILE .NOT. eof

SET FORMAT TO SCREEN
SET EJECT ON
SET PRINT ON
?? &stdform
SET PRINT OFF
SET CONSOLE ON

RELEASE ALL
RESTORE FROM holding
DELETE FILE holding.mem
SELECT SECONDARY
SET default to &dfdefault
USE ious
SET default to &pfdefault
SELECT PRIMARY
RETURN
```

## Modifications to Check Printing

Changes to the dBASE II code may be required to adapt the check writer to your check stock. The table below outlines some of the possible modifications and the changes in CHKCUT.

### Table 12-5. Some Possible Modifications and Changes in CHKCUT

| Adaptation | Change in Code |
|---|---|
| Print check stock different length. | Change form feed in INIT to length of stock. |
| Print check only. Eliminate stub. | Eliminate statements which print stub. |
| | Change form feed in INIT to length of check only. |
| Eliminate printing of check number. | Delete statements: @ 6,40 SAY "CHECK NO." @ 6,50 SAY mcheckno USING ' # # # # # ' |
| Eliminate address on check. | Delete address statements on check. |

## SPELLER and VARBAK  Convert Numerals to Words

SPELLER and the companion routine, VARBAK, convert the numeric amount of a check to the spelled out equivalent, resembling the tamper-proof output of a mechanical check writer.

The transformation of numbers to words is complex. Extensive manipulations are required to discern the 92 in the number 1921 and convert it to the "nine hundred and twenty" portion of the spelled out version. The phrase for the same digits varies greatly if enclosed in a number of a different magnitude, 19215, "nineteen thousand and two hundred."

SPELLER and VARBAK are utilities that can be used in many other financial routines. The numeric amount needs to be converted to a character variable called numr and passed to SPELLER with the command STORE STR(currchk,11,2) to numr. The spelled out amount will be returned as sd. A pause will be noticed while the conversion is being accomplished.

CODE FOR SPELLER.CMD

```
* SPELLER.CMD
SET talk OFF
* numr must be read in from calling files
* numr is character type with leading
* and trailing blanks trimed

do while $(numr,1,1)=chr(32)
    store $(numr,2,10) to numr
    store trim(numr) to numr
enddo
```

```
STORE ' ' TO zero
* check to see of last three digits the cents

IF $(numr,LEN(TRIM(numr))-2,1)= '.'
ELSE
    STORE numr+ '.00' TO numr
ENDIF $(numr,LEN(TRIM(numr))-2,1)= '.'

STORE 12-LEN(numr) TO flag

DO WHILE flag>0
    STORE '0' + TRIM(zero) TO zero
    STORE flag-1 TO flag
ENDDO WHILE flag>0

STORE zero+numr TO num
STORE TRIM(num) TO num
STORE VAL($(num,1,1)) TO m1
STORE VAL($(num,4,1)) TO m1a
STORE VAL($(num,7,1)) TO m1b
STORE $(num,10,3) TO m6
STORE 0 TO m2,m3,m4,m5,m2a,m3a,m4a,m5a,m2b,m3b,m4b,m5b
STORE ' ' TO sd

IF VAL($(num,2,1)) >= 2 .AND. VAL($(num,3,1)) = 0
    STORE VAL($(num,2,2)) TO m2
ENDIF VAL($(num,2,1)) >=

IF VAL($(num,2,1)) >= 2 .AND. VAL($(num,3,1)) > 0
    STORE VAL($(num,2,1))*10 TO m3
    STORE VAL($(num,3,1)) TO m4
ENDIF VAL($(num,2,1)) >= 2

IF VAL($(num,2,1)) = 0
    STORE VAL($(num,3,1)) TO m4
ELSE
    IF VAL($(num,2,1)) = 1
        STORE VAL($(num,2,2)) TO m5
    ENDIF
ENDIF

IF VAL($(num,5,1)) >= 2 .AND. VAL($(num,6,1)) = 0
    STORE VAL($(num,5,2)) TO m2a
ENDIF VAL($(num,5,1)) >= 2

IF VAL($(num,5,1)) >= 2 .AND. VAL($(num,6,1)) > 0
    STORE VAL($(num,5,1))*10 TO m3a
    STORE VAL($(num,6,1)) TO m4a
ENDIF VAL($(num,5,1)) >= 2

IF VAL($(num,5,1)) = 0
    STORE VAL($(num,6,1)) TO m4a
ELSE
    IF VAL($(num,5,1)) = 1
        STORE VAL($(num,5,2)) TO m5a
    ENDIF
```

```
ENDIF

IF VAL($(num,8,1)) >= 2 .AND. VAL($(num,9,1)) = 0
    STORE VAL($(num,8,2)) TO m2b
ENDIF VAL($(num,8,1)) >= 2

IF VAL($(num,8,1)) >= 2 .AND. VAL($(num,9,1)) > 0
    STORE VAL($(num,8,1))*10 TO m3b
    STORE VAL($(num,9,1)) TO m4b
ENDIF VAL($(num,8,1)) >= 2

IF VAL($(num,8,1)) = 0
    STORE VAL($(num,9,1)) TO m4b
ELSE
    IF VAL($(num,8,1)) = 1
        STORE VAL($(num,8,2)) TO m5b
    ENDIF
ENDIF

IF m1 > 0
    STORE 'M1' TO var
    STORE 'NUM1' TO var2
    DO varbak
    STORE sd + num1 + 'HUNDRED ' TO sd
ENDIF m1 > 0

IF m2 > 0
    STORE 'M2' TO var
    STORE 'NUM2' TO var2
    DO varbak
    STORE sd + num2 + 'MILLION ' TO sd
ENDIF m2 > 0

IF m3 > 0
    STORE 'M3' TO var
    STORE 'NUM3' TO var2
    DO varbak
    STORE sd + num3 TO sd
ENDIF m3 > 0

IF m4 > 0
    STORE 'M4' TO var
    STORE 'NUM4' TO var2
    DO varbak
    STORE sd + num4 + 'MILLION ' TO sd
ENDIF m4 > 0

IF m5 > 0
    STORE 'M5' TO var
    STORE 'NUM5' TO var2
    DO varbak
    STORE sd + num5 + 'MILLION ' TO sd
ENDIF m5 > 0

IF m1a > 0
    STORE 'M1A' TO var
```

```
        STORE 'NUM6' TO var2
        DO varbak
        STORE sd + num6 + 'HUNDRED ' TO sd
ENDIF m1a > 0

IF m2a > 0
        STORE 'M2A' TO var
        STORE 'NUM7' TO var2
        DO varbak
        STORE sd + num7 + 'THOUSAND ' TO sd
ENDIF m2a > 0

IF m3a > 0
        STORE 'M3A' TO var
        STORE 'NUM8' TO var2
        DO varbak
        STORE sd + num8 TO sd
ENDIF m3a > 0

IF m4a > 0
        STORE 'M4A' TO var
        STORE 'NUM9' TO var2
        DO varbak
        STORE sd + num9 + 'THOUSAND ' TO sd
ENDIF m4a > 0

IF m5a > 0
        STORE 'M5A' TO var
        STORE 'NUM10' TO var2
        DO varbak
        STORE sd + num10 + 'THOUSAND ' TO sd
ENDIF m5a > 0

IF m1b > 0
        STORE 'M1B' TO var
        STORE 'NUM11' TO var2
        DO varbak
        STORE sd + num11 + 'HUNDRED ' TO sd
ENDIF m1b > 0

IF m2b > 0
        STORE 'M2B' TO var
        STORE 'NUM12' TO var2
        DO varbak
        STORE sd + num12 TO sd
ENDIF m2b > 0

IF m3b > 0
        STORE 'M3B' TO var
        STORE 'NUM13' TO var2
        DO varbak
        STORE sd + num13 TO sd
ENDIF m3b > 0

IF m4b > 0
```

```
                    STORE 'M4B' TO var
                    STORE 'NUM14' TO var2
                    DO varbak
                    STORE sd + num14 TO sd
                ENDIF m4b > 0

                IF m5b > 0
                    STORE 'M5B' TO var
                    STORE 'NUM15' TO var2
                    DO varbak
                    STORE sd + num15 TO sd
                ENDIF m5b > 0

                IF VAL(m6)=0
                    STORE "EXACTLY" + ' ' +sd+ ' ' + 'DOLLARS' TO sd
                ELSE
                    STORE sd + 'AND ' TO sd
                    STORE sd + $(m6,2,2) TO sd
                    STORE sd + ' /100 DOLLARS' TO sd
                ENDIF VAL(m6)=0

                STORE '****' +sd+ '***' TO sd

                RELEASE numr,zero,flag,m1,m1a,m1b,m6
                RELEASE m2,m3,m4,m5,m2a,m3a,m4a,m5a,m2b
                RELEASE m3b,m4b,m5b,var,var2

                RETURN
```

## CODE FOR VARBAK.CMD

```
            * VARBAK.CMD
            * this is the subroutine of speller.cmd that will convert
            * numeric values to alphas.
            * REMEMBER: REPLACE CASE STATEMENTS WITH IF/ENDIFS
            * IF YOU ARE NOT USING DBASE VERSION 2.4 !!!!
            DO CASE

                CASE &var = 0
                    RETURN
                CASE &var = 1
                    STORE 'ONE ' TO &var2
                CASE &var = 2
                    STORE 'TWO ' TO &var2
                CASE &var = 3
                    STORE 'THREE ' TO &var2
                CASE &var = 4
                    STORE 'FOUR ' TO &var2
                CASE &var = 5
                    STORE 'FIVE ' TO &var2
                CASE &var = 6
                    STORE 'SIX ' TO &var2
                CASE &var = 7
                    STORE 'SEVEN ' TO &var2
```

```
        CASE &var = 8
            STORE 'EIGHT ' TO &var2
        CASE &var = 9
            STORE 'NINE ' TO &var2
        CASE &var = 10
            STORE 'TEN ' TO &var2
        CASE &var = 11
            STORE 'ELEVEN ' TO &var2
        CASE &var = 12
            STORE 'TWELVE ' TO &var2
        CASE &var = 13
            STORE 'THIRTEEN ' TO &var2
        CASE &var = 14
            STORE 'FOURTEEN ' TO &var2
        CASE &var = 15
            STORE 'FIFTEEN ' TO &var2
        CASE &var = 16
            STORE 'SIXTEEN ' TO &var2
        CASE &var = 17
            STORE 'SEVENTEEN ' TO &var2
        CASE &var = 18
            STORE 'EIGHTEEN ' TO &var2
        CASE &var = 19
            STORE 'NINETEEN ' TO &var2
        CASE &var = 20
            STORE 'TWENTY ' TO &var2
        CASE &var = 30
            STORE 'THIRTY ' TO &var2
        CASE &var = 40
            STORE 'FORTY ' TO &var2
        CASE &var = 50
            STORE 'FIFTY ' TO &var2
        CASE &var = 60
            STORE 'SIXTY ' TO &var2
        CASE &var = 70
            STORE 'SEVENTY ' TO &var2
        CASE &var = 80
            STORE 'EIGHTY ' TO &var2
        CASE &var = 90
            STORE 'NINETY ' TO &var2

    ENDCASE

    RETURN
```

An error message may be given when VARBAK is being used, due to a bug in some earlier versions of dBASE, which involved CASE and macro statements. Substitute IF ENDIF statements for the CASE. Delete the DO CASE and ENDCASE statements. Replace the commands CASE &var = [number] with the following:

```
IF &var = [number]
   STORE '[phrase]' TO &var2
ENDIF
```

# PAYABLES REPORT COMMAND FILES

## PAYRPTME.CMD   The Payables Report Options

The Payables offers options using the same logic as the INVOICE system. Files are closed by the use of repetitive SELECT and USE statements.
Three report options are available:

1. The daily transaction summary of several composite reports.
2. The vendor name and phone data with the total outstanding balance for that vendor.
3. The check register.

After ensuring that all previous data files are closed and an option is chosen, the operator is asked to chose if the results of the report should be sent to the printer or the screen. A macro (&) command is used to switch output between the two, by varying the contents of prntog, the *pr*in*ter tog*gle.

```
IF view = 'V'
   STORE '        ' TO prntog
ELSE
   SET CONSOLE OFF
   STORE 'TO PRINT' TO prntog
ENDIF
```

The reports that are enacted by PAYRPTME all use the following general command:

```
REPORT FORM customer [or other FORM] &prntog
```

The variable prntog will either stand for blanks ('        ') or ('TO PRINT'). The macro (&) before prntog will inform dBASE II to ignore treating prntog as a variable with data, and consider it shorthand for a command. Output will be directed to one of two destinations depending upon the earlier value of view.

```
REPORT FORM customer
REPORT FORM customer TO PRINT
```

The use of a macro to form part of the REPORT statement allows flexible direction of the output. Many reports can be generated by a multitude of REPORT commands, yet the operator has only to choose once for the screen or the printer.

================TECH TIP================

*Flexible Direction of REPORT Output*

*STORE ' ' TO variable for screen reports*
*STORE 'TO PRINT' TO variable for printer*

*Use with a macro (&) in a command:*

*REPORT FORM something &variable*

*dBASE II will see the commands as:*

*REPORT FORM something*
*REPORT FORM something TO PRINT*

CODE FOR PAYRPTME.CMD

```
* payrptme.cmd
* module purpose: allow report options to be printed
* for paybills system
* close all files before proceeding
SELECT secondary
USE
SELECT PRIMARY
USE

* set system date in report
SET DATE TO &mviewdate

DO WHILE t

    STORE ' ' TO selection2
    DO WHILE @(selection2, '0123' )=0
        ERASE
        @ 2,15 SAY ' ------ ACCOUNTS PAYABLE REPORT SUB-MENU --------'

        @ 4,15 SAY ' 0-Exit to MAIN MENU'
        @ 6,15 SAY ' 1-DAILY TRANSACTION SUMMARY '
        @ 7,15 SAY ' 2-VENDOR PHONE LIST and OUTSTANDING;
          BALANCE'
        @ 8,15 SAY ' 3-CHECK REGISTER'
        @ 10,15 SAY "Prepare Printer and Choose An Option " ;
        GET selection2 PICTURE '#'
        READ
    ENDDO WHILE @(selection1, '0123' )=0

    * return to main menu
    IF selection2 = '0'
```

```
            RELEASE selection2,rptnum,rptnum2,prntog,view
            USE
            SELECT secondary
            USE ious
            SELECT PRIMARY
            USE vendor
            RETURN
     ENDIF selection2 = '0'

* Allow choice of viewing on screen or on printer
* Note: Vendor ID may wrap around screen
ERASE
STORE 'V' TO view
@ 12,10 SAY ''Do You Wish to View (V) only or Print (P)? '' ;
GET view PICT '!'
READ
IF view = 'V'
    STORE ' ' TO prntog
ELSE
    * eliminate clutter on screen
    SET CONSOLE OFF
    STORE 'TO PRINT' TO prntog
ENDIF

DO CASE

    CASE selection2 = '1'
        * produce the variety of transaction reports
        DO transrpt

    CASE selection2 = '2'
        USE vendor
        INDEX ON lastname + firstname TO name
        * print general report
        * use compressed print code from prconfig
        * allow code to be sent to the printer
        SET PRINT ON
        ? &comprint
        SET PRINT OFF
        SET HEADING TO PHONE LIST -- ALL VENDORS
        REPORT FORM customer &prntog
        * print summary list of clients who owe money
        SET HEADING TO PHONE LIST -- VENDORS with BALANCES
        REPORT FORM customer FOR balance < > 0 &prntog
        * return to normal print pitch
        SET PRINT ON
        ? &normprint
        SET PRINT OFF
        SET INDEX TO
        DELETE FILE name.ndx
```

```
        CASE selection2 = '3'
            USE checkfil
            * Get the last check number as default
            * Last check number assumed to be at bottom of file
            GO BOTTOM
            STORE checknum TO rptnum2
            GO TOP
            SET HEADING TO CHECK REGISTER REPORT
            STORE 00000 to rptnum
            ERASE
            @ 12,10 SAY "Enter Begining Check Number for Report. " ;
            GET rptnum PICTURE '#####'
            @ 14,10 SAY "Enter Last Number or Press [RETURN]. " ;
            GET rptnum2 PICTURE '#####'
            READ
            REPORT FORM checks FOR checknum >= rptnum .AND. ;
                checknum <= rptnum2 &prntog
    ENDCASE

    SET HEADING TO
    SET CONSOLE ON
    WAIT

ENDDO t
```

## TRANSRPT.CMD  Daily Transaction Summary

The DAILY TRANSACTION SUMMARY is a composite of several reports from the transaction file, IOUS. TRANSRPT is called by the report menu to process the records, age the accounts due, and report the proper records to the screen or to the printer.

One FORM, billtran, is used to generate all the reports (see Figure 12-3). The first report is the summary of payments for all records that had an entry into the datepaid field on the logged date.

```
REPORT FORM billtran FOR datepaid = mfiledate &prntog
```

The second report details all bills posted into the computer on this date. The datein field establishes the condition upon which the records will generate the report.

```
REPORT FORM billtran FOR datein = mfiledate &prntog
```

The last reporting option is the aging of accounts. You will be able to determine which bills have been due more than 30, 60, and 90 days. The same report will be generated but only the outstanding payments for the given time period will be included on each of the three reports.

Aging uses the Date and Duration toolkit of utilites and is described in detail in Chapter Seventeen. The utilities will determine the correct

```
M=0
Y
ACCOUNTS PAYABLE TRANSACTION LIST
N
Y
Y
NAMECODE
N
N
------- VENDOR ===========>
5,BILLNUM
BILL;NUM.;====
N
8,$(DATEDUE,4,5) + '/' + $(DATEDUE,1,2)
DATE;DUE;====
8,$(DATEIN,4,5) + '/' + $(DATEIN,1,2)
DATE;REC.;=====
8,BILLBAL
BILL;BAL.;=====
Y
10,LASTPAY
LAST;PAYMENT;========
Y
10,$(DATEPAID,4,5) + '/' + $(DATEPAID,1,2)
DATE OF;PAYMENT;=======
20,DESCRIPT
;DESCRIPTION;===========
```

*Figure 12-3.* Dialog for BILLTRAN.FRM

calender date for each report and STORE it in turn to *day30, day60,* and *day90*. A conditional report statement is generated using one of these and the SET HEADING TO is revised accordingly prior to each report.

CODE FOR TRANSRPT. CMD

```
* transrpt.cmd
* module purpose: produces the daily transaction reports
* bill receipts, payments and bill status, and aged accounts
USE ious
INDEX ON namecode + datedue + STR(billnum,5) TO trans

* produce payment report
SET HEADING TO = DAILY PAYMENT SUMMARY =
REPORT FORM billtran FOR datepaid = mfiledate &prntog

* produce bill receipt report
SET HEADING TO = RECEIPT of BILLS on this DATE =
REPORT FORM billtran FOR datein = mfiledate &prntog

* Offer choice to produce aging report
STORE f TO decide
```

```
ERASE
@ 12,10 SAY "Do You Wish to Age Accounts (T/F)? " ;
GET decide
READ

IF decide
    * age accounts
    * use utility programs calint.cmd and intcal.cmd
    * see chapter on the use of date utilities
    * find the calendar dates 30, 60, 90 days from today
    * see Chapter 17 on date mechanics for details
    STORE mfiledate TO filedate
    DO calint
    STORE integer + 30 TO integer
    STORE integer TO cumdate
    DO intcal
    STORE filedate TO day30
    STORE cumdate + 30 TO integer
    DO intcal
    STORE filedate TO day60
    STORE cumdate + 30 TO integer
    DO intcal
    STORE filedate TO day90

    * print 4 reports for the aged accounts
    SET HEADING TO = Payments Due in 30 Days or Less =
    REPORT FORM billtran FOR datedue > mfiledate .AND. ;
    datedue < = day30 .AND. .NOT. pif &prntog

    SET HEADING TO = Payments Due between 30 to 60 days =
    REPORT FORM billtran FOR datedue > day30 .AND. ;
    datedue < = day60 .AND. .NOT. pif &prntog

    SET HEADING TO = Payments Due between 60 to 90 days =
    REPORT FORM billtran FOR datedue > day60 .AND. ;
    datedue < —day90 .AND. .NOT. pif &prntog

    SET HEADING TO = Payments Due 60 + days =
    REPORT FORM billtran FOR datedue > day90 ;
      .AND. .NOT. pif &prntog

ENDIF decide

* turn off index
SET INDEX TO
DELETE FILE trans.ndx

RELEASE cumdate,integer
RELEASE day30,day60,day90,decide
RETURN
```

## CALINT and INTCAL  Aged Accounts

The aging of accounts requires that 30, 60, and 90 days be added to "today's" date and converted back to the three corresponding calendar dates. CALINT and INTCAL are commands that perform the conversions. Chapter 17 details the operation of both. Once done, a REPORT command can be written to process only those records that have a due date within the given period with the code:

```
REPORT FORM billtran FOR datedue > day90 .AND. .NOT. pif &prntog
```

Records will be sent to either the printer or the screen (depending upon prntog) upon the condition that the datedue field in each is chronologically greater than the date represented by day90. The day90 date is calculated by converting today's date to an integer by using CALINT, adding 90 days to the result, and converting back to the calendar date ninety days later. All the aging reports are produced by the same method. Control is returned to the report menu once the transaction reports are produced.

## The Vendor Form  CUSTOMER.FRM Adapted to PAYABLES

INVOICE and PAYBILLS share the same FORM file that generates reports and balances—purchasers for the former and vendors for the latter. A negative number in the BALANCE field in PAYBILLS indicates debt; positive values indicate overpayments to vendors. Details on the installation of CUSTOMER.FRM can be found in Chapter 8.

## CHECKS.FRM  The Check Register

Reports are generated from the check file on the checks written on the logged day. A provision exists to print over a range of checks. The selection criterion for printing checks has been chosen as the check numbers instead of check dates. A procedure has been developed to allow the operator to enter the first and the last of the check number series to be printed. The default check number for the last check was obtained by the use of a very common technique, the use of the GO BOTTOM command to move to the last record in the file. (Dialog for CHECKS.FRM is shown in Figure 12-4.)

## EMBELLISHMENTS AND MODIFICATIONS

*Customizing the Check Stock*

The coordinates in the CHKCUT or the length of the form feed may be altered to suit your particular stock. The alterations were outlined earlier in the chapter.

```
Y
    ACCOUNTS PAYABLE CHECK PAYMENT REGISTER
N
Y
N
10,CHECKNUM
>CHECK;NUMBER;======
N
5,' '

10,$(DATEPAID,4,5) + '/' + $(DATEPAID,1,2)
DATE;PAID;====
5,' '

10,NAMECODE
<VENDOR;ID;======
10,' '

10,CURRCHK
CHECK;AMOUNT;======
Y
```

*Figure 12-4.* Dialog for CHECKS.FRM

═══════════════════════ **TECH TIP** ═══════════════════════

## To Find Characteristics about the Last Record

*USE file*
*GO BOTTOM*

*STORE a field to a variable*
*STORE # (record number) to a variable*
*GO TOP*

*(process records in the file)*

---

### Other Reports

A report to track bills by type can be implemented in the same way that one was for sales in the INVOICE system. To subtotal bills on vendor (the payments to the electric company for the year), simply REPORT from the IOUS file using BILLTRAN over the desired period. The dBASE II code:

```
REPORT FORM billtran FOR datein> ='83/12/01'
```

would print all bills that were received on or after the first of December 1983. Use the IOUS file when it is indexed on the NAMECODE field.

Additional reports can be developed for payments by using the check file, CHECKFIL. Print payments over a range of days by using the field datepaid in the conditional REPORT command.

The command

```
REPORT FORM checks FOR datepaid > = '83/12/01'
```

will report payments over the same period as bills received.


## SUMMARY

Tracking of both inflow of resources (money, due to sales) and outflow (purchases of inventory and services) is now automated by the dBASE II systems INVENT, INVOICE, and PAYBILLS. Several techniques were incorporated that are commonly used in many dBASE II financial routines. The Technical Tutorial outlines these in further detail in Chapter 13.

# 13

## WORKING WITH NUMBERS: A TECHNICAL TUTORIAL

The INVENT, INVOICE, and PAYBILLS systems used dBASE II with numbers to track financial and other resources. Several techniques are generally used with numbers:

1. Two or more linked files
2. Custom reporting from more than one file
3. Decimal rounding and truncating
4. The SAY USING command with numbers

### LINKED FILES

You would not want to store all the mailing data about each vendor in each of the check records, or retain all the company data on each purchaser in the INVOICE system's inventory file. Large segments of disk storage would be wasted repeating data that needs to be stored only once.

One of the strengths of dBASE II is that it is *relational;* comparisons can be easily made between one body of data and another. Economy often dictates that the storage of data be placed in more than one file and later merged into a report, like merging boilerplate letters with the MAIL-FORM names and addresses.

Conserve storage by CREATing a data file that will store similar data that, as a file, serves a unique need. Practice will determine the best methods of separating your fields into the two or more files, but, in general, ask the following questions while planning the databases:

- Can data items be identified and collected into a file that is rarely changed, like a name and address file of customers? All bibliographic or contact data can usually be placed in one relatively static file.
- Are there data that describe many exchanges? A transaction file may need to be organized.
- Are there exchanges of characteristically different items? One transaction file may be necessary for money (purchases) and one for materials (inventory). Separate transaction data files would be appropriate.

Multiple file processing requires that one or more fields in one file be matched or linked to fields in another file. Linked files require that records from one file be intelligently matched to records in another.

The method of matching needs to be considered from the beginning. Only the correct customer record should be matched with the proper purchase, with the resulting adjustment of the product number in the inventory file. An ID code or some other condition is used as a common field in all files as the matching device. The ID may be a customer or vendor code (namecode), Social Security number, employee code number, or some other available and convenient series of numbers or characters.

dBASE II allows more than one file at a time to be accessed. Data may be exchanged between two files once they are matched. NAMECODE is the common field for all three files in both INVOICE and PAYBILLS. LOCATE was used in the standard technique to link two of the three files.

```
USE vendor
  [now at first vendor's ID]
  SELECT SECONDARY
USE ious
LOCATE FOR s.namecode = p.namecode
```

We have asked dBASE II to examine all of the records in ious to find the first occurrence of a record that has a NAMECODE matching the vendor ID in the file vendor. Once LOCATEd, the records are linked. Data are available in the current record for both files. Data can also be passed between the two records across the two files by use of the REPLACE command.

Commands other than LOCATE may link files. PAYBILLS used SKIP in a DO WHILE loop to examine each record. The FIND command on a file works the quickest but requires that a file be always correctly indexed.

The use of multiple files is necessary for all but the simplest applications. Practice structuring the files you will need, the fields needed in each, and linking fields across files.

# CUSTOM REPORTS FROM MULTIPLE FILES

The REPORT writer has been used for many purposes on single files. Several FORMS have been used on one data file; one FORM has been used for different data files; and many reports have been written under a variety of conditions.

REPORT can access only one file at a time and cannot be used for linked files. Unfortunately, one of the main purposes of linking files is to obtain data not available from only one file. The shortcoming must be overcome by writing a custom command file.

The PAYBILLS check printer, CHKCUT, illustrates a custom reporter and is discussed in detail in Chapter 10. Although CHKCUT used a special form length EJECT, virtually all custom reports use the same logic. Files are linked and the report is generated.

A general report works like CHKCUT, except that the unique alteration of the EJECT for check stock is not necessary. An inner loop (DO WHILE .NOT. EOF) uses a driver to locate a record in one file (a payment transaction). Once found, the key upon which the files are linked is used to search the other file.

The report can be printed once the files are linked. A counter retains a number that determines the number of lines printed on the page. Test with an IF command, and EJECT when the counter equals the number of records that can be printed on one page.

The REPORT command automatically places headings, dates, and page numbers at the top of each page. You will need to do these yourself in a custom routine. The headings and dates must be placed on every page and the page number will need to be increased after the prior page is ejected.

The outer DO loop continues the search for another driver record (another transaction record, a payment, a purchase). Each record is stepped through one of the two files, linked to a corresponding record in the other file, and printed. The process repeats until all the records are printed.

Shown below is an example of a Custom Report. A version of CHKCUT, the report will print the check stubs on standard pages, print page numbers, headings, and footings. Two stubs will be printed per standard page. A sample of the printed product follows the code (see Figure 13-1).

## EXAMPLE OF CUSTOM REPORT

```
* myrpt.cmd
* module purpose: stripped down version ofchkcut.cmd
* illustrates custom reports on standard paper
SET talk OFF
SELECT PRIMARY
USE vendor
```

```
SELECT secondary
USE checkfil

ERASE
@ 12,10 SAY "**** CHECK PRINTING IN PROGRESS ***"
SET EJECT OFF
SET CONSOLE OFF
SET FORMAT TO PRINT
* initialize page number, headings, footings, date
STORE 1 TO mpage
STORE '12/23/83' TO mviewdate
STORE 'CUSTOM REPORT OF CHECK STUBS' TO HEADING1
STORE 'Stripped Down Version' TO HEADING2
STORE 'End of Page ' TO footing

* outer do loop—handles headings, date, next record
* monitors number of stubs on a page
* set up search routine for continue
LOCATE FOR unprinted
DO WHILE .NOT. eof
   * initialize number of stubs per page
   * initialize line counter
   STORE 1 TO stubs
   STORE 5 TO line
   @ line +2,5 SAY HEADING1
   @ line +2,50 SAY mviewdate
   @ line +3,5 SAY HEADING2

   * inner do loop—prints each stub, links files

   DO WHILE .NOT. eof .AND. stubs < 3

      * find the address in primary file
      SELECT PRIMARY
      LOCATE FOR p.namecode = s.namecode
      * now print check information
      SELECT secondary
      SET FORMAT TO PRINT
      * PRINT WHATEVER IS PRINTED FROM EACH RECORD
      @ line + 5,40 SAY "DATE:"
      @ line + 5,50 SAY mviewdate
      @ line + 6,40 SAY "CHECK NO."
      @ line +10,20 SAY company
      @ line +12,20 SAY street
      @ line +14,20 SAY TRIM(suite:etc)
      @ line +16,20 SAY TRIM(city) + ' ' + st + ' ' + zip
      @ line +18,20 SAY 'ATTN: ' + TRIM(mr:ms) + ' ' + TRIM(firstname) + ' ' + lastname
      @ line +20,20 SAY "AMOUNT REMITTED ON THIS DATE"
      @ line +20,50 SAY currchk USING '$$$$$$$.##'
      * end of check stub
      * signal that another stub has been printed
      STORE stubs + 1 TO stubs
      * move the next check 23 down the page or 21 plus a couple of lines
```

```
      STORE line + 23 TO line
      * Move down one record in check file to get next record as driver
      SKIP
   ENDDO WHILE .NOT. eof
   * Printing 2 stubs now done.
   * Print footing at bottom of page
   @ 60,30 SAY footing
   @ 60,45 SAY mpage USING '##'
   STORE mpage + 1 TO mpage
   EJECT
ENDDO WHILE .NOT. eof

SET FORMAT TO SCREEN
SET EJECT ON
SET CONSOLE ON
SELECT PRIMARY
RELEASE line, HEADING1, HEADING2
RELEASE Stubs, Footing, MPAGE
RETURN
```

```
CUSTOM REPORT OF CHECK STUBS        12/23/23
  Stripped Down Version

                                     DATE: 12/23/83
                                     CHECK NO.

         International Widget

         54 Floor St.

         Suite 9876

         New York NY 10098

         ATTN: Mr. Diamond Jim Brady

         AMOUNT REMITTED ON THIS DATE $$$$900.00

                                     DATE: 12/23/83
                                     CHECK NO.

         Home Handicrafters

         1 Twinkle Toes Lane

         Suite 22

         Everywhere IA 33333

         ATTN: Mr. John Doe

         AMOUNT REMITTED ON THIS DATE $$$$100.00
                        End of Page 1
```

*Figure 13-1.*   Sample of Check Stubs Using a Custom Report Writer

Besides being able to use multiple files, custom reporting also gives you other options that the REPORT writer does not. One record's data may occupy more than one line, as illustrated by the checks in Figure 13-1. More polish may be added to each report. Testing of the values of a field in each record can be performed. Once done, the printing can be handled differently, according to the value of the contents.

Assume that you have a policy that each check over the value of $5,000 must be cashed within 20 days. Other checks must be cashed within 90 days. Code may be inserted into CHKCUT as indicated:

```
* standard code here
@ line + 20 SAY "AMOUNT REMITTED ON THIS DATE"
@ line + 20,50 SAY currchk USING '######.##'

* insert special code for testing here
IF currchk >= 5000
   @ line + 21,15 SAY "Please Cash Within 20 Days."
ELSE
   @ line + 21,15 SAY "Please Cash Within 90 Days."
ENDIF
```

The instruction that matches the check amount for each check will be correctly chosen and printed. Testing and branching to an alternative print phrase is not possible with the dBASE II REPORT command.

## DECIMAL PRECISION

dBASE II and decimals sometimes don't mix, unless you know the limitations and the easy methods to overcome them. Problems arise when the results of calculations (especially dividends) are expressed. The precision, or number of decimal places, must be adjusted to reflect your needs.

### Too Little Precision

dBASE II at times does not have enough data to give you a number with enough decimal digits. Type within dBASE II the following:

| TYPE | YOU WILL SEE |
|---|---|
| ? 100/3 [RETURN] | 33 |

The dividend is correct only to two decimal places. dBASE II takes the precision from the denominator if it has not been established before from the STORE or USING commands. Two-digit precision can be obtained by dividing by a number that has two decimals:

| TYPE | YOU WILL SEE |
|------|--------------|
| ? 100/3.00 | 33.33 |

(Two zeros are added to the right of the decimal.)
(Dividend then yields two digits of precision.)

As a general rule, when numbers are to be divided, ensure that the denominator has enough decimals to force the calculation and display of the dividend to the degree of accuracy required.

## Too Much Precision

Columns of numbers need to be aligned on official forms without extraneous thousandths and ten-thousandths of a penny protruding from the columns. Two methods can be used: truncating and rounding.

### Truncating Decimals

One of the easiest methods to lob off excess decimals is to express them as a string of characters, using the STR command. The STR command takes a value and converts it to characters.

| AT THE KEYBOARD TYPE: | YOU WILL SEE: |
|-----------------------|---------------|
| STORE 123456.8999 to number | |
| ? number | 123456.8999 |
| ? STR(number,9,2) | 123456.89 |

The STR needs the variable in the parenthesis to be converted, the total number of digits that will be displayed (including decimals), and the number of decimals to be displayed. The latter is the feature that enables the technique to work. A numeric can be converted to a character string with a STR command, and any number of decimal places can be expressed.

Another conversion technique is the INT, or integer command. The INT takes any numerical variable and always lobs off every digit to the right of the decimal point. Every one of the above expressions would be a numeric of the same value: 123456.

| TYPE | YOU WILL SEE |
|------|--------------|
| ? INT(123456.8999) | 123456 |

Each technique has its benefits. The STR can express as many digits as desired, but the resultant can not be mathematically manipulated directly. The INT technique works entirely with numbers, but not even one decimal can be displayed.

One of the ways to obtain decimal data is first to multiply the variable by 10 or 100, or to what ever magnitude you wish to express the decimal, take the INT of this, then divide by the corresponding denominator. Don't forget to express the denominator to the proper degree of decimals.

For tenths:

| TYPE | YOU WILL SEE |
|------|-------------|
| ? INT(123456.8999 * 10 )/10.0 | 123456.8 |

For hundredths:

| TYPE | YOU WILL SEE |
|------|-------------|
| ? INT(123456.8999 * 100)/100.00 | 123456.89 |

Truncating is often useful when approximate amounts are listed. Accounting procedures, however, often require that subtotals across a page total down the page as well (footings and cross footings). Truncating will often result in bottom line figures that do not properly total. A consistent method for rounding is necessary.

## Rounding

Rounding is accomplished by using a variant of the same methods. To round to cents (hundredths), multiply a variable or other expression by 100. Add .5 to the result. The INTeger of the expression, divided by one hundred, gives the required result.

| TYPE | YOU WILL SEE |
|------|-------------|
| ? INT((123456.8999 * 100) + .5)/100.00 | 123456.90 |

The rounded subtotals, used in later totals, will yield a more consistent product and will foot and cross foot properly.

The truncating and rounding formulas will work in both the standard and custom reports. You may need to place them in one of the dBASE II REPORT FORMS if division is used to calculate an average.

.REPORT FORM EXAMPLE

```
Y
3 MONTH AVERAGE OF EXPENSES BY MONTH
N
N
12,JANEXPENSE
;JANUARY;EXPENSE;========
12,FEBEXPENSE
```

```
;FEBRUARY;EXPENSE;========
12,MAREXPENSE
;MARCH;EXPENSE;=======
12,(janexpense + febexpense + marexpense)/3
AVERAGE;W/O ROUNDING;===========
12,int((((janexpense + febexpense + marexpense)/3.000) * 100) + .5)- /100.00
;ROUNDED;AVERAGE;========
```

The FORM will yield the following results of the three expense fields in an example database. One of the records had a total expense of $100, the other $200, for monthly averages of $33.3333 and $66.66666, respectively (see Figure 13-2).

Rounding of financial data often becomes absolutely necessary when division is used in the REPORT writer. If not required, the shorter formula for truncating decimals may suffice.

## FORMATTING WITH THE SAY
## USING STATEMENTS

Numbers are often printed with great precision on forms, such as the running totals on an invoice (the INVOICE system) and on a report (the POSTBILLS payables screen). Numbers present special problems—they "pop over" to the right of the first coordinate that was reserved for printing. dBASE II will justify to the right any numbers, yet the coordinate you give ( @ 5,10 say num ) was for the leftmost number. Only numbers of the largest magnitude would be aligned; the others would begin printing at some coordinate on the line to the right of the tenth space. The justification problem occurs for both input and output. In dBASE II, try the following:

```
        TYPE                 YOU WILL SEE

    STORE 0 to testvar
    @ 10,5 GET testvar
    READ                     :        0 :
```

3 MONTH AVERAGE OF EXPENSES BY MONTH

| JANUARY EXPENSE | FEBRUARY EXPENSE | MARCH EXPENSE | AVERAGE W/O ROUNDING | ROUNDED AVERAGE |
|---|---|---|---|---|
| 30.00 | 20.00 | 50.00 | 33.333 | 33.33 |
| 50.00 | 40.00 | 110.00 | 66.666 | 66.67 |

*Figure 13-2.* REPORT FORM Test - Example of Rounding in REPORT

dBASE II, unless otherwise instructed, presented enough spaces between the commas to allow the entry of a ten-digit number. At times this may be unsuitable, especially if only much smaller numbers are entered and only limited space remains on the screen. Use the PICTURE statement to force only the spaces required.

| TYPE | YOU WILL SEE |
|------|--------------|

```
STORE 0 to testvar
@ 10,5 GET testvar PICTURE '# #'
READK                                       : 0 :
```

SAY USING statements can be used to force the output of data into the desired format. USING is the exact equivalent to SAY that PICTURE is to the GET command. USING is a command that is necessary if attractive financial statements are to be printed. SAY USING with numbers allows three purposes to be served: alignment, truncating, and insertion of special characters.

## Alignment

Consider a dBASE II program that produces numbers of widely varying magnitude. The program will produce the numbers and display with the use of the standard SAY statement and with the USING statement.

```
*  sayusing.cmd
*  produces numbers of
*  varying magnitude
ERASE
SET TALK OFF
STORE 10.13456 TO num
STORE 5 TO x
@ 3, 0 SAY 'UNFORMATTED'
@ 3,30 SAY 'FORMATTED WITH USING STATEMENTS'
DO WHILE num  <100000000
   *  produce unformatted printing
   @ x, 0 SAY num
   *  produce formatted printing
   @ x,40 SAY num USING '# # # # # # # # #.# #'
   STORE x + 1 TO x
   STORE num * 10 TO num
ENDDO
*  end of test program
```

This test command file produces a simulation of numbers that may appear in your financial reports. Which would you prefer to give to your boss?

### Table 13-1. Formatted versus Unformatted Printing of Numbers: Results of sayusing.cmd

| Unformatted | Formatted with Using Statements |
|---|---|
| 10.13456 | 10.13 |
| 101.34560 | 101.34 |
| 1013.45600 | 1013.45 |
| 10134.56000 | 10134.56 |
| 101345.60000 | 101345.60 |
| 1013456.00000 | 1013456.00 |
| 10134560.00000 | 10134560.00 |

The unformatted numbers appear in the raw form. No alignment is apparent, and the numbers have no consistent truncation after the decimal point. A pink slip would be the reward for your labors if the unformatted dBASE II report was handed to a superior.

The column that was formatted by the USING statement is arranged neatly and is indeed a column. Numbers are aligned and can be printed without fear of overflowing the right column.

## Truncation

The SAY USING also is a handy technique to truncate results without resorting to a formula. In the above figure, decimal information is truncated precisely at the desired number of decimal places. Any output can be expressed in dollars and cents with SAY USING by using the command:

```
@ X,Y SAY bucks USING '######.##'
```

Any averages with repeating decimals (1234.333333) will be stopped at the cent level. Any amount up to $999999.99 can be expressed in this USING expression. Greater amounts can be displayed by inserting additional #'s in the formatting statements.

## Special Characters

The # and . characters have already been used in the USING statements. The number of #'s and the placement of the .'s have forced truncation. Two other characters, the comma and the leading dollar, allow further flexibility of the USING statement. Values are not altered, nor are any digits truncated.

You probably paused to view the last number above (999999.99) and mentally inserted the commas. dBASE II will do this for you by allowing the comma between thousands and millions to be displayed to allow easier comprehension. Place the commas in the USING statement in addition to the # characters. The technique was used in the printing of the invoice and is illustrated in Chapters 7 and 8.

The other character is the leading dollar. If the $ replaces the #, dollar signs will be printed up to the first digit of a number, which hinders the tampering or alteration of the number.

To illustrate the two, replace the formatting line in sayusing.cmd:

```
@ x,40 SAY num USING '##########.##'
```

with:

```
@ x,40 SAY num USING '$,$$$,$$$,$$$.##'
```

The results will appear with Rolls-Royce splendor:

*Table 13-2. Formatted versus Unformatted Printing of Numbers: Results of Revised sayusing.cmd*

| UNFORMATTED | FORMATTED WITH USING STATEMENTS |
|---|---|
| 10.13456 | $$$$$$$$$$10.13 |
| 101.34560 | $$$$$$$$1,01.34 |
| 1013.45600 | $$$$$$$10,13.45 |
| 10134.56000 | $$$$$$101,34.56 |
| 101345.60000 | $$$$1,013,45.60 |
| 1013456.00000 | $$$10,134,56.00 |
| 10134560.00000 | $$101,345,60.00 |

The commas allowed easy reading, and the dollar signs remained packed to the left of each of the formatted numbers. The possibility of forgery is virtually eliminated.

## SUMMARY

Four techniques were discussed: Linking files, developing custom reports, printing numbers with the desired precision, and formatting. Formatting with the USING statement allows numbers to be read more easily once they are displayed on the screen or printed on your forms. Practice with these techniques, develop your own reports, and experiment with formatting the decimals and aligning the numbers. The techniques will be used in the next application, an expense manager for portable computers.

# SECTION
# FOUR

## Expense on the Go: A Portable Computer Application

# 14

# USING THE EXPENSE SYSTEM

Expense report calculations are a drudgery for the frequent business traveler. The only alternative before the advent of portable microcomputers was to return to the home office with a pocketful of receipts and reminders scribbled on scraps of paper. Each day's expenses had to be manually sorted, subtotalled by category, entered on the standard form required by the office, and totalled for the month (see Figure 14-1). Explanations of any questionable expenses had to be detailed for the boss and for IRS.

Many enterprising salespeople are now acquiring portable computers and using them while covering their territories. One of the first applications has been to record travel expenses as they occur on one of the many spreadsheet packages that comes bundled with the machines.

EXPENSE asks for general and, if needed, specific information. Daily expenses by category are entered, with the amount and location. These are subtotalled by each day and the subtotals generate category totals and a grand total.

Outlays for entertainment and unusual expenses undergo scrutiny by the IRS. If these expense categories are entered, the bottom half of the screen clears and requests further information to generate a detailed report.

The standard report is for the logged month, which can be overridden by designating a range of dates. A supplementary report is generated if any expenses for the ENT (ENTERTAINMENT) or OTH (OTHER) categories were entered during this period.

*Figure 14-1.* Expense Reports Can be a Drudgery

## OPERATION OF EXPENSE

The EXPENSE system is started by typing Do X:EXPENSE, where X is the default drive for EXPENSE. The program will check INIT on the A drive for the printer commands and the default drives. Once done, you will be asked for the first date that the expenses will be posted. The menu will appear after the date is posted (see Figure 14-2).

- Option 0 exits from dBASE II to the operating system.
- Option 1 enables the operator to add expenses.
- Option 2 allows the expenses, once added, to be reviewed and edited, starting at the logged month.
- Option 3 prints expense reports in a ledger or spreadsheet format for a given period. The default period is the logged month.
- Option 4 allows the logged date to be changed without exiting and entering EXPENSE again.

## OPTION 1: ADD TO CURRENT MONTH

The entry screen displays with the logged month and year at the top. Enter the day of the month first (see Figure 14-3).

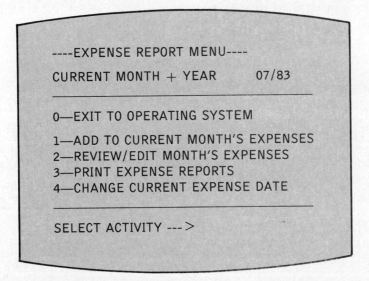

*Figure 14-2.* The Main Expense Menu

EXPENSE allows for 11 expense categories, which are outlined on the entry screen. Enter the three-digit code that corresponds to the type of expense you incurred while traveling. Enter the amount of the expense for the item and the location to finish the first phase of the entry process.

The entry would be completed if one of nine categories of expenses is chosen. The Internal Revenue Service, however, has been known to request further data about non-standard expenses. If the ENT and OTH categories are entered, the bottom half of the screen will clear and a

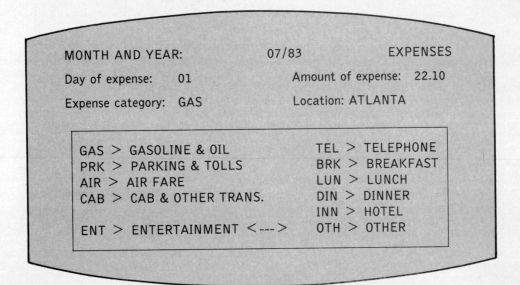

*Figure 14-3.* Illustration of Standard Entry Screen

screen will appear to request supplemental data. The ENT screen will request the restaurant name and the person who was entertained, the reason, and any other pertinent data (see Figure 14-4). The OTH screen will designate the person to whom the expense was made, the company, the reason, also the additional data (see Figure 14-5).

After the expense item has been entered, the screen asks the operator if further entries for the same day are desired. If chosen, the last entered amount and category will be cleared, but the day and location will be retained on the entry screen. If declined, a subsequent question is displayed, Continue adding expenses? (T/F). The main menu displays if no more expenses are to be added.

## OPTION 2: REVIEW/EDIT MONTH'S EXPENSES

The Edit option accomplishes the same function of revision as it has in the previous dBASE systems, but two files are reviewed at once. One is the main file with the general expense data. The second file contains the supplemental (entertainment and other) data required by the IRS.

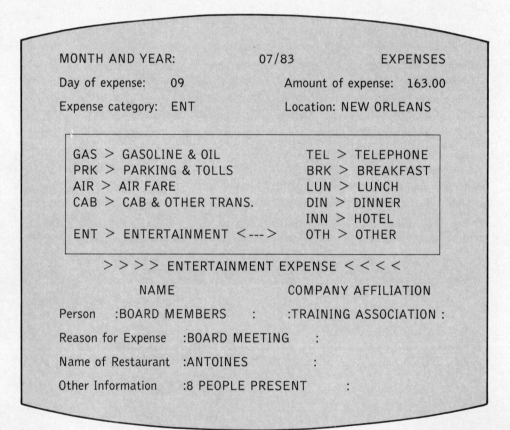

MONTH AND YEAR:              07/83                    EXPENSES

Day of expense:    09           Amount of expense:   163.00

Expense category:   ENT         Location: NEW ORLEANS

```
GAS > GASOLINE & OIL           TEL > TELEPHONE
PRK > PARKING & TOLLS          BRK > BREAKFAST
AIR > AIR FARE                 LUN > LUNCH
CAB > CAB & OTHER TRANS.       DIN > DINNER
                               INN > HOTEL
ENT > ENTERTAINMENT <--->      OTH > OTHER
```

> > > > ENTERTAINMENT EXPENSE < < < <

               NAME                    COMPANY AFFILIATION

Person    :BOARD MEMBERS     :     :TRAINING ASSOCIATION :

Reason for Expense   :BOARD MEETING      :

Name of Restaurant   :ANTOINES           :

Other Information    :8 PEOPLE PRESENT         :

*Figure 14-4.* Illustration of Entry Screen with Detail for Entertainment Category

```
MONTH AND YEAR:            07/83              EXPENSES

Day of expense:    16        Amount of expense:  50.12

Expense category:  OTH        Location: ATLANTA

 ┌────────────────────────────────────────────────────┐
 │  GAS > GASOLINE & OIL         TEL > TELEPHONE        │
 │  PRK > PARKING & TOLLS        BRK > BREAKFAST        │
 │  AIR > AIR FARE               LUN > LUNCH            │
 │  CAB > CAB & OTHER TRANS.     DIN > DINNER           │
 │                               INN > HOTEL            │
 │  ENT > ENTERTAINMENT <--->    OTH > OTHER            │
 └────────────────────────────────────────────────────┘
          > > > > OTHER EXPENSE < < < <

            Paid to :WINESTOCK'S         :

              For :FLOWERS              :

           Other :BOSS'S WIFE DIED      :
```

*Figure 14-5.* Illustration of Entry Screen with Detail for Other Category

You may notice a pause while the program searches the main file to locate the first expense for the logged month. Once found, the Review & Edit screen will be displayed (see Figure 14-6). You will be allowed to change the expense category, amount, and location, but not the date of the expense.

```
┌──────────────────────────────────────────────────────────┐
│   REVIEW & EDIT                    07/83                  │
├──────────────────────────────────────────────────────────┤
│                                                          │
│  DAY OF MONTH  :01         CATEGORY : :OTH:               │
│                                                          │
│  EXPENSE AMOUNT : :  4.00:   LOCATION : :ATLANTA      :   │
│                                                          │
├──────────────────────────────────────────────────────────┤
│                  If ENT or OTH Category:                 │
│                                                          │
│  Person : CLERK          :      Company : :POST OFFICE  :│
│                                                          │
│  Reason for expense: STAMPS            :                 │
│  Name of Restaurant:              :                      │
│  Other Information : SENT AJAX TRAIN. PROPOSAL     :      │
└──────────────────────────────────────────────────────────┘
```

*Figure 14-6.* Illustration of Editing Screen

As with the Add option, the selection of ENT or the OTH category invokes supplemental screens. Editing and review can be conducted on all expense items.

After reviewing the expenses, you will have the choice of reviewing another item or returning to the main menu. Control is restored to the main menu if you answer F to the question, the end of the file is reached, or the last record for the logged month has been displayed.

# OPTION 3: PRINT EXPENSE REPORTS

The third option allows reports to be generated about expenses. Each expense category is totalled for each day (the total of three cab fares on July 5), and total daily expenses are calculated and printed on the right. Subtotals by category for the period are printed for each of the 11 expense items on the bottom, with the grand total for all expenses printed on the lower right.

Prepare the printer before continuing. Enter start and end range dates if desired, or let EXPENSE assume the days of the logged month as the default dates of expenditures for the report. You are asked:

Report Only on CURRENT Month (T/F) :T:

Press the RETURN key to allow the report to continue. Entry of an F will signify that a range other than the logged month will be reported and the screen will clear. You will be requested to enter the first and last dates that expenses are to be reported.

The programming to transform your information from a dBASE file into a spreadsheet ledger is extensive; and a pause may be noted. The expense report is printed once the ledger is processed (see Figure 14-7).

The supplemental expense report explanation will be generated only if at least one expense entry has been entered with the ENT or OTH category. The details provided in the second report should satisfy IRS reporting requirements (see Figure 14-8).

If ENT or OTH were not used in an entry, the message, NO IRS DETAILS ENTERED FOR SELECTED PERIOD, will be printed at the bottom of the expense report. The main menu appears once the printing is finished.

# OPTION 4: CHANGE THE LOGGED DATE

You may wish to edit or add expenses to a month that is different from the currently logged month. Option 4 allows you to change the logged month.

EXPENSE REPORT

| MO/DY LOCATION | GAS OIL | PARKING TOLLS | AIRFARE | TAXI TIPS | MOTEL | MEAL BREAKFST | MEAL LUNCH | MEAL DINNER | PHONE | ENTER-TAINMENT | OTHER | DAILY TOTAL |
|---|---|---|---|---|---|---|---|---|---|---|---|---|
| 07/01 ATLANTA | 22.10 | 2.00 | 0.00 | 0.00 | 42.00 | 0.00 | 5.34 | 18.23 | 0.00 | 0.00 | 4.00 | 93.67 |
| 07/02 MONTGOMERY | 0.00 | 0.00 | 0.00 | 0.00 | 46.18 | 5.55 | 5.50 | 22.00 | 3.00 | 37.40 | 0.00 | 119.63 |
| 07/03 HUNTSVILLE | 19.32 | 0.00 | 0.00 | 0.00 | 0.00 | 2.70 | 6.60 | 17.82 | 0.00 | 0.00 | 0.00 | 46.44 |
| 07/09 NEW ORLEANS | 0.00 | 0.00 | 212.87 | 0.00 | 92.00 | 0.00 | 0.00 | 0.00 | 0.00 | 163.00 | 0.00 | 467.87 |
| 07/10 NEW ORLEANS | 0.00 | 0.00 | 233.23 | 12.00 | 0.00 | 7.90 | 0.00 | 0.00 | 18.00 | 0.00 | 0.00 | 271.13 |
| 07/16 ATLANTA | 0.00 | 3.25 | 0.00 | 0.00 | 0.00 | 0.00 | 0.00 | 0.00 | 0.00 | 0.00 | 50.12 | 53.37 |
| 07/28 DECATUR, GA | 0.00 | 0.00 | 0.00 | 0.00 | 0.00 | 0.00 | 0.00 | 16.00 | 0.00 | 0.00 | 32.00 | 48.00 |
| 07/29 ATLANTA | 0.00 | 2.00 | 0.00 | 0.00 | 0.00 | 0.00 | 0.00 | 0.00 | 0.00 | 0.00 | 0.00 | 2.00 |
| ** TOTAL ** | 41.42 | 7.25 | 446.10 | 12.00 | 180.18 | 16.15 | 17.44 | 74.05 | 21.00 | 200.40 | 86.12 | 1102.11 |

*Figure 14-7.* The General Expense Report

EXPENSE REPORT EXPLANATION

| MO/DY | AMOUNT | NAME OF PERSON | COMPANY | BUSINESS PURPOSE | NAME OF REST. | OTHER INFO |
|---|---|---|---|---|---|---|
| 07/01 | 4.00 | CLERK | POST OFFICE | STAMPS | | SENT AJAX TRAIN. PROPOSAL |
| 07/02 | 37.40 | BILL PARKS | COMPUTER DELIGHTS | DISCUSS TRAINING | SHOWBOAT LOUNGE | DBASE ORIENTED |
| 07/09 | 163.00 | BOARD MEMBERS | TRAINING ASSOCIATION | BOARD MEETING | ANTOINES | 8 PEOPLE PRESENT |
| 07/16 | 50.12 | | WINESTOCK'S | FLOWERS | | BOSS'S WIFE DIED |
| 07/28 | 32.00 | | MINI SUPPLIERS | BOX OF DISKETTES | | NEEDED FOR EXPENSE PROG |
| ** TOTAL ** | 286.52 | | | | | |

*Figure 14-8.* The Supplemental Report for the IRS

## OPERATIONS SUMMARY OF THE EXPENSE SYSTEM

Operating instructions for EXPENSE are now complete. Other uses will become evident as the record of expenses is built. Since dBASE II is a database, other reports can be developed summarizing the expenses for each client, location, and category. Decisions can be made about the profitability of visits in high-cost areas. The detailed reports that EXPENSE produces and the flexibility of dBASE II to produce other reports allow detailed analysis of expense trends. With most of the expense account paperwork eliminated by the EXPENSE program, you are free to pursue other profitable applications with your portable computer at home, at the office, or on the road.

# 15

# INSTALLATION OF EXPENSE

EXPENSE combines the storage capacity of dBASE II (65,000 records) with the convenient ledger format of a spreadsheet. Expenses are summed by the date of the expense (the major category), and by type of expense for each day. All records in the dBASE II data files are grouped and totalled on date and kind of expense.

## THE SPREADSHEET LEDGER

A report with two kinds of totals is best illustrated by a spreadsheet ledger. The dates of expenses are presented down the page with the expense categories across the top of the page. Entries for the same expense category for the same date are summarized (collapsed), and the total is shown rather than each individual record. Totals for each date are shown down the page (cross footings) in the daily total column, and totals for expense categories are shown across the page (footings). A grand total of expenses is printed where the footings and cross footings meet, in the lower right-hand corner of the report. The sum of totals down equals the sum of totals across the line on the bottom (see Figure 15-1).

Spreadsheet application software is designed to display this format much more easily than dBASE II and other database managers. The use of spreadsheets becomes awkward, however, when sufficient expenses accumulate to fill memory. Analysis of expense trends between files for several months or years may be difficult or impossible.

LEDGER FORMAT WITH FOOTINGS AND CROSS FOOTINGS

| | | V | | | |
|---|---|---|---|---|---|
| | CATEGORY OF EXPENSE | | | | DAILY |
| DATE | BRK | LUN | GAS | EMT | TOTAL |
| | | | | | |
| DAY 1 | _ | _ | 25.00 | _ | 25.00 |
| DAY 2 | 4.50 | 8.00 | _ | 40.00 | 52.50 |
| DAY 3 | 5.00 | _ | _ | _ _ | 5.00 |
| DAY 9 | 6.00 | _ | _ | _ _ | 6.00 |
| | | | | | |
| SUB TOTALS | 15.50 | 8.00 | 25.00 | 40.00 | 88.50 |

Categories listed in detail.
(expanded out)

< = Sub-totals by major category
(date) calculated at right.

< = GRAND TOTAL
Totals down and across are equal.
(Foot and cross foot)

Sub-totals
of expense
categories
listed on one line.

Two records for DAY 1 GAS
collapsed into sub-total.

STANDARD dBASE II REPORT LISTING

| | | |
|---|---|---|
| DAY 9 | BRK | 6.00 |
| DAY 1 | GAS | 10.00 |
| DAY 2 | ENT | 40.00 |
| DAY 3 | BRK | 5.00 |
| DAY 1 | GAS | 15.00 |
| DAY 2 | LUN | 8.00 |
| DAY 2 | BRK | 4.50 |
| | | |
| *TOTAL* | | |
| | | 88.50 |

One record per line.

Totals are optionally expressed
at bottom of report.

*Figure 15-1.* Standard Listings versus Ledger Format

The EXPENSE program offers spreadsheet convenience without spreadsheet limitations. Many months of expenses can be written to one file and analyzed. Unlike most spreadsheets, dBASE II is fundamentally limited by the size of the disk drive, not by the computer's memory. Each expense can be stored in a record, and all records can be reported or selectively totalled by date, category of expense, amount, or location.

The manipulations to produce a spreadsheet type report from a database like dBASE II may appear at first to be extensive. This is because dBASE II is designed to produce columns of records (with optional totals at the bottom) rather than ledgers (expense data and their totals down columns and across rows). The principles outlined by the EXPENSE system, however, can be applied with practice to your other applications.

## FILES FOR THE EXPENSE SYSTEM

EXPENSE uses three permanent data files for retaining data, one of which is used only during reporting. Four command files are used to add, edit, and manage processing. Two report FORM files configure two reports.

A new technique is the use of data files that do not reside with the permanent .DBF files but are created from the STRUCTURES of the others to prepare data files for custom reporting. The files are generated and deleted after the reporting.

*Table 15-1.   List of Files and Main Functions*

| Filename | Stands For | Function |
|---|---|---|
| MAIN.DBF | Main Data File | Holds General Expenses |
| IRSEXPEN.DBF | IRS Expenses | Holds Special Expenses |
| EXPANDED.DBF | Expanded Main File | Expands Structure |
| EXPENSE.CMD | Expense | Main Menu |
| ADD.CMD | Add | Add Records |
| ENTSCRN.FMT | Entry Screen | Entry Format File |
| EDITSCN.CMD | Edit Screen | Edit and Review Records |
| LISTOUT.CMD | List Out | Convert into Ledger |
| REPORT1.FRM | First Report Form | Form for General Report |
| REPORT2.FRM | Second Report Form | Form for IRS Report |

Utility Files Used (On the A Drive)
INIT.CMD
DTVERIFY.CMD

## DATA FILES FOR THE EXPENSE SYSTEM

### MAIN.DBF   The Main Expense Data File

The MAIN file stores data on all expenditures. The date (EDATE), type of expense (ECATEGORY), amount (EAMOUNT), and location (ELOCA-TION) are the items that provide all necessary information in the general report. The file is linked to other files by the EXpense LOCator field EXLOC. Note the categories of expenses (GAS, ENT) are stored as the contents of ECATEGORY.

```
STRUCTURE FOR FILE: B:MAIN    .DBF
NUMBER OF RECORDS: 00034
DATE OF LAST UPDATE: 00/00/00
PRIMARY USE DATABASE
FLD             NAME        TYPE    WIDTH   DEC
001             EDATE       C       008
002             ECATEGORY   C       003
003             EAMOUNT     N       008     002
004             ELOCATION   C       015
005             EXLOC       N       004
** TOTAL **                         00039
```

## IRSEXPEN.DBF  The Supplemental Database for the IRS

The IRS expense file is the other permanent data file. All supplemental data for entertainment or other expenses are retained in this file. EPERSON1 stores the name of the person entertained, ECOMPANY1 the company affiliation of the companion, EREASON displays the reason for the expense, EREST states the name of the restaurant, and EOTHER stores any other comments. The EXLOC field links IRSEXPEN to the other files.

```
STRUCTURE FOR FILE: B:IRSEXPEN.DBF
NUMBER OF RECORDS: 00008
DATE OF LAST UPDATE: 00/00/00
PRIMARY USE DATABASE
FLD             NAME        TYPE    WIDTH   DEC
001             EPERSON1    C       015
002             ECOMPANY1   C       020
003             EREASON     C       020
004             EREST       C       015
005             EOTHER      C       025
006             EXLOC       N       005
** TOTAL **                         00101
```

## EXPANDED.DBF  The Temporary File for MAIN.DBF

EXPANDED is used only when reporting is being performed. All data from MAIN is transferred to EXPANDED for conversion to a form that can be used by the REPORT FORM file in a ledger format.

Chapter 15
Installation of Expense

```
STRUCTURE FOR FILE: B:EXPANDED.DBF
NUMBER OF RECORDS: 00000
DATE OF LAST UPDATE: 07/83/00
PRIMARY USE DATABASE
FLD          NAME        TYPE    WIDTH    DEC
001          EDATE       C       008
002          ECATEGORY   C       003
003          EAMOUNT     N       008      002
004          ELOCATION   C       015
005          EXLOC       N       004
006          GAS         N       007      002
007          PRK         N       007      002
008          AIR         N       007      002
009          CAB         N       007      002
010          INN         N       007      002
011          ENT         N       007      002
012          TEL         N       007      002
013          BRK         N       007      002
014          LUN         N       007      002
015          DIN         N       007      002
016          OTH         N       007      002
** TOTAL **                      00116
```

# PROGRAM FILES FOR THE EXPENSE SYSTEM

Three command files serve the familiar functions of control (the menu EXPENSE), record addition (ADD), and record revision (EDITSCN). New techniques of data manipulation are accomplished by the fourth command file (LISTOUT). A format file arranges prompts in an attractive manner and formats operator entry and data display. Two FORM files (REPORT1 and REPORT2) configure the reports.

## EXPENSE.CMD   Main Menu

EXPENSE uses the same menu logic found in other applications in the book. The files are initialized with INIT. The date routine DTVERIFY verifies the dates of expenses. The month and year of the date are STOREd to memory variables, myear and mmonth.

CODE FOR EXPENSE.CMD

```
* expense.cmd
* Program by Michael Clifford
* Module Purpose: Allows Choice of Menu Options
```

```
* Section I - Housekeeping
DO A:INIT
SET DEFAULT TO &dfdefault
USE main
SELECT secondary
USE irsexpense
SELECT PRIMARY

SET DEFAULT TO &pfdefault

STORE "BEGINNING DATE TO POST EXPENSES" TO prompt
DO A:dtverify
STORE $(viewdate,1,2) TO mmonth
STORE $(viewdate,7,2) TO myear
STORE 'T' TO menu
STORE ' ' TO prompt


* Section II- Operator Prompting
DO WHILE menu < > 'F'
   STORE ' ' TO choice
   SET colon OFF
   ERASE

   @ 5, 15 SAY "---------- EXPENSE REPORT MENU ----------"
   @ 7, 18 SAY "CURRENT MONTH + YEAR"
   @ 7, 45 SAY mmonth + '/' + myear
   @ 8, 15 SAY "-------------------------------------------"
   @ 10, 15 SAY " 0 - EXIT TO OPERATING SYSTEM "
   @ 12, 15 SAY " 1 - ADD TO CURRENT MONTH'S EXPENSES "
   @ 13, 15 SAY " 2 - REVIEW/EDIT MONTH'S EXPENSES "
   @ 14, 15 SAY " 3 - PRINT EXPENSE REPORTS "
   @ 15, 15 SAY " 4 - CHANGE CURRENT EXPENSE DATE "
   @ 16, 15 SAY "-------------------------------------------"
   @ 18,20 SAY "SELECT ACTIVITY ===>"
   @ 18,40 GET choice PICTURE '!'
   READ

   SET colon ON

* Section III - Branching and Execution
   DO CASE

      CASE choice = '0'
         STORE 'F' TO menu

      CASE choice = '1'
         DO ADD

      CASE choice = '2'
         DO editscn

      CASE choice = '3'
         DO listout

      CASE choice = '4'
         STORE 'ENTER A REVISED BEGINNING EXPENSE DATE ' TO  prompt
```

```
        DO A:dtverify
        STORE $(viewdate,1,2) TO mmonth
        STORE $(viewdate,7,2) TO myear

      OTHERWISE
        LOOP
    ENDCASE
  ENDDO WHILE menu < > 'F'

    QUIT
```

## ADD.CMD   Routine to Add Expenses to Files

ADD, as named, allows general data to be added to MAIN and supplemental data to be added to IRSEXPEN if required. The MAIN file is prepared with the APPEND BLANK command and a format file, ENTSCRN, is issued (with the SET FORMAT TO command) to prompt the operator.

The operator must enter a valid day and expense category. A leading zero will be added to single digit days (. . .01. . .05) for consistent aligning and storing in the MAIN file.

The second third of ADD is invoked if the ENT or OTH categories are chosen. The bottom half of the screen is cleared by the use of @ statements with coordinates but no SAY statements. The appropriate entry screen for the ENT or OTH category is displayed.

━━━━━━━━━━━━━━━━━ TECH TIP ━━━━━━━━━━━━━━━━━

### Clearing of Selected Screen Portions

*Selection portions of a screen can be erased without the global use of the ERASE command.*

*All characters on or to the right of Y on line X can be erased by using the command:*

$$@ \ X,Y$$

*@ 22,0 will erase line 22*

Files are linked by first SELECTing the secondary file, IRSEXPEN. A record is prepared to hold the data with the APPEND BLANK command. Data will be entered into IRSEXPEN, which supplements the corresponding record in MAIN. The record number of the new record is STOREd to the memory variable link and the contents of link are transferred to the exloc field in MAIN. Every record number in IRSEXPEN has that record number stored in the exloc field in a corresponding record in MAIN (see Figure 15-2).

```
RECORD IN MAIN FILE
REC. #
00058    83/07/01  OTH  5.00  ATLANTA           4 <---- +
                                        EXLOC FIELD   :
                                                      :
RECORD IN IRSEXPEN                                    :
REC. #                                  EXLOC FIELD   :
00004    CLERK  POST OFFICE  STAMPS               4 ----> +
```

*Figure 15-2.* The Record Number of IRSEXPEN is Transferred to MAIN

The last third of ADD determines whether the operator wants to add another record. An affirmative answer to the first question (More expenses for same day?) will invoke the dBASE II code:

```
STORE edate TO mdate
STORE elocation TO mlocation
APPEND BLANK
CLEAR GETS
REPLACE edate WITH mdate
REPLACE elocation WITH mlocation
```

The number of the day and location in the previous record are STOREd to memory variables. Another record is prepared with the AP-PEND BLANK command, and the defaults for day and location are transferred to the new record with the REPLACE command. Use of the CLEAR GETS command eliminates problems with cursor placement.

A negative answer to the question prompts the operator to answer a second question (Continue adding expenses?). Entry of a T will display the entry screen without the last entered day and location. Entry of an F returns the operator to the menu.

CODE FOR ADD.CMD

```
* add.cmd
* Program by Michael Clifford
* COMPUTER ESSENTIALS
* Called from EXPENSE
* Module Purpose: Add to both Files

SET colon OFF

APPEND BLANK
STORE 'F' TO done
STORE '  ' TO day

DO WHILE done < > 'T'

   STORE ' ' TO more, more2
   ERASE
```

```
    SET FORMAT TO entscrn
    READ
    SET FORMAT TO screen
```

* verification of entry
* day and category checked

```
  IF day= ' '
    @ 7,22 GET day PICTURE '# #'
    READ
  ENDIF day= ' '
```

* verify that only the valid categories are entered

```
  DO WHILE ecategory=' ' .or. ;
  @(ecategory,"GAS PRK AIR CAB INN ENT TEL BRK LUN DIN OTH") =0
  CLEAR GETS
  @ 22,0
  @ 22,10 SAY "NOT A VALID EXPENSE CATEGORY. PLEASE  ENTER AGAIN."
  @ 9,23 SAY CHR(7) + "     "
  @ 9,23 GET ECATEGORY PICT '!!!'
  READ
  @ 22,0
ENDDO
```

3 spaces

* put leading zero in for days less than 10

```
  IF ' ' $(day)
    STORE '0' + STR(VAL(day),1) TO day
    @ 7,22 SAY day
  ENDIF ' ' $(day)
  REPLACE edate WITH myear + '/' + mmonth + '/' + day
```

* clear bottom half of screen for tax entries
* prepare to enter further detail into irsexpense

```
  IF ecategory = 'ENT' ;
    .OR. ecategory= 'OTH'

    @ 9,5
    @ 10,0
    @ 11,0
    @ 12,0
    @ 13,0
    @ 14,0
    @ 15,0
    @ 16,0
    @ 17,0
    @ 18,0
```

* prepare secondary file
* link the secondary file to primary
* by enclosing the record number of irsexpen
* in the exloc field of main.dbf

```
    SELECT secondary
    APPEND BLANK
    STORE # TO link
    REPLACE s. exloc WITH link
```

```
            Select Primary
            REPLACE p. exloc WITH link
            Select Secondary
            RELEASE LINK
         ENDIF ecategory

   * screen for entertainment detail
      IF ecategory= 'ENT'
         SET colon ON
         @ 9,15 SAY ">>>>>>>>"
         @ 9,25 SAY "ENTERTAINMENT EXPENSE <<<<<<<<<<"
         @ 11,20 SAY "NAME"
         @ 11,43 SAY "COMPANY AFFILIATION"
         @ 13, 5 SAY "Person "
         @ 13,15 GET eperson1
         @ 13,43 GET ecompany1
         @ 17, 5 SAY "Reason for Expense"
         @ 17,25 GET ereason
         @ 19, 5 SAY "Name of Restaurant"
         @ 19,25 GET erest
         @ 21, 5 SAY "Other Information"
         @ 21,24 GET eother
         READ
         SET colon OFF

      ENDIF ecategory= 'ENT'

      * screen for other detail
      IF ecategory = 'OTH'
         SET colon ON
         @ 9,15 SAY ">>>>>>OTHER EXPENSE"
         @ 9,35 SAY " <<<<<<<<<<<<<<<"
         @ 11, 5 SAY "Paid to"
         @ 11,13 GET ecompany1
         @ 13, 9 SAY "For"
         @ 13,13 GET ereason
         @ 15, 7 SAY "Other"
         @ 15,13 GET eother
         READ
         SET colon OFF
      ENDIF ecategory = 'OTH'

      @ 22, 0
      @ 22,10 SAY 'More expenses for same day? (T/F)' ;
      GET more PICTURE "!"
      READ
      SELECT PRIMARY

      IF more = 'T'
         STORE edate TO mdate
         STORE elocation TO mlocation
         APPEND BLANK
         CLEAR GETS
         REPLACE edate WITH mdate
```

```
        REPLACE elocation WITH mlocation

    ENDIF more = 'T'
  IF more < > 'T'
    @ 22, 0
    @ 22,10 SAY 'Continue adding expenses? (T/F)' ;
    GET more2 PICTURE "!"
    READ

    IF more2 = 'T'
      STORE '    ' TO day
      APPEND BLANK
      CLEAR GETS
    ELSE
      STORE 'T' TO done
      IF eamount = 0
        DELETE
      ENDIF eamount = 0
    ENDIF more2 = 'T'
  ENDIF more < > 'T'
ENDDO
RELEASE mdate, mlocation, more, more2,done,day

RETURN
```

Note near `STORE '    ' TO day`: **2 spaces**

## ENTSCRN.FMT  Entry Screen for Adding Expenses

ENTSCRN displays on the screen the format for the operator to enter expense data. The currently logged month and year are visible at the top of the screen. Valid expense categories are shown at the bottom. PICTURE statements further validate and format the data as it is entered.

**CODE FOR ENTSCRN.FMT**

```
* ENTSCRN.FMT
@  3, 5 SAY " MONTH AND YEAR:"
@  3,30 SAY mmonth + ' / ' + myear
@  3,50 SAY "  EXPENSES     "
@  7, 5 SAY "Day of expense:"
@  7,22 GET DAY PICTURE '99'
@  7,43 SAY "Amount of expense:"
@  9, 5 SAY "Expense category:"
@  9,23 GET ECATEGORY PICTURE '! ! !'
@  7,62 GET EAMOUNT
@  9,43 SAY "Location:"
@  9,53 GET ELOCATION
@ 10,23 SAY "\_/"
@ 11, 9 SAY " ┌───────────────────────────────────────────┐ "
@ 12, 9 SAY " │ GAS > GASOLINE & OIL        TEL > TELEPHONE │ "
@ 13, 9 SAY " │ PRK > PARKING & TOLLS       BRK > BREAKFAST │ "
@ 14, 9 SAY " │ AIR > AIR FARE              LUN > LUNCH      │ "
```

```
@ 15, 9 SAY "|CAB > CAB & OTHER TRANS.       DIN > DINNER      |"
@ 16, 9 SAY "|                               INN > HOTEL       |"
@ 17, 9 SAY "|ENT > ENTERTAINMENT <--->      OTH > OTHER       |"
@ 18, 9 SAY "|_____|"
* END OF ENTSCRN.FMT
```

## EDITSCN.CMD   Edits and Reviews Both Files

Reviewing and editing are both performed by EDITSCN. Changes can be made for all expenditures in MAIN. Supplemental data from IRSEXPEN is displayed and edited on the same screen.

The first record for the logged month in MAIN is searched with the LOCATE command. The review and edit screen allows expense data in the top half of the screen and supplemental data in the bottom of the screen to be edited.

As with the ADD routine, EDITSCN uses the record number in the exloc field in MAIN to determine where the IRS information is to be found in IRSEXPEN. A GOTO statement in IRSEXPEN allows the data to be accessed and edited. A loop and the CONTINUE command will allow editing of all expenses until the end of the month is found, the end of the file is reached, or the operator decides that no more editing is to be done.

### CODE FOR EDITSCN.CMD

```
* editscn.cmd
* Called from EXPENSE
* Module Purpose:
* Allows Edit and Review From Both Files
STORE 'T' TO repeat

* find the record for the correct date
* for undeleted record
LOCATE ALL FOR $(edate,1,5)= myear + '/' + mmonth;
 .AND. .not. * .AND. .not. EOF

ERASE

DO WHILE repeat = 'T' .AND. .not. EOF

    @ 2,15 SAY "REVIEW & EDIT"
    @ 2,45 SAY mmonth + '/' + myear
    @ 3,15 SAY "+--------------------"
    @ 3,36 SAY "-----------------------------+"
    @ 5,15 SAY "DAY OF MONTH      :"
    @ 5,30 SAY $(edate,7,2)
    @ 5,45 SAY "CATEGORY :"
    @ 5,56 GET ecategory PICTURE '!!!'
    @ 7,15 SAY "EXPENSE AMOUNT :"
    @ 7,31 GET eamount
```

```
@ 7,45 SAY "LOCATION :"
@ 7,56 GET elocation
@ 9,15 SAY "+---------------------"
@ 9,36 SAY "---------------------------+"
READ
CLEAR GETS

* verify that only the valid categories are entered
DO WHILE @(ecategory,"GAS PRK AIR CAB INN ENT TEL BRK LUN DIN OTH")=0

    CLEAR GETS
    @ 5,56 SAY CHR(7) + "   "
    @ 5,56 GET ecategory PICT '!!!'
    READ
    CLEAR GETS
ENDDO


IF ecategory= 'ENT' .OR. ecategory= 'OTH'
    * find proper record in irsexpense
    * files are linked by the value of exloc
    STORE exloc TO finder
    SELECT secondary
    GOTO finder

    * the edit portion for the other file
    @ 11,29 SAY "If ENT or OTH Category:"
    @ 13,15 SAY "Person :"
    @ 13,25 GET eperson1
    @ 13,45 SAY "Company :"
    @ 13,55 GET ecompany1
    @ 16,15 SAY "Reason for expense:"
    @ 16,35 GET ereason
    @ 17,15 SAY "Name of Restaurant:"
    @ 17,35 GET erest
    @ 18,15 SAY "Other Information :"
    @ 18,35 GET eother
    @ 19,15 SAY "+-------------------------"
    @ 19,39 SAY "------------------------+"
    READ
    SELECT PRIMARY

ENDIF ecategory= 'ENT' .OR. ecategory= 'OTH'

@ 22,15
@ 22,15 SAY "CONTINUE THE REVIEW? (T/F)? "
@ 22,45 GET repeat PICTURE '!'
READ
ERASE
CONTINUE

ENDDO repeat = 'T'

RELEASE repeat,finder

RETURN
```

The arrow points to the 3 spaces in `@ 5,56 SAY CHR(7) + "   "` with a label reading "3 spaces".

## PRINTING ROUTINES

Three files are used to generate the two reports. The LISTOUT command file produces two data files with new structures. REPORT1.FRM configures the general report, and REPORT2.FRM configures the IRS supplemental report.

The dBASE II records in MAIN must be converted into ledger format to produce the general report. The types of expenditures (GAS, OTH, BRK) must be expanded in detail for later reporting as columns across the page. Records of expenditures for the same category on the same day ( $10 for GAS in the morning, then a $15 fill-up in the evening) must be summarized ($25 for GAS on DAY 1, see Figure 15-1).

The contents of MAIN for the reported period are transferred to a temporary database structure, named EXPANDED, which has the further detail of eleven expense categories as fields. The contents of the EAMOUNT field in MAIN is transferred to one of the new eleven fields in EXPANDED that correspond to the type of expenditure listed in the ECATEGORY field in MAIN. An expenditure of $15.00 for gasoline is recorded as the phrase 'GAS' in the ECATEGORY field in MAIN. The $15.00 expense is transferred to the field GAS in EXPANDED (see Figure 15-3).

Once all the records are expanded to the new file's structure, the records need to be first subtotalled by category for each day, then totalled for all days and expense categories for the given duration. If a file is

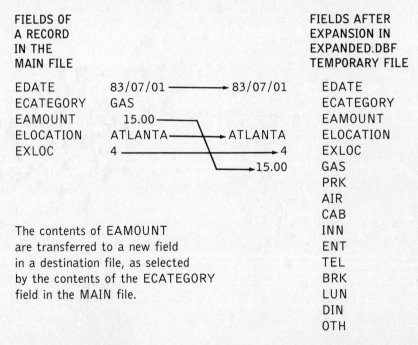

Figure 15-3 Principle of Tranfer of Contents of a Record in One Data base to Expand Fields of Another Database

indexed on the proper key, the TOTAL command performs the tabulation and stores the results in a temporary file, which can be printed with the REPORT command.

The supplemental report is easier to produce. The JOIN command will generate a temporary third file of a record from MAIN and a record from IRSEXPEN that have the same value in the exloc field. A new file will be created with a structure that combines the fields of the two source files, from which the REPORT2 form file generates the desired report for the IRS.

## LISTOUT.CMD  Generates Files for Reports

LISTOUT first establishes a date that will be printed in the report. The SET DATE TO command places the logged month and year into the reports.

Next is the establishment of the duration of expenses to be reported. The default is the logged month, with the first day of the month STOREd to begin and the last day STOREd to end. You may override this by answering F to the question:

Report ONLY on CURRENT Month? :T:

A new duration can be established by the use of DIVERIFY to enter a new beginning and ending date for records in the file. Once the duration is established, the temporary file EXPANDED is opened and the APPEND command is implemented to bring into the file only the records from MAIN that registered expenses during the duration. A review of the present contents of a record in EXPANDED reveals the contents of each record at this point (see Figure 15-4).

The file is prepared for the JOIN command by indexing on the exloc key. The SELECT secondary command returns the active work area to IRSEXPEN, which is then also indexed on the exloc key.

The JOIN command can be used once both files are indexed on the same key (exloc). The structures (up to 32 fields) are merged, and only a record in MAIN, which has the same exloc value as in IRSEXPEN, will be transferred to the JOINed temporary file, IRSRPT, the IRS RePorT file (see Figure 15-5).

The JOINED file appears with duplicate fields at the top and the bottom. dBASE II has a bug that will print a field twice if the simple version of the JOIN command is used. The word FIELDS is used in the JOIN command, followed by the list of only the fields needed, to restrict the generation to only the fields we wish to later use with the REPORT2 FORM file. The temporary file for the second report is now prepared.

Work progresses on the files for the first general report. EXPANDED is USEd, and the structure is copied to another temporary file, TOTL-

```
83/07/01      EDATE
GAS           ECATEGORY
15.00         EAMOUNT
ATLANTA       ELOCATION
      4       EXLOC
              GAS
              PRK
              AIR
              CAB
              INN
              ENT
              TEL
              BRK
              LUN
              DIN
              OTH
```

*Figure 15-4*   Sample Record in EXPANDED.DBF After Appending from Main File

| FLD | NAME | FLD | NAME | FLD | NAME |
|-----|------|-----|------|-----|------|
| 001 | EPERSON1 | 001 | EDATE | 001 | EDATE |
| 002 | ECOMPANY1 | 002 | ECATEGORY | 002 | ECATEGORY |
| 003 | EREASON | 003 | EAMOUNT | 003 | EAMOUNT |
| 004 | EREST | 004 | ELOCATION | 004 | ELOCATION |
| 005 | EOTHER | 005 | EXLOC | 005 | EXLOC |
| 006 | EXLOC | 006 | GAS | 006 | GAS |
| 006 | | 007 | PRK | 007 | PRK |
| 007 | | 008 | AIR | 008 | AIR |
| 008 | | 009 | CAB | 009 | CAB |
| 009 | | 010 | INN | 010 | INN |
| 010 | | 011 | ENT | 011 | EMT |
| 011 | | 012 | TEL | 012 | TEL |
| 012 | | 013 | BRK | 013 | BRK |
| 013 | | 014 | LUN | 014 | LUN |
| 014 | | 015 | DIN | 015 | DIN |
| 015 | | 016 | OTH | 016 | OTH |
| 016 | | 016 | | 017 | EPERSON1 |
| 017 | | 017 | | 018 | ECOMPANY1 |
| 018 | | 018 | | 019 | EREASON |
| 019 | | 019 | | 020 | EREST |
| 020 | | 020 | | 021 | EOTHER |
| 021 | | 021 | | 022 | EXLOC |

*Figure 15-5.*   The first File Joined to the Second File Yields a New File

CORE, which will be used later. Once done, the amount of each purchase in the original file is tucked into the proper field (GAS, ENT, OTH) in EXPANDED for use by the REPORT FORM with the code:

```
DO WHILE .not. EOF
   STORE ecategory to trans
   REPLACE &trans WITH eamount
   SKIP
ENDDO
```

In the example in Figure 15-3, the EAMOUNT contains the value of $15.00. GAS would be STOREd to the memory variable trans in the second line of code. With a macro symbol preceding trans, dBASE would consider the word GAS not simply contents of a field, but as a *field* named GAS. The third line of code would alter the contents of this GAS field, with the command:

```
REPLACE &trans WITH eamount
```

dBASE would process the macro as:

```
REPLACE GAS WITH eamount
```

The EAMOUNT value would be duplicated into the proper field. Once done, the record in EXPANDED is truly expanded according to the contents of one field in MAIN. All the other records in the temporary file EXPANDED are processed in the same manner (see Figure 15-6).

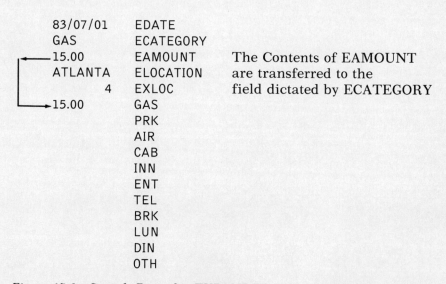

*Figure 15-6.* Sample Record in EXPANDED.DBF After Final Expansion

The next three lines of code prepare for the TOTAL command. The TOTAL command operates like the REPORT command, except that the results are placed into another database instead of printed. To subtotal properly, the source database must be indexed on the major category (date). The destination database, if not designated, will store only numeric fields; all other detail (character and logical fields) will be stripped and not carried over into the destination database. However, dBASE II will allow these to be carried if the structure of the destination database contains these fields. The structure of TOTLCORE is identical to EXPANDED and was generated by the COPY STRUCTURE TO command a few lines previously. The summary database for the general report can now be generated from the processed EXPANDED file by the code:

```
INDEX ON edate TO DATE1
TOTAL ON edate TO totlcore
```

A listing would reveal the three files and their 34 sample records that have been processed to produce the general report (see Figure 15-7).

Figure 15-8 shows the sample contents of TOTLCORE after the TOTAL command has been used. Notice that the APPEND command transferred only the records that had expenditures during the given duration. All of the records, in this case, were for the logged month. Eleven fields of detail (the expense categories) were added to EXPANDED.

Once expanded, the TOTAL command collapsed the number of records, from 34 to 8 by providing summaries of type of expenses on each day. All GAS payment records were TOTALed for each day and extraneous details were discarded. The final result was the subtotalled expenses by category for each day of the duration, with the number of records in TOTLCORE exactly equal to the number of days that expenses were incurred—eight.

The expense report can then be printed by the USE of TOTLCORE, establishing the compressed print pitch and using the REPORT1 FORM file. The FORM file provides the total expenses for each day and the totals for all expenses for the duration. Once done, the printer will stop on the last line of the report.

IRSRPT, the JOINed file necessary for the second report is then opened (see Figure 15-9). The GO BOTTOM command is used to find the last record number. If it is 0, that is, no records are in the supplemental database, a message will be printed on the bottom page of the first report.

| DATABASE FILES | # RCDS | LAST UPDATE |
|---|---|---|
| MAIN | 00034 | 07/01/83 |
| EXPANDED | 00034 | 07/01/83 |
| TOTLCORE | 00008 | 07/01/83 |

*Figure 15-7.* Files Used to Generate the General Report

244

## Figure 15-8

| 83/07/01 | GAS | 107.90 | ATLANTA | 4 | 36.33 | 2.00 | 0.00 | 0.00 | 42.00 | 0.00 | 0.00 | 0.00 | 5.34 | 18.23 | 4.00 |
|---|---|---|---|---|---|---|---|---|---|---|---|---|---|---|---|
| 83/07/02 | BRK | 119.63 | MONTGOMERY | 1 | 0.00 | 0.00 | 0.00 | 3.00 | 46.18 | 37.40 | 0.00 | 5.55 | 5.50 | 22.00 | 0.00 |
| 83/07/03 | BRK | 46.44 | HUNTSVILLE | 0 | 19.32 | 0.00 | 0.00 | 0.00 | 0.00 | 0.00 | 2.70 | 6.60 | 17.82 | 0.00 |
| 83/07/09 | AIR | 467.87 | NEW ORLEANS | 2 | 0.00 | 0.00 | 0.00 | 0.00 | 92.00 | 163.00 | 212.87 | 0.00 | 0.00 | 0.00 | 0.00 |
| 83/07/10 | BRK | 271.13 | NEW ORLEANS | 0 | 0.00 | 0.00 | 12.00 | 18.00 | 0.00 | 0.00 | 233.23 | 7.90 | 0.00 | 0.00 | 0.00 |
| 83/07/16 | PRK | 53.37 | ATLANTA | 5 | 0.00 | 3.25 | 0.00 | 0.00 | 0.00 | 0.00 | 0.00 | 0.00 | 0.00 | 0.00 | 50.12 |
| 83/07/28 | DIN | 48.00 | DECATUR, GA | 3 | 0.00 | 0.00 | 0.00 | 0.00 | 0.00 | 0.00 | 0.00 | 0.00 | 16.00 | 32.00 |
| 83/07/29 | PRK | 2.00 | ATLANTA | 0 | 0.00 | 2.00 | 0.00 | 0.00 | 0.00 | 0.00 | 0.00 | 0.00 | 0.00 | 0.00 |

*Figure 15-8* Contents of TOTLCORE Before Deletion After 34 Records in EXPANDED Are Summerized with dBASE TOTAL Command

## Figure 15-9

| 00004 | 83/07/01 | 4.00 | CLERK | POST OFFICE | STAMPS | SENT AJAX TRAIN. |
|---|---|---|---|---|---|---|
| 00001 | 83/07/02 | 37.40 | BILL PARKS | COMPUTER DELIGHTS | DISCUSS TRAINING | DBASE ORIENTED |
| 00002 | 83/07/09 | 163.00 | BOARD MEM | TRAINING ASSOC | BOARD MEETING | 8 PEOPLE PRESENT |
| 00005 | 83/07/16 | 50.12 | WINESTOCK'S | FLOWERS | | BOSS'S WIFE DIED |
| 00003 | 83/07/28 | 32.00 | MINI SUPPLIERS | BOX OF DISKETTES | | NEEDED FOR EXPENSE PROG |

*Figure 15-9.* Contents of the Temporary Data File IRSRPT Before Reporting

```
DATABASE FILES     # RCDS      LAST UPDATE

EXPANDED           00034       07/01/83
IRSEXPEN           00005       07/01/83
IRSRPT             00005       07/01/83
```

*Figure 15-10.* Files Used to Generate the Supplemental Report

```
STRUCTURE FOR FILE: B:IRSRPT .DBF
NUMBER OF RECORDS: 00005
DATE OF LAST UPDATE: 07/83/00
PRIMARY USE DATABASE
FLD              NAME       TYPE    WIDTH    DEC
001              EDATE       C       008
002              EAMOUNT     N       008     002
003              EPERSON1    C       015
004              ECOMPANY1   C       020
005              EREASON     C       020
006              EREST       C       015
007              EOTHER      C       025
** TOTAL **                          00112
```

*Figure 15-11.* The Final Structure

The supplemental report will be printed if records exist to warrant the printing. IRSRPT must now be indexed by date of expense to match the chronological order of expenses in the general report. The files that contributed towards the generation of the supplemental report are listed in Figure 15-10.

As with the general report, the JOIN command collapsed the number of records by providing summary detail. IRSRPT contains only records that had matching exloc values in each file. The FIELDS portion of the JOIN command restricted the merger to precisely the fields that are needed for the REPORT2 FORM file. The final structure (illustrated in Figure 15-11) is now ready to be printed by using the REPORT command.

After printing, housekeeping commands delete all temporary indexes and data files. All the records in EXPANDED are also deleted, retaining only the structure. Control is returned to the main menu.

CODE FOR LISTOUT.CMD

```
* listout.cmd
* Called from EXPENSE
* Module Purpose:
* prints out reports in spreadsheet form
* uses subtotal features in dbase report generator
STORE mmonth + '/' + myear TO mmyy
SET DATE TO &mmyy
RELEASE mmyy
STORE 'T' TO current
```

```
ERASE
@ 10,05 SAY "Report ONLY on CURRENT Month? (T/F)"
@ 10,40 GET current PICTURE '!'
READ

* Get range of expenditures dates to generate report
IF current < > 'T'

   STORE "BEGINNING DATE" TO prompt
   DO A:dtverify
   STORE "ENDING DATE" TO prompt
   DO A:dtverify
   STORE filedate TO end
   STORE ' ' TO prompt

ENDIF current < > 'T'

* place in default first and last day
* of logged month
IF current = 'T'
   STORE myear + '/' + mmonth + '/01' to begin
   STORE myear + '/' + mmonth + '/31' to end
ENDIF current = 'T'

* Establish temporary data base
SET DEFAULT TO &dfdefault
USE expanded
APPEND FROM main FOR edate > = '&BEGIN' ;
   .AND. edate < = '&END'
INDEX ON STR(exloc,5) TO exndx

* Prepare to JOIN second database
SELECT secondary
INDEX ON STR(exloc,5) TO exloc
JOIN TO irsrpt FOR p.exloc = s.exloc;
   FIELDS edate,eamount,eperson1,ecompany1,ereason,erest,eother

* create destination database for TOTAL
SELECT primary
USE expanded
COPY STRUCTURE TO totlcore

* Transfer eamount to proper category
* i.e., place 15.00 in GAS field
DO WHILE .not. EOF
   STORE ecategory TO trans
   REPLACE &trans WITH eamount
   SKIP
ENDDO WHILE .not. EOF

* Use TOTAL command for database
* which contains all subtotals
```

```
INDEX ON edate TO DATE1
TOTAL ON edate TO totlcore
USE totlcore
ERASE

SET DEFAULT TO &pfdefault

SET PRINT ON
? &COMPRINT
SET EJECT OFF

REPORT FORM REPORT1 TO PRINT

* Open the JOINED database
SELECT secondary
SET DEFAULT TO &dfdefault
USE irsrpt

GO BOTTOM

IF # = 0
   ?
   ?
   ? '**** NO IRS DETAILS ENTERED FOR SELECTED PERIOD. '
   ?? 'A SUPPLEMENTAL REPORT WILL NOT BE PRINTED ****'
ELSE
   * generate the supplemental report
   INDEX on edate to rpt2ndx
   EJECT
   SET DEFAULT to &pfdefault
   REPORT FORM REPORT2 TO PRINT
   SET DEFAULT to &dfdefault
   SET INDEX TO
   DELETE FILE rpt2ndx.ndx
ENDIF

* Housekeeping before exiting
? &NORMPRINT
SET EJECT ON
SET PRINT OFF

SET DEFAULT TO &dfdefault

USE irsexpense

SELECT PRIMARY
USE expanded
DELETE ALL
PACK
USE main
DELETE FILE exndx.ndx
DELETE FILE exloc.ndx
DELETE FILE date1.ndx
DELETE FILE totlcore
DELETE FILE irsrpt
```

```
SET DEFAULT TO &pfdefault

RELEASE current,begin,end,trans
RETURN
```

# THE REPORT FORM FILES

The files are now prepared for the REPORT FORMS. Totals down the page will be generated by use of answering Y to the question in the standard REPORT dialog (ARE TOTALS REQUIRED?). Daily totals of the expense categories across the page in the general report are generated by the FORM code:

```
8,GAS+PRK+AIR+CAB+INN+ENT+TEL+BRK+LUN+DIN+OTH
```

Enter REPORT1 and REPORT2 exactly in the manner that all of the FORM files have been entered in the previous applications. Note that 132 columns are needed for REPORT1.

| DIALOG FOR REPORT1.FRM | DIALOG FOR REPORT2.FRM |
|---|---|
| M=1,W=132 | W=132,M=1 |
| Y | Y |
| EXPENSE REPORT | EXPENSE REPORT EXPLANATION |
| N | N |
| Y | Y |
| N | N |
| 5,$(EDATE,4,5) | 5,$(EDATE,4,5) |
| MO/DY | MO/DY |
| 15,ELOCATION | 15,EAMOUNT |
| <LOCATION | >AMOUNT |
| B,GAS | Y |
| >GAS;OIL | 17,EPERSON1 |
| Y | <NAME OF PERSON |
| 8,PRK | 22,ECOMPANY1 |
| PARKING;TOLLS | <COMPANY |
| Y | 22,EREASON |
| 8,AIR | <BUSINESS PURPOSE |
| AIRFARE | 15,EREST |
| Y | <NAME OF REST. |
| 8,CAB | 25,EOTHER |
| >TAXI;TIPS | < OTHER INFO |
| Y | |
| 8,INN | |
| HOTEL | |
| Y | |
| 8,BRK | |

```
>MEAL;BREAKFST
Y
B,LUN
>MEAL;LUNCH
Y
8,DIN
>MEAL;DINNER
Y
8,TEL
>PHONE
Y
8,ENT
>ENTER-;TAINMENT
Y
8,OTH
>OTHER
Y
8,GAS+PRK+AIR+CAB+INN+E- NT+TEL+BRK+LUN+DIN+OTH
DAILY;TOTAL
Y
```

# EMBELLISHMENTS AND MODIFICATIONS

You may note that the fields in IRSEXPEN are named EPERSON1 and ECOMPANY1. Earlier versions of the EXPENSE system allowed for entry of a second person and company in the supplemental database. Add the two fields to the STRUCTURE of IRSEXPEN. Change the entry screen, ENTSCRN, to allow for display of the new fields. Add new code in ADD and EDITSCN to store or edit the new fields, which can be named EPERSON2 and ECOMPANY2. Use the original code for EPERSON1 and ECOMPANY1 as a guide.

# SUMMARY

The installation of the EXPENSE system is now complete. EXPENSE is another application of dBASE II to the solution of financial problems. The familiar technique of linked files and the INDEX and REPORT commands are used. The macro (&) is used once again as a powerful aid to transform data into commands.

dBASE and other database managers store data in a fashion best visualized as columns. Totals can be expressed at the bottom of the columns of data, but totals across the page are difficult to express.

A new and involved technique is the manipulation of dBASE data to emulate a ledger or spreadsheet's totals both across and down a printed page (footings and cross footings). Data is transferred from one file to another with an expanded structure. The JOIN command is used to report data resident in two files by creating a third, which is a merger of the two. TOTAL is used to sum data from one file and transfer the results to a new file.

The EXPENSE system completes the major applications in this book. Section Five will introduce utilities—command files that perform such general but useful tasks as initializing programs and managing dates.

Programs such as MAILFORM detailed the technique of using dBASE to process words. The EXPENSE and INVOICE applications processed numbers. One of the utilities in Section Five, dPLOT, will illustrate the principles of graphing results, again by utilizing the flexibility of dBASE.

# SECTION FIVE

## Useful dBase II Utilities

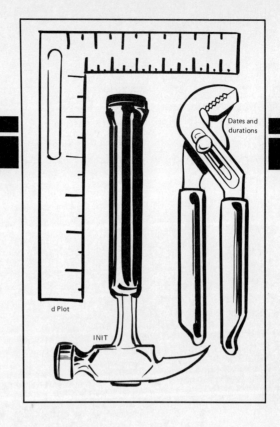

d Plot

INIT

Dates and durations

Electric, water, and gas companies provide essential services to residents. The type of service is basic and varies only by the amount delivered to every house on the block.

A subordinate computer program that provides a comparable service to larger programs is also known as a utility. Utilities are general purpose routines and can be used by a variety of other files and application programs. Many utility programs have been developed for CP/M and MS-DOS, which perform such tasks as cataloging the programs on all diskettes into a program library, rapid viewing of text files without using a word processor, and sorting large numbers of records at unsurpassed speed.

A dBASE II utility can be used with little or no modification in any other program to provide such essential services as:

- Initializing programs
- Entry and calculation of dates and durations
- Graphing summed fields in a data file

Utilities outlined in Section Five assist the operator with critical and often used operations. Each utility stands alone and can be called either from the keyboard by typing DO utilityname, or from other command files.

Each utility is very short so the operation and the installation instructions are merged into the same chapter. Utilities accomplish a basic purpose, but the techniques to do so are not necessarily simple. The TECH TIPS in the Section detail approaches and code that you can use in many of your other dBASE programs.

# 16

# INITIALIZING PROGRAMS
# WITH INIT

Software must be configured properly if a program is to operate without difficulty. The current state of both the hardware and software of your system may affect the operation of the dBASE program that is about to operate.

## THE INIT UTILITY

INIT tailors a dBASE program to a hardware configuration that you have established. Once done, the configuration of placement of programs on disk drives and printer codes are saved to a file and used when needed. You do not need to enter the codes again unless changes are made in the hardware.

INIT also ensures that the software environment is properly established. Unwanted interactions from previous programs are eliminated by the closing of previous files, the clearing of unnecessary memory variables, and the tailoring of the SET commands to ensure that your dBASE program will run without error.

Without a utility such as INIT, there are many opportunities for Murphy's Law (if anything can go wrong, it will) to avert the successful operation of a dBASE program. Some common problems include:

- *Incomplete housekeeping of files in a previous program.* Sometimes new data files cannot be opened because old data files were not closed properly.

- *Undesirable use of SETS from the previous program.* The previous program may have finished printing with the SET FORMAT TO PRINT. In addition, clutter on the screen may have been terminated with the SET CONSOLE OFF command. If not changed (SET FORMAT TO SCREEN, SET CONSOLE ON), a blank screen and frozen keyboard would greet the operator of the new program.

- *Changes of disk configuration.* You may wish to install the same command files on several machines that require a different configuration of disk drives and placement of dBASE files (one, two, and three drive systems). Yet any application program that features the SET DEFAULT TO command (for example, SET DEFAULT TO B) would need to have every one of the command files inspected by a person knowledgeable with the operation of the program. The SET DEFAULT statements may need to be changed in every command file, a tedious and error-prone process. A flexible and consistent method of changing defaults allows the code used in one machine's configuration to be easily changed to run in another.

All these problems can be eliminated if each program is established to a known state from which changes are then made. Assumptions are made that adequate housekeeping has not been accomplished previously: files closed, SETS standardized, and disk drive assumptions established for programs and data files. This process is known as initializing your new program.

INIT.CMD is a command file that initializes programs. Called at the beginning of each main command file of a system, INIT closes all open files and establishes the SET commands. Four printer code sequences are also established for compressed print, normal print, short form feed, and normal form feed. INIT will also prompt the operator for the default drives for program files and the data files. The entire configuration data is permanently saved on the A drive for future use.

## OPERATION OF INIT

The call to INIT, which is placed on drive A, is placed near the top of each main menu program.

```
* BIGPROG.CMD
* EXAMPLE OF MAIN MENU
ERASE
DO A:INIT
```

The processing of BIGPROG will continue without interruption if INIT has been properly used previously to establish configurations. All configuration data is SAVED to CONFIG.MEM, a memory file placed on the A drive. Otherwise, the screen clears and INIT prompts the operator with the screen shown in Figure 16-1.

Warning! First Time Use or CONFIG.MEM file missing.

Please Check for This File on Another Disk.
Continued Operation Will Create New Memory Variables.
Continue Operation (T/F)? :F:

*Figure 16-1.* Warning Message if CONFIG.MEM Not on Drive A

If not on the disk, a new CONFIG file is established. The file may be on another program disk and copying it to the disk currently on drive A saves time. The operator has the opportunity to stop the configuring of a new CONFIG file by answering F to the Continue Operation question.

INIT first requests printer codes. The screen clears, and the operator is prompted for each set of printer codes necessary to change print character size and page length (see Figure 16-2).

PRINTER INSTALLATION MENU

Installs ASCII Control Sequences To Alter Printer Characteristics.
Puts Numbers In CHR Commands, Which Changes Printer To;
  Compressed
Print  Or Alters FORM FEED To Print Checks. Consult Your Printer
Manual For Sequences. ENTER ONE NUMBER TO A LINE. EXAMPLE:
DBASE Needs To Send The Following Control Code Sequence To Change
For a Feed From 66 Lines to 42 Lines On An EPSON MX-80 Printer:

    ? CHR(27) + CHR(67) + CHR(42)

Enter at the 'ALT FORM' prompt the codes on each line:

              :27 :
              :67 :
              :42 :
              :   :      [RETURN] to EXIT

INIT Will Do The Rest! You Need To Do This Only ONCE!

    PRESS Any Key To Continue.

*Figure 16-2.* Detailed Printer Prompts for INIT

After the operator reads the message and presses any key, the screen displays a request to enter the control codes for restoring normal print pitch. Enter the first code. You will be allowed to enter CHR codes successively below each other until the RETURN key is used without entry of a code. The code illustrated in Figure 16-3, a single CHR sequence of 18, restores an Epson MX-80 to normal print pitch. More codes may be added if required by your printer. INIT builds the control sequence and displays it at the bottom of the screen.

The same entry process repeats for the three other control code sequences. INIT stores the codes to print reports or alternate length forms, like checks.

The default disk drives for program files and data files are established next. The screen clears and the following requests are displayed.

```
What Drive Has the Data?              : B :
What Drive Has the Programs?          : A :
```

You may override the suggested defaults by entering the correct disk drive letter over the one shown. INIT saves the configuration to drive A. Every program in this book operates as configured on the default disk drives. Defaults for your own programs are changed if the directions are followed in the INIT installation instructions (below).

## INNER WORKINGS OF INIT

INIT performs a simple task but uses techniques that the intermediate dBASE programmer will find useful. These include using a pseudo-sub-

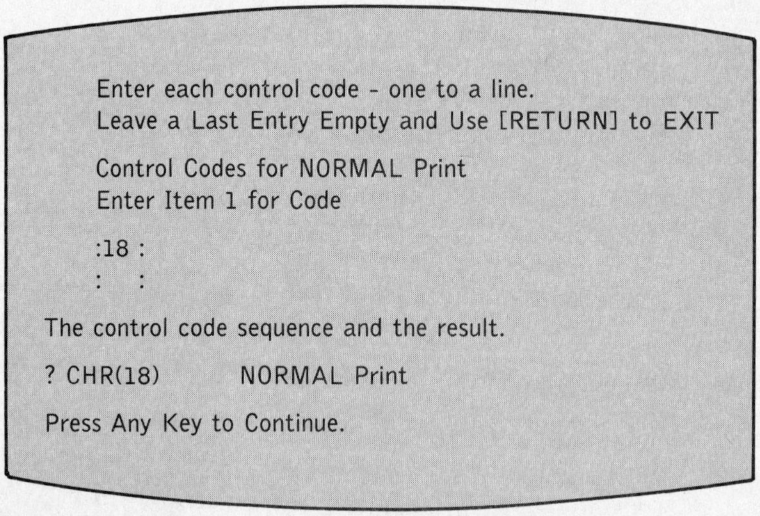

```
Enter each control code - one to a line.
Leave a Last Entry Empty and Use [RETURN] to EXIT

Control Codes for NORMAL Print
Enter Item 1 for Code

:18 :
:    :

The control code sequence and the result.

? CHR(18)        NORMAL Print

Press Any Key to Continue.
```

*Figure 16-3.*  Entry Screen for Normal Print

routine, using the FILE and TEST commands, and combining the sub-string function ($) with the substring search function (@) to remove a substring of unknown length from a larger string.

The first lines of INIT close any outstanding files. The most critical of the SET commands are established to a known state to allow operation of the console, rather than the printer, without the excess clutter of the TALK and ECHO options. INIT attempts to bring into memory the variable that affects printer operation. First, the memory file is checked on the directory for drive A with the code:

```
IF FILE("a:config.mem")
   RESTORE FROM a:config
ENDIF
```

Memory variables required for configuration are restored if config-.mem exists on drive A. If not, the IF .NOT. FILE operation is executed and the INIT error message sequence (Warning! First Time Use . . .) notifies the operator that the file is missing and allows continuation or termination of the INIT process.

Once the memory file RESTOREs the memory variables to memory, the TEST command determines if the memory file has RESTORED the necessary memory variables. The memory variable to switch to com-pressed print, comprint, is checked with the TEST command [IF 0= TEST(comprint)] to verify that comprint is in memory. No printer code initializing is done if comprint, and presumably, other printer codes are in memory.

The dBASE CHR function issues codes originally entered by the oper-ator to devices such as the screen, the bell, and notably the printer. First used in the MAILFORM application (see Chapter 5), CHR codes are used to activate four printer functions: 1) compressed print, 2) normal print, 3) alternate paper length, and 4) standard paper length. The CHR se-quences are assembled on the screen by entering individual CHR state-ments, which appear in a column down the screen, until an entire CHR sequence is built that changes printer operation. The sequence to change one of the printer functions is any number of CHR statements connected by plus signs. The process is illustrated in Figure 16-4.

The code below is the inner loop of INIT. Each repetition allows the operator to enter CHR codes and to build one CHR sequence, which is STORED to the working variable entry.

```
DO WHILE repeat
   STORE ' ' TO mentry
   @ 8,15 SAY "Control Codes for " + prompt1
   @ 9+x,15 SAY " Enter Item " + STR(x,1) + " for Code " ;
   GET mentry PICTURE '# # #'
   READ
```

```
    IF mentry < > ' '
       STORE entry + ' + CHR(' + TRIM(mentry) + ')' TO entry
       STORE x + 1 TO x
    ELSE
       STORE f TO repeat
    ENDIF mentry < > ' '

    CLEAR GETS
ENDDO WHILE repeat
```

Each repetition will increment x by one, and the resulting number determines the row to display entries successively beneath each other. The prompts are positioned down the page in the same manner as the LINE technique used in INVOICE (Chapter 10).

INIT obtains each individual CHR code entered by the operator and STOREs it to the current entry, mentry. Mentry is in turn STORED to entry. The number 27, for example, if entered and STORED to mentry, would first be fashioned into the string CHR(27). This and others would in turn be stored to entry, to build up a sequence of multiple CHR statements [CHR(27) + CHR(67) + CHR(42)].

The loop continues until the operator omits an entry, whereupon the variable mentry has a null string STORED to it. The variable repeat becomes FALSE, and the inner loop is terminated. One CHR sequence is complete.

INIT needs to initialize three other variables. The standard practice would be to place the code outlined above in another command file named, for example, CHRGET. This subordinate file could be called four times, each time returning the processed string, as in below:

```
DO CHRGET                      [CHRGET obtains CHR sequence]
STORE entry TO normprint       [Result passed to normprint]
DO CHRGET
STORE entry TO comprint        [New result passed to comprint]
DO CHRGET
STORE entry 10 stdform         [New result passed to stdform]
DO CHRGET
STORE entry TO altform         [New result passed to altform]
```

```
        Operator's View and Entry        Builds a Control Sequence

      : 27 :    — code fragment 1 —>        CHR(27) +
      : 67 :    — code fragment 2 —>        CHR(67) +
      : 42 :    — code fragment 3 —>        CHR(42)
      :    :    ----------
      Final Control Sequence = altform = "CHR(27) +
          CHR(67) + CHR(42)"
```

*Figure 16-4.*  Assembly of CHR Codes into a Control Sequence

dBASE will activate your disk drive each time CHRGET is called for a total of four times resulting in considerable delay to operate a few lines of code. A quicker method is the use of the pseudo-subroutine, which allows the same processing to be accomplished from within one command file.

The pseudo-subroutine technique processes an inner series of code for more than one repetition. The results are assigned each time to a different memory variable. Figure 16-5 outlines the pseudo-subroutine technique used in INIT to process four variables, one at a time, by the same lines of code.

Varlist stands for VARiable LIST. The variable list contains the names of variables separated by slashes or commas. The last variable is the word END. All the variable names for the four printer codes are STORED to varlist, and the respective prompts are STORED to promptlist.

The technique for the INIT pseudo-subroutine is basically simple. The outer DO WHILE loop continues until varlist is the equivalent to the word END. The routine selects from varlist the variable in the queue that will be assigned the CHR codes obtained from the operator, using the respective prompt from promptlist to facilitate entry. The subroutine code enables the CHR statements to be built until the complete CHR sequence for each printing function is constructed. A new printer function memory variable is constructed by taking another substring from varlist, fashioning the respective prompt from promptlist, and using the code in the inner loop to again construct the CHR sequence. The process repeats until the END is reached.

The first portion of the INIT code in the main loop establishes the outer loop and selects the working variables from the strings varlist and promptlist, by nesting the substring search function (@) within the substring function($).

```
DO WHILE varlist < > 'END'
   STORE $(promptlist,1,@( '/' ,promptlist)−1)      TO prompt1
   STORE $(varlist,1,@( '/' ,varlist)−1)            TO var
   STORE 1 TO x
```

dBASE processes the inner parts of parentheses first. The expression @( '/' ,varlist) returns the numeric location of the first slash character ('/') in varlist. Varlist is a larger string to which has been STORED all of the variables, separated by the slash. Once found, the value of ten (10) is returned for the slash in the smaller string 'normprint/', because the slash is in the tenth position. Substituted into the longer expression, the substring expression becomes STORE $(varlist,1,10−1) TO var.

The expression STORE $(varlist,1,9) TO var will result in the string 'normprint' being STORED to the temporary working variable var. A new memory variable has been created by selecting it from a longer one, varlist. The working prompt has been fabricated in the same manner

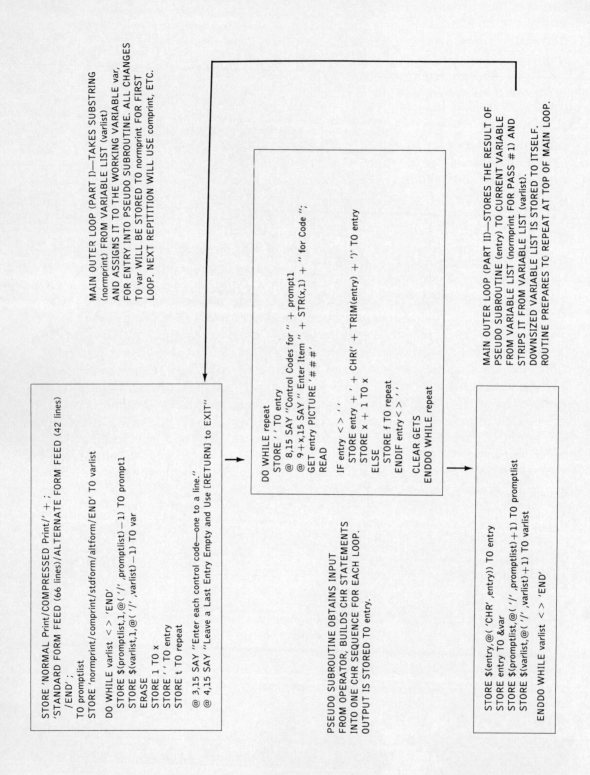

*Figure 16-5.* Diagram of the Pseudo-subroutine Technique Applied to INIT.CMD

═══════════════ TECH TIP ═══════════════

## Separating Variables from a Variable List

*To separate a variable list into variables use both the substring +
substring search functions. Nest the positional function (@) in the
substring function. Use the @ to find the delimiting character. Use
the returned value in the $(VARIABLE,START,LENGTH) sub-
string to excise the proper phrase.*

*STORE 'one/two/three/four' TO varlist*
*. ? $(varlist,1,@( '/',varlist) −1)*
*. one*

---

from promptlist. Once done, the pseudo-subroutine is called and the output, entry, is STORED to the active memory variable, which will be normprint for the first repetition. Processing exits the pseudo-subroutine and passes to part II of the main loop.

The main purpose of the second part of the main loop is to prepare for repetition. Preceding spaces are stripped from the final sequence with the STORE $(entry,@( 'CHR',entry)) TO entry command. All characters in the larger string beginning with the first occurrence of 'CHR' will be STORED back to the entry variable, which is in turn STORED to &var, the current active variable from the promptlist string. Used the first time, &var has the string 'normprint'. Therefore, the memory variable normprint now has a sequence of CHR statements STORED to it.

═══════════════ TECH TIP ═══════════════

## Stripping Used Preceding Variables from Variable List

*To strip unwanted characters or used variables from a
variable list with slash delimiters: nest the substring and
substring search functions. Store the reminder of the variable list to itself.*

*STORE 'one/two/three/four' TO varlist*
*. ? $(varlist,1,@( '/' ,varlist)−1)*
*. one*
*STORE (varlist,1,@( '/' ,varlist) +1) to varlist*
*. ? varlist*
*. two/three/four*

---

Promptlist and varlist must be prepared before the next active varia-bles are selected. The @ command always returns the first occurrence of the slash. Simply repeating the nested substring/substring search in varlist will result in normprint being used again. The characters that were used last to generate the active memory variables and precede others must be stripped from the two source strings (varlist and promptlist). The code below accomplishes the tasks before the outer loop repeats the process.

```
STORE $(promptlist,@( '/' ,promptlist)+1) TO promptlist
STORE $(varlist,@( '/' ,varlist)+1) TO varlist
```

Part II of the main loop has adequately prepared for the next repetition. One entire CHR sequence has been initialized. The pseudo-subroutine technique will continue to repeat, selecting a variable for processing, allowing the operator to assign CHR codes. More printer functions could simply be added by adding other substrings to the variable list, with each separated by slashes.

====================== TECH TIP ======================

## *Approximating a Subroutine*

1. *Store all variables to variable list. Delimit with a slash (/) character.*

2. *Enclose in an outer loop and repeat until end.*

3. *Strip current variable with use of nested substring and substring search functions. Assign to working variable (var).*
   *STORE $(varlist,1,@( '/',varlist)−1) to var*

4. *Process the working variable and store results to current variable from variable list.*

5. *Strip used phrase from varlist. Store remainder to new varlist.*

   . *? varlist*
   . *'two/three/four'*
      *STORE $(varlist,@( '/', varlist)+1) TO varlist*
   . *? varlist*
   . *three/four*

6. *Loop and continue processing until the 'END'.*

The last task that INIT accomplishes is the establishing of default disk drive locations. The variables pfdefault and dfdefault stand for Program File Default and Data File Default. Program files include command files, index files, report form files, and all other non-data files. The operator is allowed to assign the disk drive letters to each.

Command files must employ, at least once, the SET DEFAULT TO assignments, followed by the macroed variables. Every application in this book initiates the opening of files with the code:

```
SET default TO &dfdefault
USE file1
SET default TO &pfdefault
```

Used in this manner, all program files may be placed in one drive location* and all data files may be placed in another. The entire application may be transferred from a two drive system to a one drive system and operate without disturbance by simply entering the following during the last prompt by INIT:

What Drive Has the Data?              : A :
What Drive Has the Programs?          : A :

All configuration information is SAVED to the config memory file on drive A once the file defaults are entered. The dBASE II processing is RETURNED to the main menu of the application.

## CODE FOR INIT.CMD

```
* init
* module purpose: reset to initial settings
* close all files
* initialize printer and disk default drive
* check for config memory file
* config is needed for most programs in
* THE dBASE CASEBOOK OF BUSINESS APPLICATIONS

ERASE
SELECT secondary
USE
SELECT primary
USE
SET talk OFF
SET DEFAULT TO a
SET FORMAT TO SCREEN
SET PRINT OFF
SET echo OFF
SET intensity OFF
SET CONSOLE ON

ERASE
* The file config.mem retains all variables.
* Bring these in if the file is on the A drive.

IF FILE( "a:config.mem" )
    RESTORE FROM a:config
    STORE f TO savemem
```

---

*Remember: INIT and DTVERIFY must always be placed on Drive A.

```
     ELSE
         STORE f TO goahead
         ERASE
         @ 12,05 SAY "Warning! First Time Use or CONFIG.MEM file missing."
         @ 14,05 SAY "Please Check for This File on Another Disk."
         @ 15,05 SAY "Continued Operation Will Create New Memory  Variables. "
         @ 16,05 SAY "Continue Operation (T/F)? " GET goahead
         READ

         IF .NOT. goahead
             CANCEL
         ELSE
             STORE t TO savemem
         ENDIF .NOT. goahead

  RELEASE goahead
  ENDIF FILE("a:config.mem")

  * initialize printer for:
  * 1- standard and alternate pitch
  * 2- standard and alternate page legnth
  * assigns control sequences to key words in
  * programs in the dbase casebook
  * build the control codes for printer if not present
  * assume none are present if the compressed code is not.

  IF 0=TEST(comprint)

      ERASE

      ? " PRINTER INSTALLATION MENU"
      ?
      ? "Installs ASCII Control Sequences To Alter Printer Characteristics."
      ? "Puts Numbers In CHR Commands, Which Changes Printer To Compressed"
      ? "Print Or Alters FORM FEED To Print Checks. Consult Your Printer"
      ? "Manual For Sequences. ENTER ONE NUMBER TO A LINE. EXAMPLE:"
      ? "DBASE Needs To Send The Following Control Code Sequence To Change"
      ? "Form Feed From 66 Lines to 42 Lines On An EPSON MX-80 Printer:"
      ?
      ? " ? CHR(27) + CHR(67) + CHR(42)"
      ?
      ? "Enter at the 'ALT FORM ' prompt the codes on each line:"
      ?
      ? " :27 : "
      ? " :67 :"
      ? " :42 :"
      ? " : : [to EXIT]"
      ?
      ? "INIT Will Do The Rest! You Need To Do This Only ONCE! "
      ?
      ? " PRESS Any Key To Continue."

      SET CONSOLE OFF
      WAIT
```

```
SET CONSOLE ON
ERASE

STORE 'NORMAL Print/COMPRESSED Print/' + ;
'STANDARD FORM FEED (66 lines)/ALTERNATE FORM FEED (42  lines)/END' ;
TO promptlist
STORE 'normprint/comprint/stdform/altform/END' TO varlist

DO WHILE varlist < > 'END'
   STORE $(promptlist,1,@( '/' ,promptlist)-1) TO prompt1
   STORE $(varlist,1,@( '/' ,varlist)-1) TO var
   ERASE
   STORE 1 TO x
   STORE '          ' TO entry        2 spaces
   STORE t TO repeat

   @ 3,15 SAY "Enter each control code - one to a line."
   @ 4,15 SAY "Leave a Last Entry Empty and Use [RETURN] to EXIT"

   DO WHILE repeat              3 spaces
      STORE '          ' TO mentry
      @ 8,15 SAY "Control Codes for   " + prompt1
      @ 9+x,15 SAY " Enter Item   " + STR(x,1) + "  for Code   " ;
      GET mentry PICTURE '# # #'
      READ
         IF mentry < > ' '
            STORE entry + ' + CHR(' + TRIM(mentry) + ')' TO  entry
            STORE x + 1 TO x
         ELSE
            STORE f TO repeat
         ENDIF mentry < > ' '

         CLEAR GETS
      ENDDO WHILE repeat

      STORE $(entry,@( 'CHR' ,entry)) TO entry
      STORE entry TO &var
      @ 15,15 SAY "The control code sequence and the result. "
      @ 18,15 SAY &var + '          ' + prompt1
      @ 20,15 SAY "Press Any Key to Continue. "
      SET CONSOLE OFF
      WAIT
      SET CONSOLE ON
      STORE $(promptlist,@( '/' ,promptlist)+1) TO promptlist
      STORE $(varlist,@( '/' ,varlist)+1) TO varlist

   ENDDO WHILE varlist < > 'END'

   RELEASE promptlist,varlist,prompt1,var,x
   RELEASE repeat,mentry,entry

ENDIF 0=TEST(comprint)

* establish default drives if needed
```

```
* pfdefault stands for program file default
* dfdefault stands for data file default
* these will be used in all programs (except DTVERIFY and INIT) in
* THE dBASE CASEBOOK OF BUSINESS APPLICATIONS

IF 0=TEST(pfdefault) .OR. 0=TEST(dfdefault)
    ERASE
    STORE 'A' TO pfdefault
    STORE 'B' TO dfdefault
    @ 5,20 SAY "What Drive Has the Data?       " GET dfdefault PICT '!'
    @ 7,20 SAY "What Drive Has the Programs? " GET pfdefault PICT '!'
    READ
ENDIF 0=TEST(pfdefault) .OR. 0=TEST(dfdefault)

* save all information to memory file config
* this will always be on the A drive with dBASE II

IF savemem
    SAVE TO a:config
ENDIF savemem
RELEASE savemem
RETURN
```

## SUMMARY

All necessary data to assign drive defaults to program and data files, change printer codes, and tailor the program with SET commands has been permanently placed on the main disk drive and brought into memory. INIT will now initialize each program and serve as one of your most useful command files.

INIT functions as a utility, a short routine that performs a vital yet general service. Using the pseudo-subroutine technique, INIT processed several variables without calling another command file. Other utilities in Section Five will also employ this technique for efficient and speedy operation.

Chapter 17, Dates and Duration, illustrates the management of date verification and the calculation of elapsed days, from which invoices may be aged. Like INIT, all of the routines are utilities. As utilities, they can be used in virtually any dBASE application program.

# 17

# THE DATE AND DURATION TOOLKIT

## Validating and Manipulating Dates

A common problem with computing is the entry of valid dates into computers and the calculations of an elapsed duration in days between two calendar dates. Dates should be easy to enter and stored in a form useful for computing and comparison.

There are several forms of dates. The fifteenth day of March of nineteen hundred and eighty three can be expressed in these forms:

3/15/83   3/15/1983
03/15/83  March 15, 1983
83/03/15  The Ides of March

Computers are unforgiving about discrepancies. Conventions must be established about how dates are stored. You would not want your payroll check due on the 12th of July to be issued on 12/07/84.

Another problem is comparing dates. January 1 of 1984 appears to people to be greater (or later) than December 31, 1983. Precautions must be taken to instruct the computer of the correct relationship. No problems will arise for the same year if dates consistently are expressed either with six digits (010184) or with eight digits (01/01/84) in the MONTH/DAY/YEAR format.

The MM/DD/YY format, while easy to read, has one major drawback —dates with different years cannot be compared reliably by the computer and dBASE. Ask dBASE to confirm the obvious, that the first day of 1984 occurs later than the last day of 1983. At the dot-prompt, type:

ENTER THE EXPRESSION                 YOU WILL SEE

. ? '01/01/84' > '12/31/83'                    .F.

You would be told that the premise is FALSE. According to the computer, New Year's Day comes before its adjacent New Year's Eve. Don't schedule an appointment with the boss using such logic.

A remedy is to use the YEAR/MONTH/DAY order of dating. Two dates are always considered like numbers if the YY/MM/DD format is used and 84/01/01 always interprets as later than 83/12/31. Comparisons can be made between dates without difficulty if all dates are entered into a file in the YY/MM/DD format. Rearrange the dates and again conduct the test.

ENTER THE EXPRESSION                 YOU WILL SEE

. ? '84/01/01' > '83/12/31'                    .T.

While correctly interpreted by the computer, the reversed date may be unfamiliar to the operator. A software application program will allow entry of a date in the more familiar MM/DD/YY format, then convert it to the YY/MM/DD format for use by the computer. The operator never sees the reversed date.

In time, however, many members of the office will also make comparisons to dates in a data file at the dot-prompt level (i.e., LIST ALL FOR PAIDDATE > '83/12/07' .AND. PAIDDATE < '84/01/14'). The operator becomes accustomed to comparing 83/12/07 and 84/01/14. Ad hoc reporting is easily accomplished, and comparisons of dates can be made across the years with accuracy.

Note that the 1984 date had a zero in front of the ones digits. This is called a leading zero. Computers compare two numbers digit-by-digit. Unintended results can occur when a six figure date (111783) is compared with a four figure date (1184).

All applications in this book use both the MM/DD/YY and YY/MM/DD formats and require leading zeros. A variable is assigned to represent a date for each format. VIEWDATE is a variable that designates a working date arranged in the normal date viewed by people, the MM/DD/YY format. FILEDATE arranges the same date in the YY/MM/DD format for insertion into a date field in a data file. The operator is encouraged to be familiar with both.

All dates also use slashes to separate the month, day, and year portions. The addition is technically unnecessary to the functioning of the routine but promotes much greater clarity when dates are viewed or listed directly from a data file.

A second problem with the formatting of dates is the difficulty with which date calculations can be made. There comes an occasion in every enterprise when date calculations are as necessary as date comparisons. A program that ages invoices 30, 60, or 90 days requires calculation of payment deadlines for future reference. Payroll dates must be determined months in advance. Methods to post recurrent appointments (the biweekly dates for the Rotary meetings next year) prove useful to the busy executive.

Two centuries from now, a (hopefully) more enlightened civilization may opt for a date system that allows arithmetic calculations. Days and months may be based upon a uniform system, instead of the historically haphazard arrangement of 28, 29, 30, and 31 days in a month, and either 365 or 366 days in a year.

Until that time, routines are required to convert a calendar date into a form that can be added and subtracted. The most common technique is to convert a calendar date into total days elapsed from a benchmark date. All dates are converted into elapsed days from this standard. Calculations can therefore be performed, and the result converted back to calendar notation. For example, to find the days elapsed from November 12, 1983, to January 14, 1984, convert each to the number of elapsed days since a standard date of New Year's Day, 1983. One normal year (365 days) has transpired between January 1 of 1983 and January 14 of 1984, plus another fourteen days, or 379 standard days. November 12 must be converted from the number of elapsed days remaining in the year, or 316. The elapsed duration is the difference (379 minus 316), or 63 days.

Date routines use different standard dates and different transformation techniques. A routine that comes with dBASE II purchased from Ashton-Tate converts to and from Julian and Gregorian calendar notations. Conversions can be made dating back hundreds of years. Routines in Chapter 17 use January 1, 1901, as a benchmark date. All calendar dates are converted into the days elapsed from that standard.

The Date and Duration Toolkit consists of four utilities:

• DTVERIFY verifies entry of dates.
• CALINT transforms calendar dates to integer.
• INTCAL transforms integers to calendar dates.
• DAYOFWK transforms integers to the day of the week.

These routines can be used with each other, either at the dot-prompt or called from within a larger program. Combinations of the routines will fulfill virtually all your requirements. Elapsed dates can be calculated, given two calendar dates; a future calendar date can be generated from a present date and a duration; and the day of the week can be reported for a future calendar date.

# OPERATION OF THE DATE AND DURATION TOOLKIT

Toolkits carry individual tools that complement or support each other. Each tool, or utility, in the Date and Duration Toolkit can be used in one of two ways. It can be fed a calendar date or number from another program and give an answer to the operator, or pass a number or calendar date back to the larger program without disturbing the current screen.

Each date routine stands alone and can be used at the dot-prompt for ad hoc queries. The input data necessary for operation of the tool is not available from a program and so must originate from the operator. The screen will clear, and a prompt will request entry of the needed variable.

The date routines can be used without modification for both purposes because they will sense whether or not they were called from another program or invoked from the keyboard by a command. The screen will erase, and the required variable will be requested from the operator. Otherwise, the operation of the tool will not be visible on the screen.

## Operation of DTVERIFY

DTVERIFY asks the user to enter information in the MM/DD/YY format. The program repeats the request for entry until a valid month, day, and year are entered. Simple error checks are performed. The verification routine is called by the command DO dtverify. The entry screen appears, and the multi-purpose prompt line will display the default statement, DATE ENTRY SCREEN (see Figure 17-1).

The cursor is positioned at the first digit of the month entry and remains until a correctly numbered month between 01 and 12 is entered. The cursor jumps to the first digit of the day entry, and the operator is prompted to enter a day between 01 and 31, as illustrated in Figure 17-2.

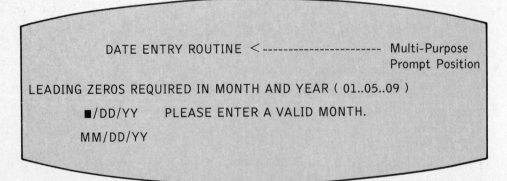

*Figure 17-1.* The Initial Dtverify Screen - Entry of the Month

```
                DATE ENTRY ROUTINE

LEADING ZEROS REQUIRED IN MONTH AND YEAR ( 01..05..09 )

        02/ ■/YY     PLEASE ENTER A VALID DAY.

        MM/DD/YY
```

*Figure 17-2.*   The Dtverify Screen - Entry of the Day

The last entry is the year. Any number greater than 82 is allowed. Note that DTVERIFY currently does not allow entry of years into the next century (see Figure 17-3). We will modify the program when the year 2000 is reached.

DTVERIFY finishes operation when a valid year is entered. The date is stored in two variables with different formats, filedate and viewdate. Both can be examined by typing DISPLAY MEMORY.

```
.DISPLAY MEMORY

FILEDATE        (C)   84/02/19
VIEWDATE        (C)   02/19/84
** TOTAL **           02 VARIABLES USED 00018 BYTES USED
```

Note that DTVERIFY does not check for Sadie Hawkins errors of entry (a February 29 in a non-Leap Year). Furthermore, DTVERIFY erases the screen before date entry, which may be awkward for some applications. DTVERIFY is otherwise suitable as a general purpose utility to enter and verify dates into a dBASE application.

```
                DATE ENTRY ROUTINE

LEADING ZEROS REQUIRED IN MONTH AND YEAR ( 01..05..09 )

        02/19/■     PLEASE ENTER A VALID YEAR.

        MM/DD/YY
```

*Figure 17-3.*   The Dtverify Screen - Entry of the Year

273

## MANIPULATING DATES

Three other utilities allow days and dates to be manipulated. CALINT converts a calendar day to integer format for calculating elapsed durations between dates. DAYOFWK transforms the integer to a day of the week (i.e., Saturday). INTCAL converts an integer to its equivalent calendar expression.

### Operation of CALINT

If needed, CALINT uses DTVERIFY to obtain a calendar date. Whether used by another program or called by an operator, CALINT returns the number of days which have transpired from January 1, 1901, to the entered date.

Unlike DTVERIFY, CALINT operates differently depending upon the source of the input variable. If called by another program, then no changes on the screen are apparent. The input variable, the calendar date, is transferred from another program to CALINT for processing. The main program continues after the RETURN statement is processed in CALINT. The integer date corresponding to the calendar date is STORED to integer.

If CALINT is called from the keyboard, the screen clears and CALINT asks the operator for the calendar date, rather than getting it from a program. The DTVERIFY screen appears, highlighted by the prompt (Enter a Calendar Date to Be Converted) in the multi-purpose prompt position (see Figure 17-4).

CALINT displays the integer value equivalent of the calendar date if the program was called by the operator or passes the value to the calling program in a memory variable called integer (see Figure 17-5).

No processing is apparent if a calendar date was passed to CALINT from a calling dBASE program. However, CALINT produces in either case the numeric memory variable integer.

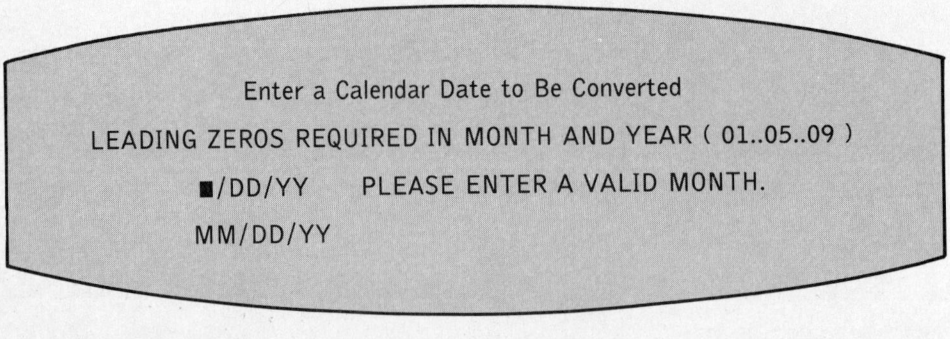

Enter a Calendar Date to Be Converted

LEADING ZEROS REQUIRED IN MONTH AND YEAR ( 01..05..09 )

■/DD/YY     PLEASE ENTER A VALID MONTH.

MM/DD/YY

*Figure 17-4.* The CALINT Entry Screen

Enter a Calendar Date to Be Converted

LEADING ZEROS REQUIRED IN MONTH AND YEAR ( 01..05..09 )

02/19/83        PLEASE ENTER A VALID MONTH.

MM/DD/YY

Integer Date      30365

*Figure 17-5.* Final CALINT Results if Calendar Date Entered by Keyboard

```
. DISPLAY MEMORY
INTEGER    (N)    30365
** TOTAL **     01 VARIABLES USED 00007 BYTES USED
```

The duration between two dates is easily calculated by using CALINT twice. First use CALINT to convert the first date to an integer and store the integer value to a memory variable. Enter the second calendar date, convert, and store the result to another memory variable. The duration is obtained by subtracting the first integer from the second.

| EXAMPLE USING THE CALINT TOOL | RESULTS |
|---|---|
| DO calint [enter February 19, 1984] | integer    = 30365 |
| STORE integer TO startdate | startdate = 30365 |
| DO calint [enter November 11, 1984] | integer    = 30632 |
| STORE integer TO enddate | enddate = 30632 |
| ? enddate — startdate | 267 |

There are 267 days between the two days. CALINT is used as necessary, always passing the converted value of integer to another variable. Comparisons are made to determine the duration. The accounts payable program in Chapter 12, PAYBILLS, used CALINT to determine bills which were outstanding 30, 60, and 90 days from the current date.

## Operation of INTCAL

INTCAL produces exactly the opposite result to CALINT. Any integer is transformed to a standard calendar date. Like CALINT, INTCAL responds according to the source of the variable to be input and no response is evident if called from another program. The operator is otherwise prompted with the statement:

What is the Integer Date? :        :

In the keyboard entry mode, the results of the entry of 30365 displays at the bottom of the screen:

Calendar Date 02/19/84

In either case, the final results are STOREd in the memory variables filedate and viewdate, and the calendar dates in the YY/MM/DD and MM/DD/YY formats.

```
. DISPLAY MEMORY
FILEDATE     (C)   84/02/19
VIEWDATE     (C)   02/19/84
** TOTAL **   02   VARIABLES USED 00018 BYTES USED
```

INTCAL has as many uses as CALINT and is most often used with CALINT after mathematical operations have been done on integer dates. For example, a calendar date is determined below from the entry of a starting date and the duration of 267 days.

| EXAMPLE USING THE INTCAL TOOL | RESULTS |
|---|---|
| DO calint [enter February 19, 1984] | integer    = 30365 |
| STORE integer        TO startdate | startdate = 30365 |
| STORE 267            TO duration | duration   =    267 |
| STORE integer + duration TO integer | integer    = 30632 |
| DO INTCAL | |
| ? filedate | 84/11/12 |
| ? viewdate | 11/12/84 |

## Operation of DAYOFWK

DAYOFWK transforms an integer into the day of the week upon which the integer falls. Either the operator is asked to enter the integer or it is otherwise obtained from another program. The integer is converted to the day of the week and the result is displayed to the operator or passed to the calling program. DAYOFWK is most commonly used after manipulations have been done by CALINT and INTCAL.

| EXAMPLE USING THE DAYOFWK TOOL | RESULTS |
|---|---|
| DO calint [enter February 19, 1984] | integer    = 30365 |
| STORE integer        TO startdate | startdate = 30365 |
| STORE 267            TO duration | duration   =    267 |
| STORE integer + duration TO integer | integer    = 30632 |
| DO INTCAL | |

```
? filedate                          84/11/12
? viewdate                          11/12/84
DO DAYOFWK
? dayofwk                           Monday
```

DAYOFWK is the last of the DATE and DURATION tools. All may be combined in many ways for several purposes. One other command file, DATEMENU, has been enclosed not to serve as a utility, but to illustrate the features of the four tools as they are combined in different ways to produce the desired results.

## Operation of DATEMENU

At the dot-prompt, type DO datemenu to produce the screen that outlines the five DATEMENU options (see Figure 17-6). Operation of each is explained by the prompts and all of the subsequent screens are identical to those previously outlined for DTVERIFY, CALINT, INTCAL, and DAYOFWK.

Option 1 prompts the operator for entry of a calendar date and responds with the day of the week. Option 2 gives the elapsed number of days between two calendar days entered at the prompts. Option 3 generates a calendar date if an originating calendar date is given with a duration. Option 4 returns with the calendar days 30, 60, and 90 days from the entered date. Option 5 exits the menu.

## INSTALLATION OF THE DATE AND DURATION TOOLKIT

The Date and Duration tools are easily installed. All but DTVERIFY are mounted on the default program drive for use by other command files. Each may be used at the dot-prompt or by larger programs.

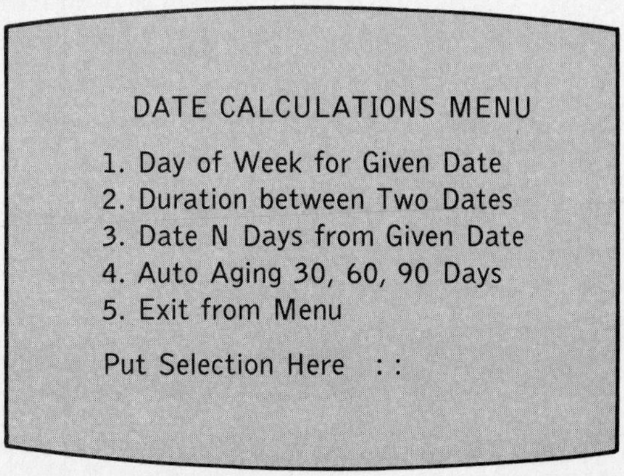

```
        DATE CALCULATIONS MENU

        1. Day of Week for Given Date
        2. Duration between Two Dates
        3. Date N Days from Given Date
        4. Auto Aging 30, 60, 90 Days
        5. Exit from Menu

        Put Selection Here  : :
```

*Figure 17-6.* Screen for DATEMENU

# FILES FOR THE DATE AND DURATION TOOLKIT

*Table 17-1.   List of Files and Main Functions*

| Filename | Stands For | Function |
| --- | --- | --- |
| DTVERIFY.CMD | Date Verify | Verifies Date Entry |
| CALINT.CMD | Calendar/Integer | Transfers Calendar to Integer |
| INTCAL.CMD | Integer/Calendar | Transfers Integer to Calendar |
| DAYOFWK.CMD | Day of Week | Transfers Integer to Day of Week |
| DATEMENU.CMD | Date Menu | Illustrates Uses of Tools |

## DTVERIFY.CMD   The Date Verification Tool

DTVERIFY uses one DO WHILE/ENDDO loop and its ancillary command, LOOP. The month is entered on the first repetition, the day is entered the second, and the year is entered last. Each of the three entries are validated before the operator is allowed to exit the routine.

As with INIT, the TEST command is used to determine if a memory variable is already in memory. The first prompt used in DTVERIFY originates either from DTVERIFY, one of the other tools, or from other command files to convey specific information.

The TEST command determines if this multi-purpose prompt, prompt, is already in memory and established by another file. If not, the default prompt DATE ENTRY ROUTINE is STORED to prompt and will be displayed centered at the top of the screen when DTVERIFY is used. The other prompts are displayed and the operator begins entering the data.

The DO WHILE loop continues until checkdate is FALSE, after the month, day, and year entries are obtained. The entry month is verified for the proper range (between one and twelve) and for the necessary presence of a leading zero for months that are less then ten. If these conditions are not met, the LOOP command returns to the last DO WHILE used in the command file. The prompt line at @10,35 is cleared and the proper prompt is again displayed.

The day, then the year, are entered and verified in turn. Once done, checkdate is set to FALSE and the loop is exited. Both filedate and viewdate are configured from the other variables. Control is returned to the dot-prompt or another command file once housekeeping is accomplished. Note that prompt is released to ensure that the TEST command will work properly the next time DTVERIFY is called.

CODE FOR DIVERIFY.CMD

```
* command files name: dtverify.cmd
* module purpose: obtain correct date
```

```
* final version

* set up housekeeping          2 spaces
SET talk OFF
SET colon OFF
STORE '          ' TO month,day,year
STORE t TO checkdate
ERASE

* check to see which prompt will be used:
* a special purpose prompt stated from another file or
* the general purpose prompt below

IF 0=TEST(prompt)
   STORE 'DATE ENTRY ROUTINE ' TO prompt
ENDIF 0=TEST(prompt)

* put prompt in center of 80 col. screen irregardless of prompt length
@ 3,(79-LEN(prompt))/2 SAY prompt
@ 6,10 SAY "LEADING ZEROS REQUIRED IN MONTH AND YEAR ( 01..05..09 )"
@ 10,25 SAY "MM/DD/YY"
@ 12,25 SAY "MM/DD/YY"

* enter and verify month, day, and year
* does not check for correct days per given month

DO WHILE checkdate

   * clear operator prompt line
   @ 10,35

   * enter and verify month
   IF month < '01' .OR. month> '12' .OR. $(month,2,1)= ' '
      @ 10,35 SAY 'PLEASE ENTER A VALID MONTH. '
      @ 10,25 GET month PICTURE '99'
      READ
      LOOP
   ENDIF month

   * enter and verify day
   IF day< '01' .OR. day> '31' .OR. $(day,2,1)= ' '
      @ 10,35 SAY 'PLEASE ENTER A VALID DAY. '
      @ 10,28 GET day PICTURE '99'
      READ
      LOOP
   ENDIF day

   * enter and verify year
   IF year < '83'
      @ 10,35 SAY 'PLEASE ENTER A VALID YEAR '
      @ 10,31 GET year PICTURE '99'
      READ
      LOOP
   ENDIF year

   * decide to loop and re-enter day,month,year
   STORE f TO checkdate
```

```
ENDDO WHILE checkdate

* arrange dates in the two formats:
* one for humans, the otherwise for computer comparisons

STORE year + '/' + month + '/' + day TO filedate
STORE month + '/' + day + '/' + year TO viewdate

* housekeeping before exiting
* note that filedate and viewdate are passed out of dtverify
RELEASE year,month,day,checkdate,prompt
SET colon ON
RETURN
```

# CALINT   Calendar to Integer Tool

CALINT like DTVERIFY uses the TEST command, but for a different purpose. After housekeeping, the origin of the input variable filedate is determined. If not in memory, TEST returns a zero. DTVERIFY obtains a calendar date from the operator, but first CALINT will STORE to prompt an identifying message for use in DTVERIFY. The variable keyboard is initialized as TRUE for later use.

Once filedate has been obtained, the number of days that have transpired since the standard year to that date is calculated. First, all but the remainder of the current year is determined with the code

```
STORE int((year-1)*365.25) TO integer
```

An interim value for the output variable integer is calculated. The remainder of the days in the year up to the filedate must also be determined. The correction for Leap Year is done to establish the correct number of days in February and STORE the result to v. The variable v is STORED with the aide of the macro to the longer string, dim, which stands for "Days in Month."

The pseudo-subroutine technique is used as it was in INIT to take each remaining whole month's days, from 28 to 31 days, and add the days in each to integer. The code below cycles through the larger string to select the smaller strings, the correct days of each month.

```
DO WHILE flag < month

   STORE integer + VAL($(dim,monrepeat,2)) TO integer
   STORE 3 + monrepeat TO monrepeat
   STORE flag + 1 TO flag

ENDDO WHILE flag < month
```

The code is simpler than that used by INIT. INIT used shorter strings of different lengths in the variable list. Each short string in dim is the same three-digit length: two characters for the number of days in the month and one for the comma. The variable monrepeat, the MONthly REPEATing counter, is equal to 1 the first time CALINT is used. Substituted into the major expression in the DO WHILE loop, the result is

```
STORE integer + VAL($(dim,1,2)) TO integer
```

The string '31' is returned from the substring function, the numeric equivalent of which is added to integer. The next month, February, operates similarly but uses v, the days corrected for the current year.

The loop continues to add days for the remainder of the whole months to integer until only a fraction of a month remains. The variable day is added to integer to yield the correct number of elapsed days since the benchmark date of January 1, 1901.

The variable keyboard determines if results should be displayed. If TRUE, the value of integer and a prompt will be placed on the bottom of the screen. The input variable filedate is RELEASED so that CALINT will again work properly. The program is exits after housekeeping, leaving the correct integer date in memory.

## CODE FOR CALINT.CMD

```
* calint.cmd
* converts filedate to integer
* base date = January 1, 1901


* set up housekeeping
SET talk OFF
STORE f TO keyboard

* check to see if an operator should be asked for
* input and results displayed on screen. otherwise,
* results are passed back to a calling program

IF 0=TEST(filedate)
   STORE "Enter a Calendar Date to Be Converted" TO prompt
   DO A:dtverify
   STORE ' ' TO prompt
   ERASE
   STORE t TO keyboard

ENDIF 0=TEST(filedate)

* segment filedate into months,days, and years
STORE VAL($(filedate,1,2)) TO year
STORE VAL($(filedate,4,2)) TO month
STORE VAL($(filedate,7,2)) TO day

* determine the number of days in whole years
STORE int((year-1)*365.25) TO integer
```

```
* find elapsed days in remaining year
* and correct for leap year

IF int(year/4)=year/4
   STORE '29' TO v
ELSE
   STORE '28' TO v
ENDIF int(year/4)=year/4

STORE "31,&v,31,30,31,30,31,31,30,31,30,31," TO dim
* dim stands for days in month

STORE 1 TO monrepeat,flag
* add the number of days in whole months to integer

DO WHILE flag < month

   STORE integer + VAL($(dim,monrepeat,2)) TO integer
   STORE 3 + monrepeat TO monrepeat
   STORE flag + 1 TO flag

ENDDO WHILE monrepeat <= 34


* add the remainder of days in the last month
STORE integer + day TO integer

* display results if the operator invoked the program
IF keyboard
   @ 15,5 SAY "Integer Date   "
   @ 15,25 SAY integer
   RELEASE filedate
ENDIF keyboard

* housekeeping before exiting
* filedate is not released if called from a program
RELEASE keyboard,year,month,day,monrepeat,v
RELEASE dim,flag,viewdate,prompt

RETURN
```

## INTCAL  Integer to Calendar Tool

The code for INTCAL is nearly identical to CALINT. Whereas CALINT built up integer from the discrete units of years, months, and days, INTCAL assembles these calendar units from the value of integer. The TEST command is also used to determine the origin of the necessary input variable, corrections are also required for the Leap Year, and the dim phrase is again used. Like DTVERIFY, a single digit days and months are expressed with leading zeroes to ensure proper placement of the digits of the calendar expression.

### CODE FOR INTCAL.CMD

```
* intcal.cmd
* converts integer to calendar
```

```
* starts days from january 1, 1901

* set up housekeeping
SET talk OFF
STORE f TO keyboard

* check to see if an operator should be asked for
* input and results displayed on screen. otherwise,
* results are passed back to a calling program

IF 0=TEST(integer)
  ERASE
  STORE t TO keyboard
  STORE 000000 TO integer
  @ 5,5 SAY " What Is the Integer Date? "  GET integer
  READ
ENDIF 0=TEST(integer)


* subtract the number of days in whole years from integer date
STORE int(integer/365.25) + 1 TO year
STORE ((integer/365.25)+1−(int(integer/365.25)+1))*365.25 TO integer
STORE int(integer+1) TO integer

* correct for leap day
IF int(year/4)=year/4
  STORE '29' TO v
ELSE
  STORE '28' TO v
ENDIF int(year/4)=year/4

* subtract the number of days in whole months from remainder
* subtract the correct number of days in each month in
* the dim phrase, and increment the number of months by one.
* dim stands for days in month

STORE "31,&v,31,30,31,30,31,31,30,31,30,31," TO dim
STORE 1 TO monrepeat,month

DO WHILE integer > VAL($(dim,monrepeat,2))

  STORE month+1 TO month
  STORE integer−VAL($(dim,monrepeat,2)) TO integer
  STORE 3+monrepeat TO monrepeat

ENDDO WHILE monrepeat < =34
* the remainder are days in the last partial month
* put leading zeros in single-digit months and days
IF month < =9
  STORE '0' + STR(month,1) TO mmonth
ELSE
  STORE STR(month,2) TO mmonth
ENDIF month < =9

IF integer < =9
  STORE '0' + STR(integer,1) TO day
ELSE
```

```
        STORE STR(integer,2) TO day
    ENDIF integer < =9

    * arrange dates in the two formats:
    * one for humans, the otherwise for computer comparisons
    STORE STR(year,2)+ '/' +mmonth+ '/' + day TO filedate
    STORE mmonth + '/' + day + '/' + STR(year,2) TO viewdate

    * display results if the operator invoked the program
    IF keyboard
        @ 15,5 SAY "Calendar Date        " + viewdate
        RELEASE integer
    ENDIF keyboard

    * housekeeping before exiting
    * integer is not released if called from a program
    RELEASE keyboard,year,mmonth,month,day,monrepeat,v,dim
    RETURN
```

# DAYOFWK   Day of Week Tool

The dBASE II code used by the other date routines converted units of months, days, and years. DAYOFWK deals in two units, weeks and the remaining days after whole weeks are subtracted. The remainder is converted to days and rounded upwards to reflect the current day. Once done, a value of from 0 to 6 will be obtained, reflecting the number of days difference between the day of the week upon which falls the standard day (January 1, 1901—a Monday) and the day of the week of the integer date.

### CODE FOR DAYOFWK.CMD

```
    * dayofwk.cmd
    * module purpose: determine day of week of
    * entry date, based upon standard date
    * january 1, 1901

    * set up housekeeping
    SET talk OFF
    STORE f TO keyboard

    * check to see if an operator should be asked for
    * input and the results displayed on screen. otherwise,
    * the results are passed back to the calling program

    IF 0=TEST(integer)
        ERASE
        STORE 0000 TO integer
        @ 5,5 SAY " What integer? " GET integer
        STORE t TO keyboard
        READ
    ENDIF 0=TEST(integer)
```

```
* subtract all whole weeks since standard date
STORE ((integer/7.000) — int(integer/7.000)) TO diff

* convert remainder to whole days and fraction
STORE diff * 7.00 TO diff
* round upwards, then take integer
* int command always truncates non-integer portion
STORE int(diff + .5) TO diff


* convert the remainder to day of the week
DO CASE

   CASE diff=6
      STORE 'Sunday' TO dayofwk

   CASE diff=5
      STORE 'Saturday' TO dayofwk

   CASE diff=4
      STORE 'Friday' TO dayofwk

   CASE diff=3
      STORE 'Thursday' TO dayofwk

   CASE diff=2
      STORE 'Wednesday' TO dayofwk

   CASE diff=1
      STORE 'Tuesday' TO dayofwk

   CASE diff=0
      STORE 'Monday' TO dayofwk

ENDCASE

* display results if operator invoked the program
IF keyboard
   @ 15,2 SAY "The Day of the Week Is    " + dayofwk
   RELEASE integer
ENDIF keyboard


* housekeeping before exiting
* integer is not released if called from a program
RELEASE keyboard,diff
RETURN
```

# DATEMENU  Illustrates the Toolkit

DATEMENU combines the Date and Duration Tools in combinations
that will perform virtually any operation desired. Any portion of this
code may be substituted in your other application programs.

### CODE FOR DATEMENU.CMD

```
* datemenu.cmd
* program by michael clifford
* module purpose: illustrate otherwise date programs
* dtverify, dayofwk, calint, and intcal

* set up housekeeping

SET talk OFF

* determine that all necessary files are on drive
* remember: The FILE command needs to check for files
* ending in 'CMD' for CPM dBASE and 'PRG' for MS-DOS
IF FILE( "CALINT.CMD" ) .AND. FILE( "INTCAL.CMD" ) .AND. ;
    FILE( "DTVERIFY.CMD" ) .AND. FILE( "DAYOFWK.CMD")

ELSE
   ERASE
   ? CHR(7)
   @ 10,05 SAY "YOU ARE MISSING ONE OF THE KEY FILES "
   @ 12,05 SAY "A:dtverify...INTCAL...CALINT...DAYOFWK"
   @ 14,05 SAY "PLEASE CORRECT BEFORE CONTINUING. "
   CANCEL

ENDIF files

* display menu, prompt choice, and execute programs
DO WHILE t

   ERASE
   CLEAR
   STORE '0' TO selection

   * display prompts
   @ 2,10 SAY "5 DATE CALCULATIONS MENU"
   @ 4,10 SAY " 1. Day of Week for Given Date"
   @ 5,10 SAY " 2. Duration between Two Dates"
   @ 6,10 SAY " 3. Date N Days from Given Date"
   @ 7,10 SAY " 4. Auto Aging 30, 60, 90 Days"
   @ 9,10 SAY " 5. Exit from Menu"

   @ 12,10 SAY " Put Selection Here " GET selection PICTURE '#'
   READ

   * execute proper program
   DO CASE

      CASE selection= '1'

         DO A:dtverify
         DO calint
         DO dayofwk
         ERASE
         @ 5,5 SAY "The Day of the Week Is " + dayofweek

      CASE selection= '2'
```

```
    STORE "Enter the Earlier Date" TO prompt
    DO A:dtverify
    DO calint
    STORE integer TO day1
    STORE "Enter the Later Date" TO prompt
    DO A:dtverify
    STORE ' ' TO prompt
    DO calint
    STORE integer - day1 TO daydiff
    ERASE
    @ 5, 0 SAY "The Duration Between the Two Dates Is "
    @ 5,40 say daydiff USING '###'
    ?? " DAYS"

CASE selection= '3'

    DO A:dtverify
    DO calint
    STORE integer TO day1
    STORE 000 TO days
    ERASE
    @ 5,0 SAY "How many Days to be Added or Subtracted? " GET days
    READ
    STORE day1 + days TO integer
    DO intcal
    ERASE
    @ 5,0 SAY "The CALENDAR DATE Is " + viewdate

CASE selection= '4'

    DO A:dtverify
    DO calint
    STORE integer TO givendate
    STORE givendate + 30 TO integer
    DO intcal
    STORE viewdate TO day30
    STORE givendate + 60 TO integer
    DO intcal
    STORE viewdate TO day60
    STORE givendate + 90 TO integer
    DO intcal
    STORE viewdate TO day90
    ERASE
    @ 10,05 SAY "AGED DATES FOR  30  60  90 DAYS "
    @ 12,22 SAY day30
    @ 12,34 SAY day60
    @ 12,46 SAY day90

CASE selection= '5'

    RELEASE selection
    CANCEL
```

```
ENDCASE

* pause execution
@ 20,10 SAY "PRESS ANY KEY TO CONTINUE..."
SET console OFF
WAIT
SET console ON
ERASE

ENDDO WHILE t
```

## SUMMARY

Used alone, with another tool, or called by other command files such as DATEMENU, the Date and Duration Toolkit will allow you to perform virtually any manipulation of dates and durations.

Several small utilities were designed to be used alone, to call each other, or be used by a larger command file. The flexibility of this toolkit approach extends the usefulness of the utilities.

The TEST command was used to determine if each routine was called by the operator at the dot-prompt or from within a larger program. If a variable was needed that was not present, entry was requested from the operator and the halting of processing was averted.

The next chapter introduces a utility that accomplishes a completely different function, the graphing of data and the transference of the results to the screen, the printer, or to a text file.

# 18

## dPLOT: THE GRAPHICS TOOLKIT

A picture is worth a thousand words as proclaimed by the many graphics software packages becoming available. Many are directly compatible with dBASE data files. Most are written in machine language for increased speed and can only be used with a particular computer and plotter.

dPLOT is a utility that plots a simple but serviceable graph and can be used either at the dot-prompt or called by another application program. The plot values may be entered by an operator or obtained from fields summed in a data file. Written entirely in dBASE code, dPLOT will work on any 80-column terminal. The drawn graphs can be saved and the entire dPLOT system can be easily modified.

Like the Dates and Durations utilities, dPLOT also takes the toolkit approach. The graphing utilities combine to produce different results. The various processing options are illustrated by an optional command file that serves as a graphics menu. With the use of dPLOT, you may be spared the additional cost of a graphics package.

## OPERATION OF dPLOT

The various tools are shown on the optional menu. Invoke by typing DO dplot. The menu screen will appear as shown in Figure 18-1.

- Option 0 exits to dBASE.
- Option 1 allows creation of a graph. Up to five fields will be summed in a given data file and plotted.

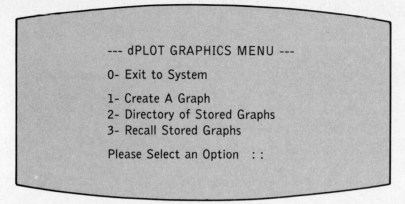

*Figure 18-1.* dPLOT Main Menu of Graphics Toolkit

- Option 2 displays a directory of the names of all graphs that are stored.
- Option 3 will recall a graph and plot it on the screen.

## Option 1: Create a Graph

The graphics toolkit has the capability to plot numbers instantly when they are entered. Option 1 obtains the plot values from numeric fields in a given file. The screen clears and prompts for the name of a data file (see Figure 18-2).

The screen shows all the numeric fields and waits for you to select up to five fields (see Figure 18-3). Enter a zero (0) and a carriage return to end entry for less than five fields.

| DATABASE | FILES | # RCDS | LAST UPDATE |
|----------|-------|--------|-------------|
| REVENUE | DBF | 00330 | 00/00/00 |
| GRAPHS | DBF | 0021 | 00/00/00 |
| CLIENTS | DBF | 0050 | 00/00/00 |
| CHECKS | DBF | 0431 | 00/00/00 |

The contents to be graphed are in what file? :REVENUE :

*Figure 18-2.* Summing Fields in the File - First Screen

```
What Field Number (Up to 5. Enter 0 to Exit) :0:

1 COMPANY1
2 COMPANY2
3 COMPANY3
4 COMPANY4
5 COMPANY5
6 CANADA
7 INTERNTL
```

*Figure 18-3.* Summing Fields in the File - Second Screen

All the numeric fields in the file display in a column down the screen. Preceding each field is a number. Select the first field you wish to be totaled and graphed. The What Title question appears to the right of the field. The title appears adjacent to the plotted field. Selection of the first field is illustrated in Figure 18-4.

Continue selecting fields and titles in any order. Up to five may be chosen. The final screen appears as in Figure 18-5.

The message —The Fields Are Now Being Summed— informs you of a delay as dBASE is totaling the fields. The screen clears, and you are asked to enter descriptions to be placed along the horizontal and vertical axis, as well as the title of the graph (see Figure 18-6).

```
What Field Number (Up to 5. Enter 0 to Exit) :1:

1 COMPANY1          What Title?   :UNIV WIDGT:
2 COMPANY2
3 COMPANY3
4 COMPANY4
5 COMPANY5
6 CANADA
7 INTERNTL
```

*Figure 18-4.* Summing Fields in the File - Third Screen

```
What Field Number (Up to 5. Enter 0 to Exit) :7:

1 COMPANY1        What Title?   :UNIV WIDGT :
2 COMPANY2
3 COMPANY3        What Title?   :TIRES       :
4 COMPANY4        What Title?   :STEEL       :
5 COMPANY5
6 CANADA          What Title?   :CANCORP     :
7 INTERNTL        What Title?   :INTERNATL  :
```

*Figure 18-5.* Summing Fields in the File - Final Screen

The fields are graphed along with the titles for each. Axes are drawn, and each numeric amount is scaled and plotted. Titles for the vertical axis appear down the side, and the title for the horizontal axis displays on the top line. The prompt for the available options will appear at the bottom right and asks you to Print the Graph (see Figure 18-7).

You are given several options after the graph appears. The first option asks the question Do You Wish to Save Graph? If you enter T, the graph is saved to the library. The prompt clears, and you are asked What Filename? The graph is saved upon entry of a filename of up to eight letters, and its name will be displayed at the top right.

The last option asks Save To Text File? If T is entered, then a standard ASCII file is saved using the name of the graph (example: REVENUE) with the extension TXT (REVENUE.TXT). The final option (Press Any Key To Continue) is displayed as illustrated in Figure 18-8. A press of any key returns you to the main dPLOT menu.

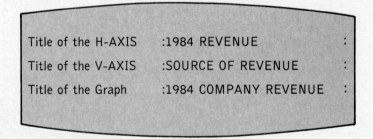

```
Title of the H-AXIS     :1984 REVENUE             :

Title of the V-AXIS     :SOURCE OF REVENUE        :

Title of the Graph      :1984 COMPANY REVENUE    :
```

*Figure 18-6.* Request for Entry of Titles

```
S   :1984 COMPANY REVENUE
O   :
U   :
R   :
C   ******************         37321.00
E   : UNIV WIDGT
    :
O   :# # # # # # # # #        37668.67
F   : TIRES
    :
R   :*********************        41280.00
E   : STEEL
V   :
E   :# # # # # # # # # #      54615.00
N   : CANCORP
U   :
E   :******************************       109230.00
    : INTERNATL
    :
    + --------------------------------------------------------------------
1984 REVENUE   Print the Graph?   :F:   <--- OPTION MESSAGE
```

*Figure 18-7.* Graph of the Summed Fields - The First Screen

# INSTALLATION AND INNER WORKINGS (OR dPLOT THICKENS)

Graphing in dBASE can be done by two methods. One is to paint a screen by use of the @ SAY commands. Any cell in the monitor's range of 80 columns by 24 rows can display a character by given a coordinate and employing the SAY command. Once your graph is plotted on the screen however, there is no easy method to save it.

dPLOT uses another method to allow the graph to be saved, printed, and edited. Why not store, in a data file, characters that represent graphic information? The LIST command can be relied upon to extract a series of records that appear to be a graph.

dPLOT stores all graphic data to a file named GRAPHS. Each record in GRAPHS has only one field, called LINE, which has a width corresponding to the width of the graph and vertical axis. Each line or row of the graph is stored to LINE as one record. A complete graph needs 21

293

```
 S   :1984 COMPANY REVENUE          GRAPH NAME: REVENUE
 O   :
 U   :
 R   :
 C   :*******************      37321.00
 E   : UNIV WIDGT
     :
 O   :# # # # # # # # #        37668.67
 F   : TIRES
     :
 R   :**********************   41280.00
 E   : STEEL
 V   :
 E   :# # # # # # # # # # #    54615.00
 N   : CANCORP
 U   :
 E   :***************************   109230.00
     : INTERNATL
     :
   + ------------------------------------------------------------------
 1984 REVENUE    Press Any Key To Continue
```

*Figure 18-8.* Graph of the Summed Fields - The Final Screen

records, and it is displayed by using the command LIST NEXT 21 OFF. Figure 18-9 illustrates a listing of the first graph in GRAPHS, with the added detail of the record numbers.

## Command Files for the dPLOT System

The command files subscribe to the toolkit approach. Some of the files are necessary for graphing, others merely assist in obtaining and saving the values to be plotted. dPLOT functions not to plot a graph but to illustrate the uses of the other command files in the graphics toolkit.

## FILES FOR THE DPLOT SYSTEM

The data file GRAPHS is used to store your graph once it is constructed. The dPLOT toolkit also requires three command files to construct a graph: 1) MAINGRAP scales the values and calls the other command files; 2) SLATEDRA draws the axes and positions the titles; and 3) PLOT

```
Record            Contents of the Field LINE in Each Record

00001 : S :1984 COMPANY REVENUE   GRAPH NAME: REVENUE                        :

00002 : O :                                                                 :
00003 : U :                                                                 :
00004 : R :                                                                 :
00005 : C :*******************     37321.00                                 :
00006 : E : UNIV WIDGT                                                      :
00007 :   :                                                                 :
00008 : O :#########      37668.67                                          :
00009 : F : TIRES                                                           :
00010 :   :                                                                 :
00011 : R :*********************     41280.00                               :
00012 : E : STEEL                                                           :
00013 : V :                                                                 :
00014 : E :#############      54615.00                                      :
00015 : N : CANCORP                                                         :
00016 : U :                                                                 :
00017 : E :*******************************     109230.00                    :
00018 : : INTERNATL                                                         :
00019 : :                                                                   :
00020 :+ ----------------------------------------------------------------   :
00021 :              1984 REVENUE
```

*Figure 18-9.* Storing Graphic Information in 21 One-field Records

draws the bars. Two other command files are optional but recommended: GRAPHOPT offers the operator the options to save and print a file, and SUMMATE totals five fields in a given file for graphing. The sample menu, dPLOT, illustrates the use of each.

## *Table 18-1.  List of Files and Main Functions*

| *Filename* | *Stands For* | *Function* |
|---|---|---|
| GRAPHS.DBF | Graphs Data File | Holds Graphs |
| MAINGRAP.CMD | Main Graphics Routine | Calls Other Tools |
| SLATEDRA.CMD | Slate Drawer | Draws Axes |
| PLOT.CMD | Plotting Routine | Plots Values |
| GRAPHOPT.CMD | Graphics Options | Prints and Saves Options |
| SUMMATE.CMD | Summation Routine | Totals Fields in File |
| dPLOT.CMD | dBASE Plotting | Menu of Plotting Tools |

## GRAPHS.DBF  The Graphs Library

The file GRAPHS.DBF contains all of the saved graphs. As a dBASE file, the 21 records that comprise a graph can be EDITed, SAVED, or RE-PLACEd.

```
STRUCTURE FOR FILE: GRAPHS
NUMBER OF RECORDS: 0021
DATE OF LAST UPDATE: 00/00/00
PRIMARY USE DATABASE
FLD           NAME    TYPE WIDTH      DEC
001           LINE         075
** TOTAL **                76
```

## MAINGRAP.CMD  The Main Graphing Routine

Coordination of the subordinate graphing routines is accomplished by MAINGRAP. As presently written, MAINGRAP uses SUMMATE to provide up to five totals to be graphed. Whether provided by SUMMATE or from the keyboard, MAINGRAP requires that values to be plotted be STORED to memory variables FN1 to FN5. Titles must be STORED in the form of FTITL1 to FTITL5. Moreover, another memory variable barnum must provide the number of values to be plotted. For the REVENUE example above, the working variables are listed below.

```
FN1     37321.00     FTITL1    UNIV WIDGT
FN2     37668.67     FTITL2    TIRES
FN3     41280.00     FTITL3    STEEL
FN4     54615.00     FTITL4    CANCORP
FN5    109230.00     FTITL5    INTERNATL
```

GRAPHS is opened and the GO BOTTOM command is used. The last record number in the file is incremented by one to determine the first record that retains data about your new graph. The last record number in the new graph is also calculated by adding 21 to the existing bottom record in the file.

MAINGRAP next determines the largest of the five possible plot values. The use of the macro allows each of the FN variables to be considered in turn. A temporary working variable max retains the numeric value of first FN1, then FN2 so on up to FN5 if five plot values are present. The operation is illustrated by the code below.

```
CODE USED IN MAINGRAP              VALUES ON FIRST PASS
STORE 1 TO counter                 counter = 1
STORE fn1 TO max                   max = 37321
DO WHILE counter <= barnum − 1     DO WHILE 1 <= 4
```

296

```
STORE counter + 1 TO counter          counter = 2
STORE STR(counter,1) TO scount        scount = '2'
IF fn&scount > max                    IF fn2 (37668.67) > 37321
   STORE fn&scount TO max                max = 37668.67
ENDIF fn&scount > max
ENDDO WHILE COUNTER < = barnum - 1
```

The routine repeats until the largest of the plot values is determined and the value is STOREd to max, which is used by the plotting routine PLOT.

MAINGRAP next calls another subordinate routine SLATEDRA to prepare the records for the graph and to draw the axes. Each value can be plotted once the graph is prepared. An equation is used to position the first plot:

```
GOTO graphtop + 2 + int((20 - (barnum * 3))/2)
```

The variable graphtop is the first record number or the top of the graph. The expression spaces down at least two more records to start the plot. The last part of the expression adds more spaces (record numbers) according to the total number of plot values as stated by barnum.

Once properly positioned at the correct record number, the first plot can be drawn. A loop and a macro are again used to cycle through the five FN variables. The routine plot plots each. A title is positioned beneath the graph with the use of the SKIP and REPLACE commands. Two more lines are added and the loop repeats and draws the next plot value. The graph is completed once the loop finishes.

The graph can be viewed by simply going to the first record and listing the 21 records with the record number suppressed. The code, used throughout, is:

```
GOTO graphtop
LIST next 21 TRIM(line) OFF
```

The graph may be listed again, printed, or sent to a text file. The choices are presented by an optional command file, graphopt. Once the variables are RELEASEd, the routine is terminated. Control will be returned to dPLOT if it was originally used.

## CODE FOR MAINGRAP.CMD

```
* maingraph.cmd
* graphs up to five values in form of
* fn1..fn2..fn5 with matching titles ftitl1...ftitl5
* also need barnum, the number of bars to be graphed.

SET talk OFF
```

```
DO summate
USE graphs
GO BOTTOM
STORE # + 1 TO graphtop
STORE # + 21 TO graphbot

* determine maximum plot value
STORE 1 TO counter
STORE fn1 TO max
DO WHILE counter <= barnum - 1
   STORE counter + 1 TO counter
   STORE STR(counter,1) TO scount
   IF fn&scount > max
      STORE fn&scount TO max
   ENDIF fn&scount > max
ENDDO WHILE counter <= barnum - 1

* draw axes
DO slatedra

* plot each value (up to five)
STORE 1 TO counter
GOTO graphtop + int ((20 - (barnum * 3))/2)
DO WHILE counter <= barnum
  STORE STR(counter,1) TO scount
  STORE fn&scount TO fieldplot
  DO plot
  STORE counter + 1 TO counter
  SKIP
  REPLACE line WITH TRIM(line) + '  ' + ftitl&scount
  SKIP + 2
ENDDO WHILE counter <= barnum

* present the graph
ERASE
GOTO graphtop
LIST next 21 TRIM(line) OFF

* offer options to save and print
DO graphopt
@ 21,35
@ 21,35 SAY 'Press Any Key To Continue'

* housekeeping
RELEASE graphtop,graphbot,counter,barnum,scount,fieldplot
RELEASE fn1,fn2,fn3,fn4,fn5,ftitl1,ftitl2,ftitl3,ftitl4,ftitl5
RELEASE gfile,asterisks,pounds,max
RETURN
```

# SLATEDRA.CMD  Draws Axes and Prepares Titles

SLATEDRA prepares the GRAPH data file to retain the graphic information on the current graph, draws the axes, and obtains the titles and descriptions from the operator. The 21 records are each prepared by use of the APPEND BLANK command within a DO WHILE loop repeats until the last record number graphbot is reached.

The characters for drawing (===, ***, and ###) are then used to build the horizontal axis and the maximum values to be plotted. Alternate plots are drawn with different characters on the graph for better visibility.

Titles are next obtained from the operator for assignment to the horizontal axis (htitle), vertical axis (vtitle), and the title of the graph (gtitle). The letters of the titles are assigned in sequence to the graph by use of the REPLACE command.

The first task is the drawing of the vertical title down the graph and the vertical axis. One character at a time is selected from vtitle and placed in the first position of the records in order that the title is read vertically. One dBASE expression draws both.

```
REPLACE next 20 line WITH $(!(vtitle),# —graphtop+1,1) + '    '

- - - - - - - - - - -          - - - - - - - - - - - - - -              - - -
Action and Range               vertical title character                 axis
```

Starting at the first record number graphtop, each record number is used to assist a substring function to take the correct character from vtitle. Assume that we have already stored ten graphs in GRAPHS. Graphtop for the eleventh graph would be (10×21) plus one or record number 211. The first vertical character of the graph (S in SOURCE OF REVENUE) can be drawn by using the current record number function (#).

```
REPLACE next 20 line WITH $(!(vtitle),# —graphtop+1,1) + ' ¦'
```

First REPLACEMENT . . . . ( # = Record Number = 211)

```
              $(!(SOURCE OF REVENUE),211—211+1,1) + ' ¦'
yields        $(!(SOURCE OF REVENUE),1,1) + ' ¦'
or            'S ¦'
```

Second REPLACEMENT . . . (Record Number = 212)

```
              $(!(SOURCE OF REVENUE),212—211+1,1) + ' ¦'
yields        $(!(SOURCE OF REVENUE),2,1) + ' ¦'
or            'O ¦'
```

The powerful REPLACE command goes through each of the 20 records, uses the substring function ($) and current record function (#) to select the proper letter from vtitle, and draws the upslash ( ¦ ) character. The vertical title and the axis appears as designed when all the 21 records are listed.

The remaining titles and the horizontal axis are drawn by first using the GOTO or SKIP commands to determine the proper record number, and using the REPLACE command to either draw the axis or insert the title. The following expression adds a + where the two axes intersect and ensures that the REPLACE command, which inserts the horizontal axis, doesn't write over and erase the vertical data previously written to that record.

```
REPLACE line WITH $(line,1,1) + ' +' + axis
```

SLATEDRA has now drawn all but the plots and their titles. Control is returned to MAINGRAP after housekeeping.

### CODE FOR SLATEDRA.CMD

```
* slatedra.cmd
* module purpose: draws axes, positions titles

* prepare the blank slate of 21 records
DO WHILE # < graphbot
   APPEND BLANK
ENDDO WHILE # < graphbot

* build up drawing characters
* you may substitute your own
STORE '==================================' TO b35

STORE b35 + b35 TO axis
STORE '*****************************' TO c30
STORE c30+c30 TO asterisks
STORE '##############################' TO d30
STORE d30 + d30 TO pounds

* draw axis and titles
STORE '                    ' TO vtitle,htitle,gtitle
ERASE
@ 10, 5 SAY 'Title of the H-AXIS ' GET htitle
@ 12, 5 SAY 'Title of the V-AXIS ' GET vtitle
@ 14, 5 SAY 'Title of the Graph '   GET gtitle
READ

* position the vertical title and axis
GOTO graphtop
REPLACE next 20 line WITH $(!(vtitle),#-graphtop+1,1) + ' ¦'
```

20 spaces

```
* position the graph title
GOTO graphtop
REPLACE line WITH TRIM(line) + !(gtitle)

* position the horizontal axis
SKIP + 19
REPLACE line WITH $(line,1,1) + ' +' + axis

* position the horizontal title
SKIP
REPLACE line WITH TRIM(line) + '    ' + !(htitle)

RELEASE c30,d30,b35,htitle,vtitle,gtitle
RELEASE axis,spacer
RETURN
```

## PLOT.CMD  Plots the Current Value

PLOT takes the current value (FN1 to FN5), scales the value, and uses one of the two drawing characters to REPLACE into a record a plot with correct number of characters.

PLOT first chooses the character to be used to draw the plot. The plots are alternatively composed of either the pounds character ( # # # ) or the asterisk ( *** ) and are STOREd to charplot the CHARacter PLOTted. The variable counter, which is used in MAINGRAP, retains the number of plots to be drawn. The expression int(counter/2) is even when counter is even, and the # # # will be used for the even plots. All odd values use the asterisk.

================= TECH TIP =================

### Test for an Even Number

*To test for an even numbered numerator, divide by two and use the INT function. Compare result to simple division by two. Both expressions will be equal only for even denominators.*

```
. STORE 50 TO counter
? INT(counter/2) = counter/2
. .T.
. STORE 51 to counter
? INT(counter/2) = counter/2
. .F.
```

The next step is to actually draw the plot for the current value, the number STOREd to fieldplot. The largest value max is used to scale the plot correctly so that the largest plot does not exceed a width on the screen of 60 characters. The correct number of characters as a proportion of 60 is calculated, and the substring function selects from a large string of 60 drawing characters precisely the correct number to be used as a smaller string. Again, one powerful expression does most of the graphing.

```
STORE $(charplot,1,int((fieldplot * 60)/max)+1) TO plotbar
```

Using the first value (37321) of the REVENUE graph, a plot can readily be developed. One is added to the expression to ensure that even zero plots has one token plot character.

```
STORE $(charplot,1,int((37321) * 60)/109230)+1) TO plotbar
```

yields

```
STORE $(charplot,1,int(20.5000412 + 1) TO plotbar
```

or

```
STORE $(charplot,1,21) TO plotbar
```

The expression $(charplot,1,21) selects 21 characters from the 60 asterisk characters STOREd to charplot and in turn STOREs them to plotbar. The actual numeric value is converted into a string and added to plotbar. The final result is REPLACEd into the record that later displays this plot. Control is returned back to MAINGRAP.

CODE FOR PLOT.CMD

```
* plot.cmd
* module purpose: draws plot

* alternate drawing characters
IF int(counter/2) = counter/2
    STORE pounds TO charplot
ELSE
    STORE asterisks TO charplot
ENDIF int(counter/2) = counter/2

* plot correctly scaled value
* add one so that a zero value will also be plotted
STORE $(charplot,1,int((fieldplot * 60)/max)+1) TO plotbar

* add numeric amount to right of plotted bar
STORE plotbar + '   ' + STR(fieldplot,10,2) TO plotbar
* place plotted value into the correct record
```

```
REPLACE line WITH TRIM(line) + TRIM(plotbar)
RELEASE charplot,plotbar
RETURN
```

# GRAPHOPT.CMD  Graphing Options Routine

The optional GRAPHOPT asks the operator for the desired options to save the graph or print to a choice of a printer or to a text file. The 21 records comprising the graph are LISTed with set PRINT ON if a print-out is desired.

GRAPHOPT saves the graph unless answered otherwise and requests a filename for the graph. The filename is preceded by the words 'GRAPH NAME: ' and inserted into the first record of the graph. DELETE and PACK are used to eliminate the 21 records if the graph is not desired.

Another available option is to save the graph to a text file. The SET ALTERNATE ON command echoes the results of most dBASE processing to a text file that can be used by word processors. The main name of the text file is the same as the name given to the graph with the suffix TXT appended to it. Control is returned back to MAINGRAP after unwanted variables are RELEASEd.

CODE FOR GRAPHOPT.CMD

```
* graphopt.cmd
* module purpose: provides options to print graph or
* save to a text file or data base

GOTO graphtop

STORE f TO gprint,savegraph,output
@ 21,35
@ 21,35 SAY 'Print the Graph? ' GET gprint
READ

IF gprint
    SET PRINT ON
    LIST next 21 OFF
    SET PRINT OFF
    GOTO graphtop
    ERASE
    LIST next 21 TRIM(line) OFF
ENDIF gprint

@ 21,35
@ 21,35 SAY 'Do You Wish to Save Graph? ' GET savegraph
READ

IF savegraph
```

8 spaces

```
        GOTO graphtop
            STORE '            ' TO mgraphname
            @ 21,35
            @ 21,35 SAY 'What Filename ? ' GET mgraphname
            READ
            REPLACE line WITH $(line,1,25) + '        GRAPH NAME: ' +;
              !(mgraphname)
            @ 21,35
            @ 21,35 SAY 'Save to Text File? ' GET output
            READ

            IF output
                SET ALTERNATE TO &mgraphname
                SET ALTERNATE ON
            ENDIF output

            ERASE
            LIST next 21 TRIM(line) OFF
            SET ALTERNATE OFF
        ENDIF savegraph

        IF .NOT. savegraph
            DELETE next 21
            PACK
        ENDIF .NOT. savegraph

        RELEASE mgraphname,output,gprint,savegraph
        RETURN
```

## SUMMATE.CMD   Sums Fields in a Data File

SUMMATE totals up to five fields in a data file and fashions them into the form that MAINGRAP can subsequently graph. SUMMATE uses a provision of the SUM command that retains up to five subtotal and assigns each to a memory variables. Specifically, SUMMATE will prompt the operator to select the desired fields in the REVENUE graph and will yield the command:

```
SUM company1,company3,company4,canada,interntl TO  FN1,FN2,FN3,FN4,FN5
```

After first LISTing the data files, the operator is prompted to select a file that has numeric fields to be totalled and graphed. The file REVENUE in the example is opened.

One of the features of dBASE allows a command file to access a data file and determine its structure: the number of fields, type, width of each, and the decimal places if any. REVENUE or any other data file yields this information to SUMMATE or any other command file by use of the COPY STRUCTURE EXTENDED TO command. A new data file is created that contains not the records of the first file, but the data about its structure. Consider the example shown in Figure 18-10.

```
. USE revenue
. COPY STRUCTURE EXTENDED TO temp

00011 RECORDS COPIED
. USE temp
. DISPLAY STRUCTURE

STRUCTURE FOR FILE: B:TEMP .DBF
NUMBER OF RECORDS: 00011
DATE OF LAST UPDATE: 00/00/00
PRIMARY USE DATABASE
FLD         NAME          TYPE      WIDTH      DEC
001         FIELD:NAME     C         010                  Name of field in        REVENUE
002         FIELD:TYPE     C         001                  Type of Field in        REVENUE
003         FIELD:LEN      N         003                  Length of Field in      REVENUE
004         FIELD:DEC      N         003                  Decimal Places in       REVENUE
** TOTAL **                          00018

. DISPLAY ALL

Record      FIELD         FIELD     LEN        DEC
Number      NAME          TYPE
00001       COMPANY1       N         8          2         First Field's Structure in REVENUE
00002       COMPANY2       N         8          2         Last Field's Structure in Revenue
00003       COMPANY3       N         8          2
00004       COMPANY4       N         8          2
00005       COMPANY5       N         8          2
00006       CANADA         N         8          2
00007       INTERNTL       N         8          2
00008       PURPOSE        C         2          0
00009       DATE           C         8          0
00010       PAID           L         1          0
00011       PRINTED        L         1          0
```

*Figure 18–10.* Example

TEMP now mirrors the structural information about REVENUE. Each record in TEMP contains the structural data for one of the eleven fields in the hypothetical REVENUE database. Only the records in TEMP referring to numeric fields in REVENUE are used, and the others are removed from TEMP by use of the expression DELETE ALL FOR field-:type < > 'N'. After a Pack is issued, only records in TEMP that contain the names of numeric fields in REVENUE remain.

```
. DISPLAY ALL

00001       COMPANY1       N         8          2
00002       COMPANY2       N         8          2
00003       COMPANY3       N         8          2
00004       COMPANY4       N         8          2
00005       COMPANY5       N         8          2
00006       CANADA         N         8          2
00007       INTERNTL       N         8          2
```

Starting at the fifth line on the screen, a DO WHILE loop displays each of the records in TEMP. The last two numbers of the record number [STR(#,2)] are displayed with the name of the field. The code below accomplishes the task of display of the TEMP fields.

```
* display the numeric fields
STORE 5 TO line
DO WHILE .NOT. eof
   @ line,5 SAY STR(#,2)+ ' ' + field:name
   STORE line + 1 TO line
   SKIP
ENDDO WHILE .NOT. eof
```

The SUM phrase (SUM company1,company2 . . . TO FN1,FN2) is next built. A DO WHILE loop repeats until up to five fields are tallied. The field flag is set to 1, and the loop is terminated. Otherwise, the first of up to five fields are entered. The code below builds the first part of the SUM phrase.

```
GOTO num
* assign entry to uniquely named variable
STORE barnum + 1 TO barnum
STORE 'FN' + STR(barnum,1) TO sumsub
STORE 0 TO &sumsub
STORE begphrase + TRIM(field:name) + "," TO begphrase
STORE endphrase + sumsub + "," TO endphrase
* obtain title for graph and assign to unique variable
STORE 'FTITL' + STR(barnum,1) TO ttlsub
STORE '         ' TO &ttlsub
@ 5 + # − 1,25 SAY "What Title? " GET &ttlsub PICTURE '!!!!!!!!!!'
READ
```

The principle uses a loop and a macro to increment actions upon variables as was used in MAINGRAP. A variant is used in the pseudo-subroutine technique in the INIT routine (Chapter 16). The GOTO command positions dBASE to the record number (num) in TEMP, which retains the structural data corresponding to a field in REVENUE. The counter barnum starts at zero and is incremented by one for each repetition. The name of the first variable ('FN1') is initialized and zero is STORED to FN1.

The cumulative portion of the SUM phrase (SUM company1,company2 . . .) is STOREd to begphrase. The trailing portion of the SUM phrase (TO FN1..FN5) is STOREd to endphrase. Each repetition builds both the prefix and suffix portions of the SUM commands until complete.

Two passes are shown below.

## CODE TO BUILD THE SUM COMMAND LINE

```
GOTO num
* assign entry to uniquely named variable
STORE barnum + 1 TO barnum
STORE 'FN' + STR(barnum,1) TO sumsub
STORE 0 TO &sumsub
STORE begphrase + TRIM(field:name) + ',' TO begphrase
STORE endphrase + sumsub + ',' TO endphrase
```

## CODE TO BUILD THE SUM COMMAND LINE

```
GOTO num
* assign entry to uniquely named variable
STORE barnum + 1 TO barnum
STORE 'FN' + STR(barnum,1) TO sumsub
STORE 0 TO &sumsub
STORE begphrase + TRIM(field:name) + ',' TO begphrase
STORE endphrase + sumsub + ',' TO endphrase
```

## RESULTS ON THE FIRST PASS

Record Number 1 in Temp

```
barnum = 1
sumsub = "FN1"
STORE 0 TO FN1
begphrase = "" + "COMPANY1" + "," = " COMPANY1,"
endphrase = "" + "FN1" + "," = " FN1,"
```

## RESULTS ON THE SECOND PASS

Record Number 3 in Temp

```
barnum = 2
sumsub = "FN2"
STORE 0 to FN2
begphrase = " COMPANY1," + "COMPANY3," = "COMPANY1,- COMPANY3,"
endphrase = " FN1,FN2,"
```

307

```
BEGPHRASE   (C)   COMPANY1,COMPANY3,COMPANY4,
                  CANADA,INTERNTL
ENDPHRASE   (C)   FN1,FN2,FN3,FN4,FN5,
BARNUM      (N)   5
FLAG        (N)   0
FTITL1      (C)   UNIV WIDGT
FTITL2      (C)   TIRES
FTITL3      (C)   STEEL
FTITL4      (C)   CANCORP
FTITL5      (C)   INTERNATL
```

*Figure 18-11.* Major Memory Variables Produced by Summate after Exiting Loop

The three other possible field names are constructed into the SUM command in the same manner. A title for each plot is obtained from the operator with each pass and assigned to the variables of FTITL1 to FTITL5. Two portions of the SUM phrase, begphrase and endphrase, are completed and the loop is terminated.

Examine the major memory variables in SUMMATE after emerging from the DO WHILE loop. The command to invoke the SUM command is almost complete (see Figure 18-11).

The SELECT PRIMARY command is issued to switch to the REVENUE file. One last line of code prepares the SUM command is:

```
STORE 'SUM ' + begphrase + ' TO ' + endphrase TO sumall
. ? sumall

SUM COMPANY1,COMPANY3,COMPANY4,CANADA,INTERNTL TO
FN1,FN2,FN3,FN4,FN5
```

The final application of the macro &sumall turns the contents of sumall into a command. Applied to the REVENUE data file, the five fields are summed, and the subtotals applied to FN1 through FN5. Titles have also been stored, and the counter barnum registers the number of fields totalled. An operator who possibly has no knowledge of dBASE has been prompted to use one of the most powerful commands in the language. As shown in Figure 18-12, all the necessary memory variables have been initialized and SUMMED for use by the graphics toolkit.

Control is returned to MAINGRAP after housekeeping, notably the closing and deletion of TEMP. A graph will be produced within seconds after the RETURN.

```
BEGPHRASE    (C)    COMPANY1,COMPANY3,COMPANY4,
                        CANADA,INTERNTL
ENDPHRASE    (C)    FN1,FN2,FN3,FN4,FN5,
BARNUM       (N)    5
FLAG         (N)    0
FTITL1       (C)    UNIV WIDGT
FTITL2       (C)    TIRES
FTITL3       (C)    STEEL
FTITL4       (C)    CANCORP
FTITL5       (C)    INTERNATL
FN1          (N)    37321.00
FN2          (N)    37667.74
FN3          (N)    41280.00
FN4          (N)    54615.00
FN5          (N)    109230.00
```

*Figure 18-12.* Major Memory Variables Produced by Summate after Macro

## CODE FOR SUMMATE.CMD

```
* summate.cmd
* program by michael clifford
* module purpose: establishes sums from
* fields to be summed upon.

SET talk OFF
ERASE
STORE '        ' TO gfile
LIST files
?
?
@ 22,0 SAY "The contents to be graphed are in what file? " ;
GET gfile PICTURE '!!!!!!!!'
READ
USE &gfile

* ask the data base about its structure
* determine the fields of numeric type
COPY STRUCTURE extended TO temp
SELECT secondary
* eliminate all but numeric fields
* in the temporary file

USE temp
DELETE ALL FOR field:type < > 'N'
PACK
ERASE

* display the numeric fields
STORE 5 TO line
```

8 spaces

```
DO WHILE .NOT. eof
    @ line,5 SAY STR(#,2)+ '    ' + field:name
    STORE line + 1 TO line
    SKIP
ENDDO WHILE .NOT. eof

* obtain up to 5 fields to be summed and graphed
STORE ' ' TO begphrase,endphrase
STORE 0 TO barnum,flag
DO WHILE flag = 0 .AND. barnum < 5
    STORE 00 TO num
    @ 2,5 SAY "What Field Number (Up to 5. Enter 0 to Exit) " ;
    GET num PICTURE '# #'
    READ

    IF num = 0
        STORE 1 TO flag
    ELSE
        GOTO num
        * assign entry to uniquely named variable
        STORE barnum + 1 TO barnum
        STORE 'FN' + STR(barnum,1) TO sumsub
        STORE 0 TO &sumsub
        STORE begphrase + TRIM(field:name) + "," TO begphrase
        STORE endphrase + sumsub + "," TO endphrase
        * obtain title for graph and assign to unique variable
        STORE 'FTITL' + STR(barnum,1) TO ttlsub
        STORE '          ' TO &ttlsub
        @ 5 + # - 1,25 SAY "What Title? " GET &ttlsub PICTURE '!!!!!!!!!!'
        READ
    ENDIF num=0
ENDDO WHILE flag = 0 .AND. barnum <=5

SELECT PRIMARY

STORE 'SUM ' + begphrase + ' TO ' + endphrase TO sumall
* the grand finale. turn the phrase into a powerhouse
* sum the five fields and store to the five memory variables
* inform the operator of a delay
ERASE
@ 10,15 SAY '== The Fields Are Now Being Summed=='
&sumall

SELECT secondary
USE
SELECT PRIMARY
USE
DELETE FILE temp
RELEASE trans,sumsub,ttlsub,num,flag,line
RELEASE endphrase,begphrase,sumall,gfile
RETURN
```

*9 spaces*

## dPLOT  The Toolkit Menu

A final and optional command file is dPLOT. Three options may be chosen: 1) creating a graph, 2) viewing a display of the names of graphs in the GRAPHS, and 3) reviewing a graph once its name is entered. The first option, creating a graph, simply calls MAINGRAP.

Option 2 uses the LOCATE command to first determine if GRAPHS has ever been used. If so, the following code presents the directory:

```
DISPLAY ALL '    ',$(line,43) FOR 'GRAPH NAME:'$line OFF
```

This extended DISPLAY command displays only the contents of records having the string 'GRAPH NAME:' in the field LINE ('GRAPH NAME:'$line). Only these records are candidates to have contents displayed. We do not wish to display the unwanted characters to the left of the filename; part of the horizontal axis and the phrase 'GRAPH NAME' are unnecessary clutter. Only characters to the right of the 42nd character in line are displayed, corresponding to only the filename and blanks.

The third and last option uses the LOCATE command to find the filename of a desired graph among all of the records in GRAPH. The graph is presented by use of the LIST command once found.

CODE FOR DPLOT.CMD

```
* dplot.cmd
* module purpose: menu for graphics toolkit programs
SET talk OFF
USE graphs
DO WHILE t
   STORE ' ' TO option,ready
   DO WHILE @(option, '0123' )=0
      ERASE
      @ 3,15 SAY "=== dPLOT GRAPHICS MENU ==="
      @ 5,15 SAY '0- Exit to Menu'
      @ 7,15 SAY '1- Create A Graph'
      @ 8,15 SAY '2- Directory of Stored Graphs'
      @ 9,15 SAY '3- Recall Stored Graph'
      @ 12,15 SAY 'Please Select an Option ' GET option PICTURE '#'
      READ
   ENDDO WHILE @(option, '0123' )=0

   ERASE
   DO CASE
      CASE option= '0'
         RELEASE option,mgraphname,ready
         CANCEL
```

```
      CASE option= '1'
         DO maingrap

      CASE option= '2'
         LOCATE FOR 'GRAPH NAME:' $line
         IF eof
            @ 10,05 SAY ' NO GRAPHS ON FILE. PRESS ANY KEY TO CONTINUE'
         ELSE
            @ 5,0
            DISPLAY ALL '      ', $(line,43) FOR 'GRAPH NAME:' $line  OFF
         ENDIF eof

      CASE option= '3'
         STORE '           ' TO mgraphname
         @ 10,05 SAY 'What Is the Name of the Graph? ' ;
         GET mgraphname PICTURE '!!!!!!!'
         READ
         LOCATE FOR '&mgraphname' $line

         IF .NOT. eof
            ERASE
            LIST next 21 TRIM(line) OFF
            @ 21,35 SAY 'Press Any Key To Continue'
         ELSE
               @ 12,05 SAY 'Not Found. Press Any Key To Continue'
            ENDIF .NOT. eof
      ENDCASE
      @ 23,75 GET ready
      READ
ENDDO WHILE t
```

*7 spaces*

# MODIFICATIONS AND EMBELLISHMENTS

Unlike a graphics package that is written in machine language, the dPLOT code can be easily altered to serve a wide array of purposes. Several modifications are possible to enhance your own customized graphics system.

*More Error Checking.*   The dPLOT system is not bomb proof. If using SUMMATE, you may choose a file having no numeric fields or express a negative sum. An error message will result.

*Other Drawing Characters.*   Many computers have special graphics characters that are printed with CHR statements. The characters can be grouped together to appear as an unbroken histogram, rather than a series of asterisks or other characters. Implementation, however, depends upon the mechanical characteristics of your computer or terminal.

*Alternate Scaling Formulas.* The maximum plot value determines the scaling factor in the dPLOT system. More complex relationships between the plot values cannot be expressed without the use of mathematical functions currently not available in dBASE II. Later upgrades should allow graphing in instances when one plot value is several times larger than the others.

*Use by Other dBASE Applications.* You may wish to graph numeric results produced by a financial program. SUM fields or accumulate the results of other expressions and STORE them to FN1 through FN5. STORE the respective titles to FTITL1 through FTITL5. Determine the number of plots and STORE to barnum. Remove the call to SUMMATE (DO summate) in MAINGRAP. In addition to the GRAPHS data file, only three files are needed: MAINGRAPH, PLOT, and SCALEDRA. The graph may optionally be called from a menu or your application may graph the values directly.

## SUMMARY

Whether changes are made to the graphics tools or used unchanged, the dPLOT system underscores the versatility of dBASE to work with images as well as numbers and words. The utility serves the basic but crucial purpose of highlighting the results of other dBASE programs.

The dPLOT system is the last of the Useful Utilities. Programs can be initialized without worry with INIT. The Date and Duration Toolkit allows verified entry of dates and calculates durations. Continue to collect utility command files into a library to be used to support other dBASE business applications. You will be well rewarded for your efforts.

# APPENDIX

# NOTES ON THE
# OPERATING ENVIRONMENTS

The programs in the book were developed to run on Version 2.4 for the CP/M operating environment. Testing was performed on others as listed:

| Version | Operating System | Computer(s) Used |
|---------|------------------|------------------|
| 2.3 B   | CP/M             | Zorba, Osborne   |
| 2.4     | MS-DOS           | Compaq           |

The MS-DOS or PC-DOS software version of dBASE II differs from the CP/M version in one significant manner: all command files ending in the file extension of .CMD in CP/M must be changed to .PRG in MS-DOS. For example, the first program, MAILFORM.CMD must be entered as MAILFORM.PRG to run on the machines which are running MS-DOS or PC-DOS as the operating system. Only the command files need to be changed.

The change from CMD to PRG will require one other alteration. The DATEMENU program, (Chapter 17), uses the following code to verify that four files ending in CMD are on the disk.

```
IF FILE ("CALINT.CMD") .AND. FILE("INTCAL.CMD") .AND. ;
    FILE ("DTVERIFY.CMD") .AND. FILE("DAYOFWK.CMD")
```

Change the code to work with files ending in PRG.

```
IF FILE ("CALINT.PRG") .AND. FILE("INTCAL.PRG") .AND. ;
    FILE ("DTVERIFY.PRG") .AND. FILE("DAYOFWK.PRG")
```

# A RESOURCE LIST

User Groups can be an economical source of detailed dBASE information. Many computer user groups can be found in metropolitan areas which have a dBASE SIG (special interest group).

Commercial classes or consultants can also provide dBASE information. Look for instructors or consultants who not only can explain concepts clearly, but who are proficient in dBASE applications.

The following resource list has been provided courtesy of Ashton-Tate. The user groups, consultants, and classes have not been reviewed by Ashton-Tate and their inclusion does not represent an endorsement by Ashton-Tate nor the author.

## Arizona

PHOENIX DATABASE USER'S GROUP
Robert Reed
4800 N. 68th Street
Scottsdale, AZ 95251
(602) 949-9353

## California

dBASE II Users Group (started 6/16/83).
Shirley Anne Anderson
34 Lassen Lane
Novato, CA 94947
(415) 499-7207 days
(415) 892-0522 eves

dBASE USERS GROUP
Robert Davies
SBT
11140 Mt. View-Alviso Road
Sunnyvale, CA 94089
(408)-980-8880

D BASERS
Hank Lautenbach
5244 Edgepark Way
San Diego, CA 92124
(619) 560-4583

GREATER SOUTH BAY IBM-PC USERS GROUP
Hank Parker
28814 Leah Circle
Rancho Palos Verdes, CA 90274
(213)-970-4560 or (213) 970-2329

NORTH COUNTY dBASE II USERS GROUP
Walt Parkman
DATABASE INDUSTRIES INC.
330 W. Felicita, Suite D5
Escondido, CA 92025
(619) 480-9616

NORTH ORANGE COUNTY IBM PC USERS
GROUP (DB-SIG)
John Buckle or Glenn Emigh
P.O. Box 665

La Mirada, CA 90637
(213)-944-9651

OSBORNE KOMPUTER OWNERS KLUB (db II SIG)
Lionel Sorraco
P.O. Box 40429
Pasadena, CA 91104
(213)-794-3243

POMONA HEATH USERS GROUP-SIG dBASE II
Jeff Joyce (contact for dBASE SIG)
205 N. Encinitas
Monrovia, CA 91016
(213) 357-6061

## Georgia

ATLANTA DATABASE USER'S GROUP
(ADBUS) (1 year old)
Keith Plossl
c/o George Plossl Educational Service
P.O. Box 19817
Atlanta, Georgia 30325
(404) 355-3610

## Illinois

CHICAGO AREA DATABASE USER GROUP (started 6/83)
Jim Graham
P.O. Box 86
Deerfield, Ill. 60015
(312) 940-1010

## New York

IBM PC USERS GROUP (DB SIG)
Jean-Pierre Baccarat
Cabin Ridge Road
Chappaqua, NY 10514
(914)-762-3391

N.Y. OSBORNE USERS GROUP (2 yrs)
Paul B. Wiske
46 W. 37th Street #3FW
New York, NY 10018
(212) 868-4082—home

## North Carolina

TRIANGLE dBASE USERS GROUP (2 mos.)
Dr. Richard Slatta
2618 Davis Street

Raleigh, No. Carolina 27608
(919) 737-2483 Hist. Dept. N.C. State Univ.
(919) 782-8926 Afternoons

## Pennsylvania

PHILADELPHIA AREA COMPUTER SOCIETY (dBASE SIG)
Mike Tankle-dBASE SIG
Steve Longow (215) 924-7935 or 951-1255

## Tennessee

MEMPHIS dBASE II USERS GROUP
James Barker
571 Buck Street
Memphis, Tennessee 38111
(901)-327-2158

## Texas

DALLAS/FT. WORTH dBASE USERS GROUP
Doug Stone
1490 W. Spring Valley Rd.
Richardson, TX 75080
(214) 644-5043

## Virginia

CAPITAL PC USERS GROUP
Jerry Schneider
9523 Burdett Road
Burke, Virginia 22015
(703) 827-4883

# CLASSES AND CONSULTANTS

## Eastern States

FENTON ASSOCIATES LTD.
Contact: Christiae Blauchard
78 Meadowood Road
Storrs, CT 06260
(203) 429-6971

dBASE II seminars

PERSONAL COMPUTER SUPPORT INC.
Seth Lewis
18 Rief Road
Fairfield, CT 06430
(203) 254-0243

ADVANTAGE BUSINESS STORE
Contact: Sherry Dunhom
208 Lisbon Street
Leviston, ME 04240
(207) 783-1003
dBASE II hands-on experience

FRIEDMAN & FULLER
Contact: Dewayne Newell
11140 Rockville Park, #350
Rockville, MD 20852
(301) 468-2121
dBASE II classes

THE COMPUTER FORUM
Contact: Joel Skolmick
Langley Place
10 Langley Road
Newton, MA 02159
(617) 244-4710

COMPUDEX CORPORATION
13 Mark Street
Natick, MA 01760
(617) 235-5152

IRA H. KRAKOW & ASSOCIATES, INC.
Contact: Ira H. Krakow
12 Clearview Road
Stoneham, MA 02180
(617) 438-6335

Introduction to IBM PC database design using dBASE II. Advanced IBM PC database design using dBASE II. Seminars one day each. $100 per person for 1st 25 attendees and $75 for each subsequent attendee, with minimum of 15 attendees. Customer must provide meeting room, and pay instructor's traveling expenses. Advantage: onsite training, substantial savings in travel expenses for attendees.

COMPUTER TUTOR
Contact: Michael Coppolino
554 Washington Street
Wellesley, MA 02181
(617) 326-3561
Home: 259-0299

SOFTWARE BANC
Contact: Adam Green
661 Massachusetts Ave.
Arlington, MA 02174
(617) 641-1235
(800) 451-2502

THE COMPUTER LEARNING CENTER
1200 Haddonfield
Cherry Hill, NJ 08003
(609) 665-7426
dBASE II introductory computer classes

UNIVERSITY OF NEW YORK
Contact: Stewart Finks
11 W. 42nd Street
New York, NY 10036
(212) 598-7771
dBASE II classes

THE COMPUTER SCHOOL
21 West 86th Street
New York, NY 10024
(213) 580-1335
dBASE II classes

ALLIED COMPUTER SERVICE
255 W. 98th Street
New York, NY 10025
(212) 222-5665
On-site dBASE II training
One day seminars on dBASE II

ONE STOP COMPUTER SHOPPE
Contact: Joanne
65 North Fifth Street
Lemoyne, PA 17043
(717) 761-6752
dBASE II classes

## Southern States

MICRO INSTRUCTIONAL, INC.
Contact: Lenny Bayer
3452 N.W. 55th Street
Fort Lauderdale, Fla. 33309
(305) 485-6880
Offers dBASE II instructional cassette and tape. Carried in Xerox stores, various Computerlands, Heathkit Electronics Centers.

COMPUTER ESSENTIALS
Contact: Michael Clifford
2746 Dover Rd.
Atlanta, GA 30327
(404) 351-9755
Full range of dBASE II classes

---

(Source: dNEWS, Volume I, No. 7. December, 1983, page 32. A publication of Ashton-Tate.)

THE COMPUTER STORE
Contact: Joe Dean
4820 Highway 42
Louisville, KY 40222
(502) 423-0690
Give instructions payable by the hour in dBASE II.

NEW TECHNOLOGY, INC.
Contact: Jack Morrow or Steve Abbott
20 Tussock Road
Greenville, SC 29615
(803) 244-4442

WARD AND SON, INC.
Contact: E.C. Marzo
115 Pheasant Road
Box 2941
Spartanburg, SC 29302
(803) 583-6028
Home: 583-5113
dBASE II classes

COMPUTER ASSISTED SERVICES, INC.
Contact: Jane R. Frazier
1012 Chateaugay Road
Knoxville, TN 37923
(615) 691-1515
Seminars on dBASE II

SIMTEC
13717 Welch Road
Dallas, TX 75234
(214) 458-9544
dBASE II classes

SEMINAR CORPORATION
Contact: Judy Good
1616 S. Voss Suite 900
Houston, TX 77057
(713) 780-8649
Hands-on training in dBASE II

DOUG STONE SOFTWARES
1490 W. Spring Valley Road
Richardson, TX 75080
(214) 644-5043

SOFTWARE DISCOUNT SOFTWARE SOURCE
Contact: Doug Stone
1490 W. Spring Valley Rd.
Richardson, TX 78080
(214) 644-5043
dBASE II classes

SOFTWARE ENGINEERING OF DALLAS
1905 Colgate Drive
Richardson, TX 75081
(214) 530-7170

DEN BAR ASSOCIATES
Contact: Dennis Smith
4215 Middlebrook Street
Fairfax, VA 22032
(703) 978-1260
dBASE II consultant who also offers introductory and advanced seminars.


## Midwest

CONCEPT DYNAMIC
Contact: Tim O'Brien
900 Ridge Road
Suite F
Munster, IN 46321
(219) 836-9090

ADRIAN MECHANICAL
Contact: Dave Burke
904 N. Main Street
Adrian, MI 49221
(517) 263-5025
dBASE II classes

COMPUTER MANAGEMENT SYSTEM
Contact: Burl Shadden
1628 N.E. Washington Street
Minneapolis, MN 55413
(612) 788-0504
dBASE II seminar

OVERLAND COMPUTER SERVICE
Contact: John Larkin
4814 Douglas Street
Omaha, NE 68132
(402) 551-9444
dBASE II classes

THE BLUE CHIP COMPUTERS
Contact: Larry Sung
4017 Marshall Road
Kettering, OH 45429
(Dayton area)
(513) 299-4594

COMPUTRAIN
Contact: Mark Pultusker
7000 Fracci Court
Mentor, OH
(216) 255-6433
Hands-on dBASE II training

## Western States

COMPUTER OPTIONS
198 Amherst Ave.
Berkeley, CA 94708
(415) 525-5033

FUNDAMENTALS OF dBASE II
Instructor: Richard Shaw
1900 Avenue of the Stars
Century City, CA 90067
(213) 651-0220

ACCELERATED COMPUTER TRAINING
12057 Jefferson Blvd.
Culver City, CA 90230
(213) 821-1245
dBASE II classes. Beginning and advanced

ALPHA COMP DATA SERVICES
Contact: Peter
6120 Bristol Parkway
Suite 206
Culver City, CA 90230
(213) 215-9471

COST PLUS COMPUTERS
Contact: Phyllis Carota or Dan Mellhorn
11162 Trask Avenue
Garden Grove, CA 92643
(714) 638-9802
(619) 445-9126

ACCELERATED COMPUTER TRAINING
Contact: Chris Jutte
18201 W. McDurmott, Suite B
Irvine, CA 92714
(714) 660-0455

COMPUTER TUTOR
Contact: Richard Mansfield
2179 Magnolia
Long Beach, CA 90806
(213) 591-4624

RICK SHAW
10920 Wilshire Boulevard
Suite 680
Los Angeles, CA
(213) 651-0220

NIVCOM MICROSYSTEMS
Contact: Leo Sigman
341 N. Sweetzer Ave.
Los Angeles, CA 90048
(213) 658-8602
Instructor: Meir Niv

JOE RAKOW
3770 Highland Ave., Suite 202
Los Angeles, CA 90266
dBASE II disk tutorial

COMPUTORIAL, INC.
Contact: Loretta Vau-Valen
4520 Wilshire Blvd.
Los Angeles, CA 90010
(213) 933-8268

PERSONAL COMPUTER TRAINING
Contact: Mary Nason
1920 La Cienega Blvd.
Los Angeles, CA 90035
(213) 558-3000

SERVICE OF EDUCATIONAL COMPUTER (SEC)
1147 S. Hope
Los Angeles, CA 90015
(213) 749-5060
Teach corporations how to use dBASE II

U.C.L.A. Extension
(213) 825-7031
dBASE II classes. Call for current information

SOURCE OF EDUCATIONAL COMPUTER
Contact: Samantha White
1147 S. Hope Street
Los Angeles, CA 90015
(213) 749-5060
dBASE II classes

ADVIN SYSTEMS
Adrienne Vincent
924 No. Sierra Bonita
Los Angeles, CA 90046
(213) 876-4048

In-office dBASE II training. To reduce disruption of office routine, instruction is provided at user's place of business. Classes may consist of one person or a small group. Mailing Membership program with tutorial documentation included at no extra cost. Cost: $195 per day.

ADC ASSOCIATES
960 San Antonio Road
Palo Alto, CA 94303
(415) 493-5500

IQUAL PICHONE
4170 Wallis Court
Palo Alto, CA 94306
(415) 493-0463
dBASE II Consultants

PHOTO AND SOUND
Contact: John Wallsner
1791 Tribute Road, Suite A
Sacramento, CA 95815
(916) 920-2421
Teaches dBASE II

ALEX SYSTEMS
Agricultural Building, Suite 200
Embarcadero at Mission Street
San Francisco, CA 94105

Computer Instruction, System Analysis, Design and Implementation. dBASE II Training Firm. Classes held: weekdays and weekends 8:30–1 PM, 1:30–6 PM. Cost $150 per person (discounts for multiple enrollments available)

ANDERSON SOFTEACH
Contact: Warren Anderson
2161 Blossom Valley Drive
San Jose, CA 95124
(408) 356-3552

TSL INDUSTRIES
Contact: Barry J. Hammond
800 North Tustin Avenue
Suite C
Santa Ana, CA 92701
(714) 953-1488

Classes held frequently in Santa Ana and Orange County areas. Extensive and in-depth dBASE II classes. Four course programs, four hours each. Cost: $100.00/session.

CENTER FOR ADVANCED PROFESSIONAL EDUCATION
1820 E. Garry Street, Suite 110
Santa Ana, CA 92705

OMENTARAMICS
Contact: Scott Bryan, Pres.
1107 N. Fair Oaks Ave.
Sunnyvale, CA 94086
(408) 356-3552
Teaches dBASE II classes

THE LAYMAN'S COMPUTER CLINIC
25550 Hawthorne Blvd. Suite 105
Torrance, CA 90505
(213) 373-8720
Classes in dBASE II

COMPUTER EDUCATORS IN THE VALLEY
14411 Vanowen Street #218
Van Nuys, CA 91405
(213) 908-1484
dBASE II classes

THE COMPUTER SCHOOLS
Contact: Carolyn S. Rigiero,
Manager
2929 N. Mari Street
Walnut Creek, CA 94596
(415) 943-1200

COMPUTERS & CLASS
Contact: Jerome L. Wilski
807 Tampico
Walnut Creek, CA 94598
(415) 944-0563

COMPUTERS & CLASS
Contact: Jerome L. Wilski
807 Tampico
Walnut Creek, CA 94598
(415) 944-0563
Teaches dBASE II classes

PIKES PEAK
Contact: Raymond Jenkins (Datamax)
318 E. Caramillo Street
Colorado Springs, CO 80907
dBASE II classes

COMPUDATA SYSTEMS
Contact: Dick Shoop or
Ron Sweeny
P.O. Box 9032
614 Stadium Way
Tacoma, WA 98403
dBASE II classes

## Alaska

SMITH DESIGN CONSULTING
Contact: Ben Smith
P.O. Box 80582
Fairbanks, AL 99708
(907) 455-6695
dBASE II seminars. Six 2-hour sessions: $75

## International

GREG BOYCE
V.S. Cheng & Assoc., Inc.
Five Ross Street
Toronto Ontario M5TLZ8
Canada
(416) 979-1038
dBASE II classes

THE ANSWER
Contact: Rick Chaudler
Mgr. Learning Center
Acc. Answer Compu. Center Corp.
Corolation Playa
14310-1111 Ave.
Edmonton, Alberta T5M3Z7
Canada
(403) 451-9111

# Index